MW01519211

Literary Theories of Uncertainty

Literary Theories of Uncertainty

Edited by
Mette Leonard Høeg

BLOOMSBURY ACADEMIC
LONDON • NEW YORK • OXFORD • NEW DELHI • SYDNEY

BLOOMSBURY ACADEMIC
Bloomsbury Publishing Plc
50 Bedford Square, London, WC1B 3DP, UK
1385 Broadway, New York, NY 10018, USA
29 Earlsfort Terrace, Dublin 2, Ireland

BLOOMSBURY, BLOOMSBURY ACADEMIC and the Diana logo are trademarks of
Bloomsbury Publishing Plc

First published in Great Britain 2021
Paperback edition published 2023

Copyright © Mette Leonard Høeg and contributors, 2021

Mette Leonard Høeg and contributors have asserted their right under the Copyright,
Designs and Patents Act, 1988, to be identified as Author of this work.

Cover design: Eleanor Rose

All rights reserved. No part of this publication may be reproduced or transmitted
in any form or by any means, electronic or mechanical, including photocopying,
recording, or any information storage or retrieval system, without prior
permission in writing from the publishers.

Bloomsbury Publishing Plc does not have any control over, or responsibility for, any
third-party websites referred to or in this book. All internet addresses given in this
book were correct at the time of going to press. The author and publisher regret any
inconvenience caused if addresses have changed or sites have ceased to exist,
but can accept no responsibility for any such changes.

A catalogue record for this book is available from the British Library.

A catalog record for this book is available from the Library of Congress.

ISBN: HB: 978-1-3501-4604-4
PB: 978-1-3502-5970-6
ePDF: 978-1-3501-4605-1
eBook: 978-1-3501-4606-8

Typeset by Deanta Global Publishing Services, Chennai, India

To find out more about our authors and books visit www.bloomsbury.com and
sign up for our newsletters.

For Thomas

Selbst die kleinste Unsicherheit in der geringfügigsten Sache ist doch immer quälend.

– Franz Kafka, *Der Prozeß* (1925)

Contents

Figures

Contributors

Mieke Bal is a cultural theorist, critic, video artist and occasional curator who works in cultural analysis, literature and art, focusing on gender, migratory culture, psychoanalysis and the critique of capitalism. Her forty books include a trilogy on political art. Her video project, MADAME B, with Michelle Williams Gamaker, is widely exhibited, in 2017 combined with paintings by Edvard Munch in the Munch Museum in Oslo. After *Reasonable Doubt*, on René Descartes and Queen Kristina (2016), she made a sixteen-channel video installation *On Quijote: Sad Countenances*, and the short essay film *It's About Time! Reflections on Urgency*.

Patrick ffrench is Professor of French at King's College London, where he works on twentieth-century French literature, film and thought and on critical theory. He is the author of five books: *The Time of Theory: A History of Tel Quel* (1995); *The Cut: Reading Georges Bataille's* Histoire de l'œil (2000); *After Bataille: Sacrifice, Exposure, Community* (2007); *Thinking Cinema with Proust* (2018) and *Roland Barthes and Film: Myth, Eroticism and Poetics* (2019). He is also the co-editor (with Roland-François Lack) of *The Tel Quel Reader* (1998). His current work includes projects on Deleuze and Proust and on the legacies of Félix Guattari.

Christopher Fynsk is Chief Academic Officer of the European Graduate School and Dean of the Division of Philosophy, Art and Critical Thought. His publications include the following monographs: *Heidegger: Thought and Historicity* (1986) (Expanded Edition, 1996); *Language and Relation: . . . that there is language,* (1996); *Infant Figures* (2000); *The Claim of Language: A Case for the Humanities,* (2006); *Last Steps: Maurice Blanchot's Exilic Writing* (2013); *Philippe Lacoue-Labarthe's Phrase* (2017). He is also the editor of Philippe Lacoue-Labarthe's *Typography: Philosophy, Mimesis, Politics* (1989). His forthcoming work bears the working title, *The Rhythmic Figure*.

Mette Leonard Høeg is Junior Research Fellow at the University of Oxford. She wrote her PhD on the notion of undecidability in twentieth-century literary theory and literature, in particular in the works of Ford Madox Ford and Robert Musil. She studied at the University of Copenhagen, Humboldt University, UC Berkeley and King's College London, and is a Fulbright scholar. Her research focuses on uncertainty of meaning and the blending of fiction and non-fiction in Modernist and contemporary literature. She has previously published 'Swinging of the Breath Undecidability and Zones of Indistinction in Herta Müller's *Atemschaukel*' (2020).

Christopher Norris is Emeritus Professor in Philosophy at Cardiff University. In his early career he taught English Literature, then moved to Philosophy *via* literary theory, and has now moved back towards creative writing. He has published widely on the topic of deconstruction and is the author of many books on aspects of philosophy, literature, the history of ideas and music. More recently, he has turned to writing poetry in various genres, among them – unusually – that of the philosophical verse-essay. His collections include *The Cardinal's Dog* (2014), *For the Tempus-Fugitives* (2017), *The Matter of Rhyme* (2018) and *A Partial Truth* (2019).

Bruce Robbins is Old Dominion Foundation Professor of the Humanities at Columbia University. His most recent book is *The Beneficiary* (2017). *Cosmopolitanisms*, co-edited with Paulo Horta, also came out in 2017. His other books include *Perpetual War: Cosmopolitanism from the Viewpoint of Violence* (2012), *Upward Mobility and the Common Good* (2007), *Feeling Global: Internationalism in Distress* (1999*)*, *Secular Vocations: Intellectuals, Professionalism, Culture* (1993) and *The Servant's Hand: English Fiction from Below* (1986). He is the director of two documentaries, 'Some of My Best Friends Are Zionists' and 'What Kind of Jew Is Shlomo Sand?'.

Nicholas Royle is Professor of English at the University of Sussex. His books include *Telepathy and Literature: Essays on the Reading Mind* (1991), *E. M. Forster* (2000), *Jacques Derrida* (2003), *The Uncanny* (2003), *How to Read Shakespeare* (2005), *Veering: A Theory of Literature* (2011), *An Introduction to Literature, Criticism and Theory* (Fifth edition, 2016, co-authored with Andrew Bennett) and *Hélène Cixous: Dreamer, Realist, Analyst, Writing* (2020). He has also published two novels, *Quilt* (2010) and *An English Guide to Birdwatching* (2017), as well as *Mother: A Memoir* (2020).

Max Saunders is Interdisciplinary Professor of Modern Literature and Culture at the University of Birmingham. He was Director of the Arts and Humanities Research Institute at King's College London. He studied at Cambridge and Harvard, and was a Fellow of Selwyn College, Cambridge. His books include *Ford Madox Ford: A Dual Life* (1996), *Self-Impression: Life-Writing, Autobiografiction,* *and the Forms of Modern Literature* (2010) and *Imagined Futures: Writing, Science, and Modernity in the To-Day and To-Morrow Book Series, 1923-31* (2019). He was awarded an advanced grant from the ERC for a five-year collaborative project on digital life-writing called 'Ego-Media'.

Hannah Vinter is a doctoral candidate in the German department at King's College London. She researches contemporary authors who write about traumatic histories using collage techniques and other fragmentary forms. Her research focuses on Herta Müller, Nora Krug, Katja Petrowskaja and Emine Sevgi Özdamar. She has previously published 'Herta Müller, Oskar Pastior and *Atemschaukel* as poetic assemblage' (2020).

Introduction

Towards a conception of 'literary theory of uncertainty'

Mette Leonard Høeg

Uncertainty of meaning is a fundamental dimension and quality of literature and constitutive of what renders some literary works accessible, appealing and engaging across time and in different contexts. Uncertainty is a precondition for literature, indeed for any stabilization of meaning. A greater or lesser degree of authorial and readerly awareness of this precondition and fundamental trait is possible, and, thus, uncertainty can also form part of a narrative strategy and function as a literary device, used either to disrupt the seeming naturalness of a narrative or as a mimetic method to authentically render the uncertainty of reality and human perception. And uncertainty can be integrated into a critical reading strategy or interpretational attitude by which the fundamental uncertainty of narrative is acknowledged and the uncertainties and inherent tensions of a literary narrative are kept open and unresolved.

The notion of uncertainty of meaning has always existed and been relevant, if not in the form of explicitly recognized and theorized concepts, then implicitly present as the defining opposition of certain and decided meaning. In this sense, all theory of literature, interpretation and meaning is also theory of uncertainty. However, in the nineteenth century through the twentieth, the ideas of, and thinking about, uncertainty begin to consolidate into a more distinct branch in literary theory. This growing preoccupation in literature and literary theory with uncertainty of meaning and interpretation is linked to a general shift in how the world and human existence is perceived and to developments in the fields of physics, philosophy and psychology. As a new scientific view of the physical world emerges in the beginning of the twentieth century, notions of uncertainty become increasingly prevalent in all spheres of society, and scientific truth about the world and the human perception of it as well as the artistic representations and explorations of these undergo a noticeable change.

Uncertainty comes to function as a structuring principle and primary conveyor of meaning in literature in the late nineteenth and early twentieth century. The uncertainty of knowledge, epistemology and phenomenology are key issues in the impressionist and Modernist works of this period. Forms of uncertainty are used as subversive devices and strategies to challenge established literary conventions and to explore and develop novel philosophical and existential ideas, and the notion of uncertainty of meaning is established as a criterion of authenticity and truth in the literary representation of reality and human experience. This foregrounding of uncertainty in Modernist literature has had a radical and lasting effect on narrative, and uncertainty continues to hold a vital position through the postmodern period and into contemporary narrative where it still functions as a criterion for credibility in both fictional and nonfictional narrative.

Literary theory also becomes increasingly preoccupied with notions of uncertainty of meaning, representation and interpretation in the late nineteenth century. A variety of subforms and related terms such as 'undecidability', 'indeterminacy', 'ambiguity', 'indistinction', 'obscurity', 'vagueness', 'opacity' and 'indiscernibility' appear at the heart of some of the most central discussions about the meaning and nature of literature. The literary theories of uncertainty in the nineteenth and twentieth centuries vary in their focus, emphases, terminology and explanations, and indeed they are often developed in explicit opposition to the conceptions of uncertainty that precede them. They are, however, aligned in their view of uncertainty of meaning as an inherent textual feature and a fundamental literary property. They share the perspective that the most interesting meanings in a literary text are linked to its uncertainty; indeed, that uncertainty is constitutive of the very meaning of literature. They recognize that uncertainty is that from which meaning springs and on which reader engagement hinges.[1]

There seems to be in literary theory and culture an implicit understanding of the significance and centrality of the notion of uncertainty, in literature fundamentally and in Modernist literature in particular. But there is curiously little conscious awareness or deliberate investigation of the notion of literary and interpretive uncertainty and few detailed and focused meta-studies on the theory of uncertainty. The present volume attempts to make up for this. It represents an exploration of uncertainty both as a fundamental dimension of all literary theory and a continuation of the strand of 'theory of uncertainty' that runs through late nineteenth- and twentieth-century literary theory. The volume draws attention to and expands this implicitly recognized, yet underexplored area of literary theory, as it looks at uncertainty of meaning and interpretation from a variety of perspectives, with a focus on the modern and postmodern period. It reinstates, investigates and further develops a number of concepts of uncertainty, unleashing some of the analytical force and potential of notions of uncertainty for the study of literature. And it emphasizes the link between literary appeal and uncertainty of meaning, thereby shedding light on the fundamental appeal and effect of interpretive challenge and recalcitrance.

'Uncertainty', 'undecidability', 'indeterminacy', 'obscurity' and so on are contested terms, words with 'bad vibes' as Geoffrey Hartman has pointed out,[2] often associated with meaning-relativism, nihilism and the prejudices against deconstruction. This volume springs from the view that a conceptualization of uncertainty need not, however, be vague, that the notion of uncertainty is not as elusive as is often presumed, and that it is both possible and desirable to explore a literary theory of uncertainty. The volume counteracts the existing conceptual vagueness with theorizations of uncertainty as a fundamental dimension of literature and offers analyses of the types and modes, uses and strategies and functions and effects of uncertainty in twentieth-century and contemporary literature. In nine diverse chapters by some of the most prominent, inquiring minds of the disciplines of literary, cultural and critical theory today, the volume thus draws the contours of the field of a literary theory of uncertainty.

Inevitably, several uncertainties are at play in the volume itself. The chapters are all to some degree determined by the very uncertainty that precedes language and discourse and which is also their object of study. There is a clear self-awareness in the volume of its inherent uncertainty as an attempt at textual fixation of meaning, and several chapters engage demonstratively with this feature. The volume arises from the zone of indistinction between theory and literature on which it also sheds light. As one contributor notes in the form of a rhetorical question, it is impossible to clearly separate theories of uncertainty in literature from theories of uncertainty that are literary. These are connected, and the volume deals in both, demonstrating exactly the literary nature of theory and the theoretical quality of literature.

The present chapter functions as an introduction, both to the volume itself and to theory of uncertainty as a literary-theoretical strand more generally. Its aim is to establish the theoretical-historical background for the volume by introducing some of the most significant points in the history of theory of uncertainty and relating these to the broader scientific and cultural context and to relevant theories and trends in other fields than the literary. My focus is mainly on the first half of the twentieth century, which is characterized by a particularly strong inventive and productive theoretical energy, and which appears as a period of culmination for literary theory of uncertainty.

Nineteenth-century notions of uncertainty

The authorial, critical and readerly awareness of the fundamental uncertainty of meaning in literature and its meaning-productive function and potential grows notably in the last half of the nineteenth century, but notions of productive forms of uncertainty are also present in literary theory and narrative before the more explicit theories take form in the early twentieth century. In 1817, Keats uses the term 'negative capability' to designate the special ability of great writers such as Shakespeare to accept uncertainties, doubt and mystery. In a letter to his brothers, Keats reflects on the insight he has had during a discussion with Charles Dilke that a prerequisite for literary greatness is an ability to accept uncertainty of meanings: 'several things dovetailed in my mind, & at once it struck me, what quality went to form a Man of Achievement especially in Literature & which Shakespeare possessed so enormously – I mean *Negative Capability,* that is when a man is capable of being in uncertainties, Mysteries, doubts, without any irritable reaching after fact & reason.'[3] Uncertainty also clearly appears as an important aspect in early Modernist literature such as the works of Gustave Flaubert, Thomas Hardy, Henry James and Joseph Conrad. In *The Uses of Obscurity: The Fiction of Early Modernism,* Allon White shows how obscurity in the last decade of the nineteenth century began to function as a significant and positive aspect of English fiction. And Jonathan Culler, in his study *Flaubert: The Uses of Uncertainty,* sheds light on the undecidable point of view in *Madame Bovary* (1856), demonstrating how the novel obstructs the identification of a single narrator and how the narrative strategy of irony creates an uncertainty of meaning and undermines conventional reading strategies.

The authorial and readerly awareness of the undecidability between the domains of fiction and nonfiction, which is one of the most immediately obvious forms of uncertainty, is also fundamental and dates back much further than the twentieth century.[4] In the first edition of *Robinson Crusoe* (1719), Daniel Defoe credited the protagonist of the work as its author, which led many to read the novel in the referential mode as a true travelogue. This undecidability between autobiography and fiction in life-writing has been a particularly contentious form of uncertainty. Generic blurring of the boundaries between the autobiography and the novel is generally perceived as dating back to Rousseau's *Confessions* (1782–9) and even Saint Augustine's *Confessions* (397–400), but the question of whether something has been made up or is true (in the sense of being in accordance with the real, external life of the author) has arguably been relevant to readers for as long as the form of the autobiography has existed.[5]

Literary experiments with the uncertainty between the autobiographical and the fictional mode begin to increase with literary impressionism around the turn of the century. In the late nineteenth century, literature begins to reject the reading strategies of Romanticism, in particular the attempt to identify literary works with their author, and uncertainty is applied as a means to avoid identification in life-writing. Max Saunders's comprehensive study of the fusing of life-writing and fiction by modern and Modernist writers, *Self Impression*, which looks at the movement from literary impressionism in the late nineteenth century to Modernism in the early twentieth, thus shows how the conventional modes of autobiography, biography, fiction and criticism begin to blend and to disrupt each other, in works by writers such as Conrad, Ford, Proust, Joyce, Woolf, Stein, Mann, Sartre and Nabokov.[6]

Another highly conspicuous form of literary uncertainty is related to the representation of speech and thought. In third-person narration, there are always two voices and, thus, potentially two perspectives at play, namely that of the narrator and that of the represented character, which may or may not be aligned. The narrative mode of free indirect discourse is particularly emblematic of this uncertainty.[7] This form of narration by which the speech or thought of a character is rendered in the idiom of the character but with the grammatical discourse of a third-person narrator, which was later to become a standard style in fiction and an integral part of the narration in Modernist works by Woolf, Joyce, Mann, Kafka and many others, also becomes more prevalent in the nineteenth century and forms part of what has been termed the 'inward turn' of narrative. It was first used extensively by Jane Austen in *Emma* (1815) and in France by Flaubert in *Madame Bovary* (1856), where it famously formed part of the central argument in Flaubert's defence in the trial against him for obscenity; and it comes to play a central role towards the end of the century as an effective technique for rendering impressions. The inherent uncertainty of Free Indirect Discourse was also used strategically to trick the reader, for instance in the works of Henry James where the perspective of the narrator is made to coincide closely with that of the character in order to confuse the reader. Indeed, the narrative undecidability of *The Turn of the Screw* (1898) has fuelled a variety of differing and even contradictory interpretations.

The work of Joseph Conrad is another prominent example of early but evident uncertainty, as is demonstrated, for instance, by the obscurity and fragmentation of *The Heart of Darkness* (1902) and its assertion of the uncertain nature of subjective understanding. James and Conrad are representative of the broader preoccupation with the notion of the impression in which uncertainty plays a central part (and the two are often discussed as 'impressionist writers', although both were ambivalent towards the term). This focus on subjective sensory experience and epistemological uncertainty of impressionism in the late nineteenth and at the turn of the century anticipates certain major scientific, philosophical and cultural changes. Impressionism can thus be seen as laying the ground for Modernism in which the deep engagement with the notion of the inherently uncertain and subjective impression is continued and elaborated.

There are also significant non-literary precursors to the specifically literary concepts of uncertainty developed in the twentieth century. At the end of the nineteenth century, a new position of uncertainty and the ethical vacuum resulting from a growing agnosticism put writers under pressure to look for alternative meanings. The dissolution of the religious meaning-system opened up a vast field of uncertainty to investigation, and writers engaged with this new field of uncertainty through formal and aesthetic experiments as well as ethical and existential explorations.

The notion of uncertainty of meaning forms an important part of the existential theory of Kierkegaard and the epistemology developed by Nietzsche, and both had a distinctive influence on the literary theories and works of uncertainty in the twentieth century. In Kierkegaard's existential theory, it plays a significant role in relation to the concepts of possibility, actuality and necessity and to his description of the human condition and of a viable existential position, which he characterizes in terms of tension and unresolved movement between finitude and infinitude and between necessity and possibility. While Kierkegaard does not offer a theory of interpretation as such (at least not explicitly), he uses literature to demonstrate his theories and deploys strategies of uncertainty in his philosophical writings, including the use of pseudonyms and unreliable narration. His philosophical works are characterized by a multiplicity of perspectives that form part of a poetic practice aimed at reorienting the understanding of readers and at activating and inciting them to read in a participatory manner. With their narrative strategies of uncertainty and playful use of pseudonyms and the autobiographical mode, his philosophical works are evident early examples of a generic uncertainty which was to become prevalent with later, in particular post-structuralist critical positions, as they undermine the borders between criticism, fiction and autobiography.[8]

Uncertainty also features prominently in Nietzsche's theory and is entailed in his theory of perspectivism, the claim of the contingency of human knowledge and the notion of multiplicity of truth. According to Nietzsche, epistemology is necessarily determined and limited by our human perspective which we cannot escape, and there is no stable or objective point of reference by which a distinction between wrong and right perspectives can be determined. For Nietzsche, then, there is no 'real' reality which is simply contaminated and blocked by our perspective, but only perspectives. As a consequence, he argues, we should acknowledge the impossibility of acquiring undistorted knowledge and, instead, consciously multiply our subjective perspectives on reality in order to attain a more multifaceted view of things. This philosophical position of perspectivism and theory of the uncertainty of epistemology are manifested through his famously contradictory and obscure writing, which also makes use of the autobiographical mode to demonstrate the subjectivity of perspective.

Similarly, the notion of the unconscious, which is one of the central conceptualizations of uncertainty in the twentieth century, is an idea that manifests itself throughout the nineteenth century, long before Freud.[9]

Twentieth-century notions

Religious uncertainty appears to be at least in part what drives the writer Stephen Reynolds to launch the term 'autobiografiction' in his 1906 essay of the same title. Autobiografiction designates a contemporary literary genre in which fiction, autobiography and essayism are blended in order to obtain and convey in an adequate, authentic and engaging manner experiences of a spiritual nature (in a broad and secular sense). Apparently unaware of the potential width and inclusivity of the concept and unsuspecting of the predominance that this conspicuously postmodern-sounding literary form was to have in Modernist literature later in the same century, as well as in the following, Reynolds presents autobiografiction as a 'minor literary form'. He explains the undecidable nature of autobiografiction by comparing it to sulphur in its state of equilibrium:

> So long as the very definite temperature and pressure are unchanged, the sulphur remains in that indefinite state of neither solid, nor liquid, nor gas, but something between the three. So with autobiografiction. It is so indefinite, and

shades off so gradually into better marked, well-known forms, that its existence as a distinct literary *genre* appears disputable. At the same time it is the outcome of definite tendencies and has a very definite position on the literary chart. Where the three converging lines – autobiography, fiction, and the essay – meet, at that point lies autobiografiction.[10]

'Autobiografiction' is one of the earliest examples of an explicitly formulated literary-theoretical concept of uncertainty and remarkably captures a literary form the prevalence of which has since only increased. It anticipates both Serge Doubrovsky's coining of the term 'autofiction' in 1977[11] as well as more recent terms such as 'autotheory' (which designates the blending of autobiography and theory in contemporary literature).

The growing awareness of the literary potential of uncertainty in the early twentieth century is further demonstrated by Ford Madox Ford's 1914 essay 'On Impressionism'. Here Ford describes literary impressionism both as a genre that is based on the recognition of the productive potential of uncertainty of meaning and as a method in which uncertainty is used as a narrative and stylistic device in order to mimic life and persuasively render its distinctive character of 'odd vibration' and 'haze' and its quality of 'shimmering'.[12] Impressionism is represented by Ford as a form of psychological or epistemological realism in literature and as a method that takes seriously the fundamental insight that a writer, as any other human being, is determined by a particular subjectivity and a naturally restricted memory. Ford's literary impressionism is based on the view that 'the general effect of a novel must be the general effect that life makes on mankind'.[13] Ford thus explains that he and his friend and collaborator Joseph Conrad accepted the label 'impressionists' because they recognized that life appeared to them in a certain way, namely through impressions; they 'saw that Life did not narrate, but made impressions on our brains. We in turn, if we wished to produce on you an effect of life, must not narrate but render . . . impressions'.[14]

The theories of Reynolds and Ford are examples of early signs of authorial awareness of the significance and potential of uncertainty as a literary device as well as a fundamental and unavoidable element in literature. They entail a view of uncertainty not as a problem or obstacle to interpretation but, on the contrary, as a quality and a possibility. Their appreciation of uncertainty as a strategy for production of meaning illustrates a general shift in the cultural attitude towards uncertainty in the first half of the century and a first step in the solidification of the notion of uncertainty in literary theory and culture.

Ford's approach to literary uncertainty is, then, indicative of a general shift in how the world and human existence in it are perceived in the twentieth century. The recognition and the ideas of uncertainty and undecidability begin to challenge and irrevocably reshape epistemological and ontological categories and change the way the world is experienced, conceptualized and represented. The increase of uncertainty in the literature of the first half of the century thus corresponds and is connected to an increasing awareness of the significance of uncertainty in society and culture more broadly. In the twentieth century, the notion of uncertainty appears at the centre of some of the most influential theories, playing a crucial role in science and technology as both an object of groundbreaking discoveries and a driving force for new developments. In physics, the theory of quantum mechanics is established, building on Einstein's theory of relativity of time and space. Wave/particle duality is discovered. And with the Uncertainty Principle, Heisenberg proves that the position and the momentum of a particle cannot be measured with absolute precision, and that the more accurately one of these values is measured, the less accurately we know the other, thereby showing that the act of observation affects the observed object and thus pointing to the uncertainty of scientific knowledge. Other ideas that significantly undermine the classical realist and logical positivist positions are developed, such as the notion of observer-induced retroactive causal influence. In 1931, Gödel publishes his Incompleteness Theorems which show the limits of provability in formal axiomatic theories as they demonstrate that in any sufficiently complex and coherent formal system there exist propositions which cannot be proved or disproved within that system. And in early computational theory the 'undecidable problem' is formulated in accordance with Gödel's incompleteness results.

In psychology, Freud further opens up the already–partly registered space of uncertainty and obscurity between the conscious and unconscious with his explicit formulation of a theoretical distinction between these two levels of the human mind. With the establishment of psychoanalysis, concepts of uncertainty such as ambivalence, overdetermination, the latent (vs the manifest), the uncanny and the repressed are introduced. These fundamental psychoanalytical categories soon become widely adopted and used in contemporary culture. In the field of philosophy, phenomenology develops a definition of reality from an experiential vantage point as it investigates the appearance of objects and the process of perception of the human mind. Thereby it includes the notion of subjectivity in the description of reality, rejects the logical positivist conception of an objective reality and the notion of the unity of science. In the study of language, Saussure undermines the notion of the referentiality of language and the idea that meaning arises in a relation between signs and the world as he puts the notions of the arbitrary and the differential character of the sign at the centre of linguistics and semiology, showing that the meaning of a word is a value that is delimited by the other words in the same enclosed, self-organizing and non-referential language system.

The recognition of the incompleteness and uncertainty in all seemingly consistent and complete systems and of the potential unresolvable ambiguity of (physical) phenomena, then, also gains influence in the humanistic scientific fields, particularly in relation to the accounts of the system of language and of linguistic representation. Roman Ingarden develops a phenomenological theory of literature in which the concept of 'Unbestimmtheitsstellen' designates a fundamental form of literary uncertainty. And with New Criticism, theorists such as William Empson and Cleanth Brooks put uncertainty of meaning at the centre of investigation in literary studies, albeit with attention primarily to poetry. Here uncertainty becomes the primary and explicit focus of a broader literary-theoretical movement, primarily in the form of the concept of ambiguity and with particular attention to the notion of overdetermination and condensation of many meanings around a particular word (or image or sentence). In New Criticism, poetic language is presented as defined by its inherent ambiguity as well as its deliberate use of this form of uncertainty. Brooks thus writes, 'Even the apparently simple and straightforward poet is forced into paradoxes by the nature of his instrument.'[15]

As philosophy, linguistics, art, political and literary theory begin to merge into the field of critical theory in the second half of the twentieth century, uncertainty remains a central notion, and the emphasis is shifted from inherent textual uncertainties to the uncertainty of interpretation. The concept of the 'text' is widened to include all forms of discourse. Interpretive and critical strategies of uncertainty are developed by a range of theorists, and a variety of terms of uncertainty are developed. Building on Ingarden's term of spots of indeterminacy or indistinction, Wolfgang Iser posits the concept of 'Leerstelle' or 'gaps of indeterminacy', and argues that 'The indeterminate elements of literary prose – perhaps even of all literature – represents the most important link between text and reader.'[16] Giorgio Agamben develops the concept of 'zones of indistinction' in his politico-theoretical theory of the state of emergency. Gilles Deleuze works with the notion of indiscernibility. Derrida introduces the concepts of 'undecidability' and 'undecidabilities', distinguishing these from the notion of 'indeterminacy'.[17] Paul de Man too uses the term 'indeterminacy' in his analyses of the tension between the rhetorical and grammatical in literature. And Geoffrey Hartman argues for a particular 'hermeneutics of indeterminacy' as he uses the concept of indeterminacy to develop his theory of literary criticism, arguing that 'Indeterminacy, as a concept, resists . . . the complicity with closure'.[18]

At the same time, uncertainty is, as already mentioned, foregrounded in Modernist literary narrative. In the post-impressionist and through the Modernist period writers such as Ford, Proust, Kafka, Woolf, Musil and Joyce use uncertainty extensively, as a structuring principle and a guiding philosophical idea in their literary-philosophical explorations of fundamental categories of epistemology, reality, subjectivity, representation and interpretation. And uncertainty continues to feature prominently in late Modernism in works by writers such as Beckett and Blanchot.

Towards the end of the century, a general, albeit implicit understanding seems to form in literary theory of uncertainty as a crucial twentieth-century notion and as particularly characteristic of Modernist literature. Uncertainty of meaning and interpretation is theoretically somewhat naturalized and appears as a central notion in several prominent theories and conceptualizations, including Wayne C. Booth's concept of the unreliable narrator, Julia Kristeva's perspectives on the undecidability of poetic language, Shlomith Rimmon-Kenan's structural theory on the concept of ambiguity, J. Hillis Miller's deconstruction-based notion of 'unreadability', Allon White's study of early Modernist 'obscurity' and Umberto Eco's notion of the 'open work'. The terms 'undecidability' and 'indeterminacy' also begin to be used pejoratively in the critical responses to deconstruction and the relativism that some consider it to entail. Defending the notion of 'determinacy', Charles Altieri writes critically of 'indeterminacy theories' and states that '[i]f there is any doctrine that constitutes a shared ideology in recent literary studies, it must be the belief that substantial aspects of literary meaning are indeterminate'.[19] And Stanley Fish, defending his own claim of the instability of the text, includes himself among what he calls the 'accused apostles of indeterminacy and undecidability'.[20] While these theories do not grow clearly out of a collective critical movement, as is arguably the case with New Criticism and the post-structuralist concepts, they nevertheless mark significant points in the further development of theory of uncertainty and demonstrate a continued theoretical interest in the notion and a sustained, although largely implicit, understanding of uncertainty as fundamental and fundamentally meaning-productive in literature.

Uncertainty in contemporary literature and beyond

Uncertainty continues to be a defining feature in postmodernist and contemporary literature, although the more productive forms appear to morph into more problematizing forms that challenge meaning altogether in late Modernism and postmodernism, and literary experiments with epistemology seem to be replaced with experiments with undermining ontological categories. In today's literary environment, the belief in the ability of nonfictional narrative to objectively represent reality has been severely reduced, and at the same time the status of fiction has been radically altered. As a result, the dichotomy between nonfiction and fiction is in decline, the relation between referentiality and construct is being reshaped, and the conception of truth and truthful representation is changing. The conventional notions of truth and objectivity have largely been rendered vacuous, and nonfiction has gained a reputation of being naïve, based on the illusion of objective and direct presentation of reality. Fiction, in turn, has come to be perceived as being detached from reality and thus irrelevant and futile, and there has in recent years been a growing disinterest in conventional fictional narrative. At the same time, contemporary literature and readership are characterized by impatience with postmodern meaning-relativism and a longing for literary commitment to truth and authenticity. In this context, uncertainty appears as an increasingly central notion on which credibility and truthfulness hinge.

Uncertainty has come to play a particularly significant role in the recent trend in life-writing of blending of fictional and autobiographical modes and in the literary forms that are often branded as 'autofiction'. Contemporary works of autofiction entail a move away from the postmodern condition and indicate a return of a need for meaning and truth in literary culture. Instead of reviving an outdated concept of truth or reality, contemporary literary works of generic uncertainty, however, imply a concept of truth based on honesty and authenticity for which the indistinction or undecidability between fiction and fact becomes a precondition. There is thus a tendency in contemporary literature to combine referentiality and construct, fiction and fact, and thus to use uncertainty to obtain a more credible expression in tune with today's conception of truth and reality.

This movement has morphed into the recent trend of 'autotheory' in which theory and essayism are fused with autobiography, as in works by Karl Ove Knausgård, Chris Kraus and Maggie Nelson.[21] Although generally perceived as a new phenomenon, this contemporary blending of philosophy, criticism, theory and personal experience and narrative clearly invokes Reynolds's concept of 'autobiografiction' as well as the merging of the philosophical work and the essayistic with fictional or nonfictional life-narrative that is so characteristic of Modernist literature (for instance, Proust, Woolf, Musil, Kafka and Joyce). This testifies to the continued relevance of theory of uncertainty. In an era where new notions of truth and credibility are being challenged by genres and forms of 'post-truth', new dimensions of uncertainty of meaning and interpretation are coming into light. In this context it is becoming more critical to distinguish between productive forms of uncertainty in literature and other, more cynical forms and genres of uncertainty such as fake news.

The notion of uncertainty clearly has relevance beyond the field of literature and for the study of meaning and interpretation in a much broader sense. It has traction in other media, including visual arts, film and performance, and in other disciplines, such as philosophy, critical theory and cultural studies. Recognizing the significance of the notion of uncertainty in the field of literature specifically, the volume also points to the relevance of the notion in the study of meaning and interpretation in general. This volume on literary theories of uncertainty, then, represents one path in a critical exploration of a general theory of uncertainty.

Connections and tensions in theory of uncertainty

With New Criticism, uncertainty of meaning is brought to the fore of literary theory, and as the post-structuralist theories later engage with the role of uncertainty in the production of meaning, they enter into an already-established discussion. This theoretical relation is explicitly expressed in several of the post-structuralist theories. Hartman presents his hermeneutics of indeterminacy as being both in opposition to and based on New Criticism. He recognizes certain elements of New Criticism as valuable but rejects the primacy given to art over criticism.[22] De Man too presents his views on formal analysis as partly developed in extension from and partly in opposition to New Criticism, arguing that New Criticism reproduces the false metaphorical model that explains literature in terms of an inside/outside opposition which has long been governing criticism.[23] And Derrida also distances himself from New Criticism, though more implicitly so, as he denounces undecidability in the sense of 'lexical richness' and polysemy and argues for a radically extended notion of undecidability as a precondition for all language and discourse.[24]

Even though the post-structuralist theories of uncertainty do not in any unified manner present a clear and delimited definition of a concept of undecidability, they all to some extent contest the definition of meaning as determined by the text only and emphasize the role of the reader and critic in the production of meaning and thus in the very formation of literature. In this way they represent a dismissal of the delimited focus on textual (in a conventional, narrow sense) and poetic ambiguity that characterizes New Criticism and a radical widening as well as destabilization of the concept of meaning, since meaning is made to hinge on interpretation. And they reflect a shift in the view of the system of language as they emphasize the instability and incoherence in this system and its elements of arbitrariness. Their aim is, however, not simply to reveal the dysfunctions of the system and criticize the existent models of literary analysis that assume its coherence and decidability. They also show a strong interest in investigating and illustrating the effect of meaning production and readerly stimulation of the instability and undecidability in the literary system. And notably, the conception of uncertainty as the crucial point of meaning production and reader engagement in a literary text is maintained in the post-structuralist theories of uncertainty. As the notion of uncertainty as a meaning-productive device and a fundamental literary quality thus appears as a clear link between these two theoretical movements, it also becomes evident how the question of uncertainty runs through literary theory in the twentieth century as a central line, structuring the discussions about the meaning and nature of literature. While the notion of uncertainty itself is generally not granted thorough or focused attention in post-structuralist theories of uncertainty,[25] the notion of uncertainty functions as an indispensable element in the arguments.

The conflicts between the theoretical positions of twentieth-century theory of uncertainty arise not so much out of fundamentally contradictory conceptions of the nature of literature and interpretation; rather the tensions between New Criticism and post-structuralist theory, on the one hand, and between structuralism and post-structuralist theory, on the other, reflect a difference in focus and emphasis in the theorizations of literature and uncertainty. In fact, certain similarities and shared interests point to a co-implication of New Criticism and deconstruction and challenge the general assumption of their opposition and contradiction. The New Critical definition mainly determines ambiguity as a textual phenomenon, and the deconstructive definition of indeterminacy establishes this form of uncertainty primarily as an interpretive problem. As such, their definitions are not contradictory but rather oriented towards different areas of meaning. It is thus possible to view the two as part of the same conceptual movement and as marking a sequence of steps from a focus on text to a focus on interpretation in the production of meaning, as Timothy Bahti has showed.[26] Similarly, the view that theories of ambiguity in New Criticism focus on polysemy and plurisignation and that post-structuralism is, in contrast, generally interested in the impossibility of deciding on meaning in texts, and the resulting view that uncertainty in New Criticism is conceptualized in relation to the *presence* of meanings in texts and in post-structuralism in relation to the *absence* or impossibility of meaning, neglects a certain feature of post-structuralism. There is also in post-structuralist theory clear awareness of the potential production of meanings by uncertainty. The claim of the absence of certainty and decidability of meaning that is present in some form or other in the theories formulated by de Man, Hartman and Derrida is linked to a simultaneous assumption of the presence of several possible meanings in the literary text. The notion of uncertainty in this sense designates the impossibility of deciding *between* several potential meanings and thus does in fact entail a notion of plurisignation.

The main difference between New Criticism and the post-structuralist position is better explained as an epistemological one: New Criticism views plurisignation as actually manifested, realized and objectively present in the text, whereas the post-structuralist theories tend to view the multiple meanings of a text as present as a 'potential', the realization of which depends on the reading and interpretation of the text. The most obvious and significant divergence of the post-structuralist theories of uncertainty from New Criticism, then, is the radical extension of the notion of uncertainty of meaning as they use it not only to designate a fundamental feature of poetic language but of literature, literary criticism and discourse as such.

Another theoretical tension which is often misread as a contradiction is at play between the structuralist conceptualization of uncertainty as ambiguity, as represented, for instance, by Rimmon-Kenan's formalist-inspired approach in *The Concept of Ambiguity – the Example of James*,[27] and the post-structuralist concepts of uncertainty, for instance as represented by the concept of 'unreadability' in J. Hillis Miller's comment 'A Guest in the House', which is written as a direct critical response to Rimmon-Kenan's logics- and linguistics-based reading of James's 'The Figure in the Carpet'.[28] This is the tension between, on the one hand, the view of uncertainty as a deliberately applied literary device and, as such, a specific historical and context-dependent feature, and, on the other, uncertainty as a fundamental characteristic of and precondition for all literature. The main difference between Rimmon-Kenan's theory and the post-structuralist approaches is that while deconstruction typically makes claims about the area of uncertainty that concerns the fundamental nature of language and thus the fundamental uncertainty of all texts, Rimmon-Kenan looks at the forms of uncertainty that are deliberately and strategically employed by the author. Miller thus develops 'unreadability' as a form of uncertainty that is fundamental to literature; and Rimmon-Kenan is interested in the notion of ambiguity as an authorial strategy rather than as an inherent literary feature. Rimmon-Kenan's approach is, however, not incompatible with an awareness and acknowledgement of the inherent uncertainty and undecidability in language and literature. And although her focus is on a different area of meaning, her method is not contradictory of the deconstructive emphasis on the unresolvability of uncertainty of meaning in literature. Although Miller, arguably quite rightly, criticizes Rimmon-Kenan's approach for being reductive, simplifying and mistakenly trying to 'master' the interpretation of literature, thereby failing to recognize the fundamental unreadability of all literature, Rimmon-Kenan does in fact accept the possibility of sustained and unresolved uncertainty in literature. She thus writes that '[a]mbiguity exists in the in-between land of hesitation'[29] and that ambiguous works 'teach us the nearly impossible lesson of being capable of belief and doubt at the same time'.[30]

While the theories of uncertainty differ in their views and emphases, and there are tensions and disagreements both within and between the critical positions, they are all founded in the view that uncertainty of meaning is a fundamental trait and a constitutive element of literature, and that it is from the points and sites of uncertainty in a text that its most interesting meanings spring. As such, the post-structuralist theories clearly continue the theoretical line which began to take shape already in the nineteenth century and which was brought to the fore of literary criticism with New Criticism. To Iser, the production of meaning and thus the formation of literature happen through the reader's engagement with the text's points of undecidability; de Man, not unlike Cleanth Brooks, views the contradictions and undecidability between grammar and rhetoric as the defining feature of literature and proposes to 'equate the rhetorical, figural potentiality of language with literature itself';[31] Hartman makes his idea of an adequate critical approach hinge on the application of indeterminacy in the engagement with the literary work; and Derrida views undecidability as a precondition not only for literary expression but for language and all discursive expression. Similarly, the theories of Rimmon-Kennan and Miller clearly build on the existing theory of uncertainty and are explicitly positioned in relation to both New Criticism and post-structuralism, and they testify to the continuation of the line of theory of uncertainty into the late twentieth century.

On the volume

The present volume sheds light on uncertainty as an intrinsic literary aspect, a specific device in literature, a reading strategy and a prevalent notion in twentieth-century and contemporary literature and literary theory. Its content is characterized by a considerable degree of experimentation and inventiveness and by a theoretical and conceptual variation which will hopefully trigger in the reader a stimulating bewilderment. A certain diversity in perspectives and variety of approaches follow naturally from the topic of uncertainty of meaning and interpretation which itself entails obvious tensions and (seeming) paradoxes and contradictions. Uncertainty appears, consequently, as a highly complex and flexible notion in the volume, at once elusive and evident and of relevance and at play on several different levels and in different stages of the formation, communication and reception of the literary and the literary-theoretical text.

The volume is structured into three parts. In Part I on the 'Poststructural legacies of uncertainty', Patrick ffrench first looks at the notion of 'suspension', which he presents as a problematic strategy of uncertainty in deconstructive thought that draws its force and its sense from the phenomenological register and literary representations. He explains the double nature of suspension, describing it as a mode of uncertainty that oscillates between the decision and its other, and which is both the suspension of a decision and a decision to suspend. ffrench looks at the deployment of the motif of suspension and its effect in literary examples in which the phenomenological and corporeal aspects of suspension are foregrounded. Assembling a number of instances of suspension, he sheds light on the heretical phenomenology of Bataille and explores how existential states of contingency and improbability in Bataille's work translate themselves into tropes of physical suspension that entail a negative critique of groundedness, meaning and subjectivity. With Blanchot he shows how suspension as a mode of decisive undecidability pertains particularly acutely to the instance or event of death.

Norris, in the third chapter, revives the conception of poetry as a mode of critical discourse and, as such, not strictly distinct from the discourses of the disciplines of philosophy, history and science. With a series of poems or 'verse-essays', he foregrounds some of the central scientific ideas of uncertainty which became predominant with quantum theory in the early twentieth century, such as Heisenberg's Uncertainty Principle and Gödel's Incompleteness Theorems, which inspired Derrida's formulation of deconstruction. Undecidability functions both as a theme and as an operative formal strategy in Norris's exploration of the status of such ideas when they are transposed from a broadly scientific or logico-mathematical context to that of literature, the arts or humanities.

In Part II on uncertainty in the context of life-writing, Christopher Fynsk first looks at the profoundly indeterminate writing of Robert Antelme in a letter to Dionys Mascolo, written a little over a month after Mascolo had helped rescue him from Dachau, underscoring in his reading Antelme's strong ambivalence regarding the knowledge he relays in the letter concerning his experience in the camp and his return to the world. Juxtaposing Antelme's letter with Mascolo's commentary on the letter four decades later and a text by Blanchot, Fynsk in this chapter investigates uncertainty in the form of the infinite in the human relation to speech and the bounds of linguistic freedom in social usage and sheds light on the significant impact of Antelme on Mascolo and Blanchot.

In Chapter 5, Max Saunders uses examples from Proust's *À la recherche du temps perdu* – a work he defines as an autobiografiction – De Quincey's *Confessions of an English Opium Eater*, Ford's *The Good Soldier* and the *To-Day and To-Morrow* series of predictions from the 1920s and 1930s in his investigation of temporal uncertainty. Juxtaposing the retrospective narrative of autobiography and its hybrid forms with the prospective narrative of futurology, Saunders shows how these two apparently incommensurable forms of writing share a kind of temporal dislocation, relocation or 'time-shifting' which disturb the reader's sense of time and place and demonstrates how such converse temporal dislocations of both modes can be mutually illuminating.

Rejecting the notions of 'authorial intention' and 'implied author', Mieke Bal, in Chapter 6, nevertheless sets out to complicate the potential presence of authorship in a narrative. Juxtaposing two different instances of novelistic undecidability, namely Cervantes *Don Quixote* and her own video installation MADAME B, which explores the narrative uncertainty of Flaubert's novel, she develops a notion of the author as a ghostly presence that appears at the points or moments of undecidability in a text, not to determine or dictate what the text means, but as a presence and a spectral after-effect that make readers think beyond the obvious narrative plot. To the uncertainty of the author's ghost, Bal adds and sheds light on two other forms of uncertainty: between linguistic and visual imaginative thinking, and between showing and invoking trauma.

In the volume's Part III on uncertainties in contemporary literature, Bruce Robbins, in Chapter 7, investigates the uncertainty that results from the current sociopolitical circumstances in which our confidence in sovereignty and in the authority of the deciders of society has been shaken. He defines this as a contextual and relative undecidability, rather than a philosophical one, and he illuminates it through a discussion of the Nordic noir *The Keeper of Lost Causes* by bestselling Danish crime author Jussi Adler-Olsen. As Robbins shows, in this novel the essential task of the state of assigning responsibility for a murder has succumbed to a form of undecidability that is specific to the Scandinavian welfare society, and he derives from the analysis a specific and conspicuous kind of Scandinavian welfare undecidability.

In Chapter 8, Hannah Vinter sheds light on the inherent uncertainty of the collage form as she explores how the heterogeneity of Turkish-German author Emine Sevgi Özdamar's novel *Seltsame Sterne starren zur Erde* relates to the author's practice of creating theatre collages. Through an analysis of Özdamar's *Hamlet* collages – some of which are shown for the first time here – Vinter shows how the disruptive aesthetics and anti-authoritarian politics of the collages illuminate Özdamar's novel; and she sheds light on how Özdamar uses the material ambiguity of the collage form to challenge political ideologies and historical interpretations that impose fixed images of the world.

The volume ends with Nicholas Royle's dialogic Chapter 9, set out in two parts: one interrogative and one reflective. By means of the quintessential uncertain linguistic form of the question, and with reference to Padgett Powell's *The Interrogative Mood* (2009), Royle challenges the fundamental premise of the very anthology in which his text participates, sheds light on the irreducible uncertainty of metafiction and demonstrates the literary dimension of theoretical writing. Uncertainty is then explored in the form of the double, the undecidable and the double bind and as the single word 'twilight', in Royle's own novel *An English Guide to Birdwatching*, in the work of Hélène Cixous and as a figure in Derrida's reading of William Collins's 'Ode to Evening' and Thomas Gray's 'Elegy Written in a Country Churchyard'.

Divergent in their views on the nature of interpretation and uncertainty, the theories of and on uncertainty in this volume, as in the twentieth century generally, are nonetheless connected in that uncertainty plays a fundamental and indispensable role in their conception of the meaning of literature. Uncertainty is consistently presented as constitutive of meaning and as a defining feature of literature.

Notes

1   Moreover, literary theories of uncertainty tend to accentuate the unresolvedness of uncertainty and its effect of producing and nurturing meanings as particularly significant qualities, thereby evoking the notion of a distinct sustained and productive form of uncertainty. In my PhD dissertation *Undecidability and Uncertainty of Meaning and Interpretation in Twentieth-Century Literature and Literary Theory*, I investigate this specific form of uncertainty which I term 'undecidability' and distinguish from the notion of 'indeterminacy' – the latter designating an unlimited and unproductive form of uncertainty. The present introduction is in part based on and uses extracts from my thesis.

2   Geoffrey Hartman, *Criticism in the Wilderness: The Study of Literature Today* (New Haven: Yale University Press, 1980), 265.

3   'Letter to George and Tom Keats, 21 December 1817', in John Strachan (ed.), *The Poems of John Keats* (London and New York: Routledge, 2003).

4   I do not wish to conflate 'undecidability' with 'uncertainty', and in fact I view the two as distinct, but related. My distinction in this chapter is based on an understanding of undecidability as a specific form of uncertainty of meaning, as explained in note 1.

5   As Paul de Man remarks in 'Autobiography as De-Facement', 'the distinction between fiction and autobiography is not an either/or polarity but . . . is undecidable'. 'Autobiography as De-Facement', *Modern Language Notes*, 94, no. 5 (1979): 919–30, 926.

6   On the basis of this synthetization of modernism and life-writing, Saunders study challenges the description of Modernist literature as impersonal and redefines Modernism as a period that engaged with the auto-/biographical by reinventing it, rather than rejecting it. *Self Impression* (Oxford: Oxford University Press, 2013).

7   Various terms are used for this mode of representation in the study of narrative. In German it is usually referred to as 'erlebte Rede' and in French as 'style indirect libre', while 'free indirect discourse' is used in the *Handbook of Narratology*, where it is also described as 'the most problematic and, no doubt for that very reason, still the most widely discussed form for representing speech, thought, and perception'. Brian McHale, 'Speech Representation', in Peter Hühn, Wolf Schmid, Jörg Schönert and John Pier (eds), *Handbook of Narratologoy* (Berlin: Walter de Gruyter, 2009), 435.

8   And Kierkegaard arguably exercises a form of narrative deconstruction, undermining canonical works and conventional readings, for example as he rewrites the biblical story of Abraham in *Fear and Trembling* (published in 1843).

9   Indeed, literature played a seminal role for the formation of psychoanalysis – see, for instance, Meg Harris Williams and Margot Wadell's *The Chamber of Maiden*

Thought in which the authors explore the literary sources for the psychoanalytical ideas, starting with Shakespeare and including Romantic and nineteenth-century writers such as Blake, Wordsworth, Coleridge and George Eliot.

10 'Autobiografiction', in 'Speaker', new series, 15, no. 366 (6 October 1906): 28–30, 28.

11 On the cover of his novel *Fils* (Paris: Edition Galilée, 1977).

12 That is, to capture 'The Complexity, the Tantalization, the Shimmering, the Haze, That Life Is', *Joseph Conrad: A Personal Remembrance* [1924] (New York: Cambridge University Press, 2013), 191.

13 Ibid., 180.

14 Ibid., 182.

15 Cleanth Brooks, *The Well-Wrought Urn. Studies in the Structure of Poetry* (New York: Reynal and Hitchcock, 1947), 10.

16 Wolfgang Iser, 'Indeterminacy and the Reader's Response in Prose Fiction', in J. Hillis Miller (ed.), *Aspects of Narrative* (New York: Columbia University Press, 1971), 1–38, 43.

17 Derrida thus firmly rejects the notion of undecidability as an unlimited form meaning that has often been associated with deconstruction and presents undecidability as a restricted form of uncertainty, contrasting it to the notion of indeterminacy in order to refute the common accusation of deconstruction that it leads to relativism of meaning: 'I do not believe I have ever spoken of "indeterminacy", whether in regard to meaning or anything else. Undecidability is something else again . . . . I want to recall that undecidability is always a *determinate* oscillation between possibilities (for example, of meaning, but also of facts). These possibilities are themselves highly *determined* in strictly *defined* situations . . . . They are *pragmatically* determined. The analyses that I have devoted to undecidability concern just these determinations and these definitions, not at all some vague "indeterminacy". I say "undecidability" rather than "indeterminacy" because I am interested more in relations of force, in differences of force, in everything that allows, precisely, determinations in given situations to be stabilized through a decision of writing (in the broad sense I give to this word, which also includes political action and experience in general). There would be no indecision or *double bind* were it not between *determined* (semantic, ethical, political) poles, which are upon occasion terribly necessary and always irreplaceably singular. Which is to say that from the point of view of semantics, but also of ethics and politics, "deconstruction" should never lead either to relativism or to any sort of indeterminism'. *Limited Inc.* (Evanston, IL: Northwestern University Press, 1988), 148–9.

18 Hartman, *Criticism in the Wilderness*, 272.

19 'Literary Procedures and the Question of Indeterminacy', in Hazard Adams and Leroy Searle (eds), *Critical Theory Since 1965* (Tallahassee: Florida State University Press, 1986), 545–58, 545.

20 'Is There a Text in this Class?' in Hazard Adams and Leroy Searle (eds), *Critical Theory Since 1965* (Tallahassee: Florida State University Press, 1986), 525–35, 525.

21 'Auto-theory' was used by the writer and philosopher Paul B. Preciado to describe his book *Testo Junkie* (2008) and picked up by Maggie Nelson to designate the hybrid form of her work *The Argonauts* (2015) on the book jacket of the same work. Since then it has been used in literary journals and circulated in online literary criticism as a description of an emerging genre.

22 *Criticism in the Wilderness: The Study of Literature Today* (New Haven: Yale University Press, 1980), 180.

23 *Allegories of Reading. Figural Language in Rousseau, Nietzsche, Rilke, and Proust* (New Haven and London: Yale University Press, 1979).

24 *Dissemination*, trans. Barbara Johnson (London and New York: Continuum, 1981), 229.

25 Iser is an exception as his theory of 'gaps of indeterminacy' is developed directly from Ingarden's concept of 'sites of indeterminacy' ('Unbestimmtheitsstellen'). And as noted earlier, Derrida too insists on the importance of clear terminology as he establishes the distinction between undecidability and indeterminacy, although tellingly under pressure in the context of an interview where he is confronted with the accumulation of charges of nihilism made by critical readers against his theory of deconstruction.

26 'Ambiguity and Indeterminacy: The Juncture', *Comparative Literature*, 38, no. 3 (1986): 209–23, 210.

27 *The Concept of Ambiguity – The Example of James* (Chicago and London: University of Chicago Press, 1977).

28 'A Guest in the House: Reply to Shlomith Rimmon-Kenan's Reply', *Poetics Today*, 2, no. 1b (1980–1): 189–91.

29 *The Concept of Ambiguity*, 15.

30 Ibid., 16.

31 *Allegories of Reading*, 10.

Works cited

Altieri, Charles, 'Literary Procedures and the Question of Indeterminacy', in Hazard Adams and Leroy Searle (eds), *Critical Theory Since 1965*. Florida, TN: Florida State University Press, 1986, 545–58.

Bahti, Timothy, 'Ambiguity and Indeterminacy: The Juncture', *Comparative Literature*, 38, no. 3 (1986): 209–23.

Brooks, Cleanth, *The Well-Wrought Urn. Studies in the Structure of Poetry*. New York: Reynal and Hitchcock, 1947.

de Man, Paul, *Allegories of Reading. Figural Language in Rousseau, Nietzsche, Rilke, and Proust*. New Haven and London: Yale University Press, 1979.

de Man, Paul, 'Autobiography as De-Facement', *Modern Language Notes*, 94, no. 5 (1979): 919–30.

Derrida, Jacques, *Dissemination*, trans. Barbara Johnson. London and New York: Continuum, 1981.

Derrida, Jacques, *Limited Inc.* Evanston: Northwestern University Press, 1988.

Doubrovsky, Serge, *Fils*. Paris: Edition Galilée, 1977.

Fish, Stanley, 'Is There a Text in this Class?´ in Hazard Adams and Leroy Searle (eds), *Critical Theory Since 1965*. Florida, TN: Florida State University Press, 1986, 525–35.

Ford, Ford Madox, *Joseph Conrad. A Personal Remembrance* [1924]. New York: Cambridge University Press, 2013.

Hartman, Geoffrey, *Criticism in the Wilderness: The Study of Literature Today*. New Haven: Yale University Press, 1980.

Iser, Wolfgang, 'Indeterminacy and the Reader's Response in Prose Fiction', in J. Hillis Miller (ed.), *Aspects of Narrative*. New York: Columbia University Press, 1971, 1–38.

Keats, John, 'Letter to George and Tom Keats, 21 December 1817', in John Strachan (ed.), *The Poems of John Keats*. London and New York: Routledge, 2003.

McHale, Brian, 'Speech Representation', in Hühn, Peter Wolf Schmid, Jörg Schönert and John Pier (eds), *Handbook of Narratologoy*. Berlin: Walter de Gruyter, 2009, 434–46.

Miller, J. Hillis, 'A Guest in the House: Reply to Shlomith Rimmon-Kenan's Reply', *Poetics Today*, 2, no. 1b (1980–81): 189–91.

Reynolds, Stephen, 'Autobiografiction', *Speaker*, new series, 15, no. 366 (6 October 1906): 28–30.

Rimmon-Kenan, Shlomith, *The Concept of Ambiguity – The Example of James*. Chicago and London: University of Chicago Press, 1977.

Saunders, Max, *Self Impression*. Oxford: Oxford University Press, 2013.

Part I

Post-structuralist legacies of uncertainty

Suspended sentence

Experience of the undecidable

Patrick ffrench

In the 'Introduction' to *Parages* (1986), which assembles essays written on and around the work of Maurice Blanchot, Jacques Derrida invents the verb *to undecide* (*s'indécider*) as a qualification of the ways in which his writing shifts between performative and constative modes, between the 'event' of citation and the desire for something or someone to arrive or to come (*venir*): 'It regularly undecides itself between the event of the citation, in advance divisible and iterable, and the desire of it/her coming itself' (*Elle s'indécide regulièrement, entre l'événement de la citation, d'avance divisible et itérable, et le désir de la venue elle-même, avant toute citation*).[1] Critical writing, commentary, analysis here dislocate themselves from a secure relation to the work they critique, comment or analyse and play out in an uncertain space between the reiteration of what the text says, through citation, and an invocation to let the text come, to allow it to arrive or to go where it will. A writing that 'undecides itself' produces the undecidability of what it addresses and of its own mode of address. It starts from an 'experience of the undecideable', as Derrida makes clear in the sentence that follows: 'But the event – encounter, decision, call, appeal, nomination, initial incision of a mark – can come to pass (*advenir*) only from the experience of the undecidable, not the undecidable that is still of the order of calculation, but the other, the one that no calculation would know how to anticipate.'[2] The writing that 'undecides' begins from an experience of radical undecidability, outside a calculable or programmable causality.

The writing that undecides, moreover, also *suspends*, and the lexis of suspension is recurrent throughout what Derrida writes on or with or around Blanchot in *Parages*. Here again, however, we must distinguish between a decisive suspension, a suspension that 'merely' defers the event, the final and definitive arrival of the decision, and a more fundamental experience of suspension or of being suspended. Suspension, in this context, sits uneasily between decision and undecidability; to suspend (a judgement, a sentence) is a decision; what it suspends, defers; what it leaves hanging in the air, remains undecided; and as long as the suspension endures, it is undecidable. To suspend a judgement is to decide not (yet) to decide, yet for all that this suspension remains decisive. Such a suspension, however, comes afterwards – the decision has already been made; a *suspensive* writing, on the other hand, (re-) introduces undecidability and equivocation into language, starting from the experience of radical improbability, beyond calculation.

These observations may be self-evident to readers of deconstructive writing. It is perhaps less obvious to suggest that as with other conceptual personae in the arena of deconstructive criticism such as the trace, *espacement* and, to some extent, *différance*, the topos or figure of suspension draws its force and its sense from the phenomenological register; without appealing to any sense of origin or centrality in the realm of experience (yet can that *appeal* be so decisively warded off?), the figure draws on the gestural, physical instance of suspension, across its many variations. What I want to begin to explore here are the ways in which the deployment of the motif and effects of suspension, which I propose as a problematic strategy of undecidability in deconstructive thought, draw some of their force and impetus from literary instances in which the phenomenological and corporeal registers of suspension are foregrounded. It is an aspect of the specificity and rhetorical distinctiveness of deconstruction, as well as of its conceptual rigour, however, that its gestural thematics recurrently appeal to an *aberrant* phenomenology, to a phenomenology of the heterogeneous body or to what Georges Bataille proposed, in unpublished work of the 1930s, to call 'heterology'; it is not an orthodox phenomenology or conception of the body that is at work here.[3] What *is* at stake is a heretical phenomenology which departs quite radically or which takes or lifts off from the Cartesian grounding of phenomenological experience in the thinking subject as it works through Husserl and Merleau-Ponty or as it manifests itself, for example, in the latter's appeal to a Gestalt of the 'whole' figure of the body.[4] This is not, moreover, a merely ornamental, experimental or phantasmatic transgression of the normative phenomenology of the body, but one which hovers specifically over the limit of a phenomenology of the body as a living presence, that is, in one instance, over the threshold between life and death: suspension as a mode of decisive undecidability pertains acutely to the instance or event of death, as we will see with Blanchot. For Derrida, this threshold, its imminence and its relation to law and time will come into particular focus around the question of the death penalty and the death sentence, a matter of particular concern for Derrida in the seminar of 1999–2001 but also elsewhere and earlier in his work, and particularly around the work of Blanchot, whose *récit L'Arrêt de mort* provides the basis for a key text by Derrida from 1979, the essay 'Living On. Border Lines'.

In this chapter, I will assemble a number of instances of suspension: the suspension that lifts or defers a judgement or a sentence, and in its acute form a death sentence; the strange form of suspension that pertains to the corpse; and figures of physical modes of suspension. Different forms of decision and indecision relate to each instance, and it may be overambitious to aim to weave them together or to tabulate them, synthetically or systematically.

We may start somewhat abstractly, however. In the interview with Derek Attridge published as 'That Strange Institution called Literature', Derrida proposes, broadly speaking, that literature suspends, and that deconstruction has a 'suspensive' effect. In response to Attridge, Derrida says, 'The law of literature tends, in principle, to defy or lift the law'.[5] This is not, however, a straightforward question of a suspension of reference, with the effect that the text refers only to itself. 'These texts', Derrida writes, referring to texts which instigate a '*critical* experience of literature', are 'not only reflexive, specular or speculative, [nor do they simply] suspend reference to something else, as is so often suggested by stupid and uninformed rumour'.[6] What is suspended, rather, is the transcendent reading 'which means going beyond interest for the signifier, the form, the language (note that I do not say "text") in the direction of meaning or the referent (this is Sartre's rather simple but convenient definition of prose)'.[7] Derrida adds that

> it is not enough to suspend the transcendent reading to be dealing with literature, to read a text as a literary text. One can interest oneself in the functioning of language, in all sorts of structures of inscription, suspend not reference (that's impossible), but the thetic relation to meaning or referent, without for all that constituting the object as a literary object.[8]

There is an equivocation here: literature 'suspends', in the sense of pausing or arresting the tendency to read 'for' reference, transcendence, the thetic, but this suspension is 'not enough' to qualify the literary. The critical experience of literature is in this sense a suspension which also suspends or arrests, and hovers over its own nomination, its own categorization, its own qualification as a mode of suspension. *Literature suspends*, but this definitive proposition is itself also suspended.

Derrida continues, however: 'There is no literature without a *suspended* relation to meaning and reference. *Suspended* means *suspense*, but also dependence, condition, conditionality. In its suspended condition, literature can only exceed itself.'[9] Here Derrida brings out the double, split nature of suspension: it is both interruption, deferral, delay, arrest on the one hand, and, on the other hand, de-pendence, pendency, a condition of dependency. It is the conflation of these two senses of arrest and conditionality which is expressed in the notion and the gestural thematics of suspension. Derrida clarifies further:

> to pick up again the deliberately equivocal expression I just used, literature's *being-suspended* neutralizes the 'assumption' which it carries; it has this capacity, even if the consciousness of the writer, interpreter or reader (and everyone plays all these roles in some way) can never render this capacity completely effective and present. First of all, because this capacity is double, equivocal, contradictory, *hanging on* and *hanging between*, *dependent* and *independent*, an 'assumption' both assumed and suspended.[10]

What emerges clearly here is the importance of 'literature's *being-suspended*', and the dual sense here of de-pendence, *to be hanging from*, and in(ter)-dependence, *to hang between*. I want to underline this effect of hanging, of hanging from (conditionality), of hanging over (in the sense of having a sentence hanging over you, a suspended sentence), but in any case of not being on the ground, not being grounded, of being in some sense above the ground, in the air. This also links suspension to a 'lifting', which echoes the proposition that literature, in principle, 'lifts' the law, as noted earlier.

This lifting is also a suspension, a taking of something out of its place, an arresting. Later in the Attridge interview, Derrida considers the issue of the 'lifting' of repression: 'This lifting or simulacrum of a lifting of repression, a simulacrum which is never neutral and without efficacity, perhaps hangs on this being-suspended (hyphenated here, as before), this *épochè* of the thesis or the "metaphysical assumption" which we were talking about just now.'[11] He adds that the suspension 'produces a subtle and intense pleasure'.[12] To 'lift' repression, to suspend it, to suspend the law or the interdiction, which in this context is made equivalent to the suspension of the thesis, the transcendent idea and the underlying, inevitable 'metaphysical assumption', yields pleasure, a pleasure of transgression. If the pleasure of deconstruction, and the pleasure deconstruction procures from literature and from a certain mode of literature, 'is linked to this game which is played at the limit, to what is suspended at this limit', as Derrida writes, we can say that this transgression is suspensive; it is a transgression, a play at the limit, which suspends (rather than annulling or destroying).[13] It is thus conditional, *hanging on and hanging over*, provisional (in the sense that a suspension is not definitive), and yet at the same time aerial, ungrounded. There is a yield of pleasure in being ungrounded and in suspense, in *lifting off*.

The double sense of suspension – as an act of law, a decree, and as an arrest, a pause or delay – is at work in the text that Derrida writes on Blanchot's *récit Death Sentence* (*L'Arrêt de mort*), and it is indeed already also at work in this title, which is not only the death sentence (as it has been translated) but also the suspension of death, the arrest of death.[14] Derrida writes, in 'Living On: Border Lines', where the body of the text is *suspended over* the 'Journal de Bord', the place of the translator's footnote: 'In French an *arrêt* comes at the end of a trial, when the case has been argued and must be judged. The judgement that constitutes the *arrêt* closes the matter and renders a legal decision. It is a sentence. An *arrêt de mort* is a sentence that condemns someone to death.'[15] The arrest is both decision and suspension, in this case of that very decision, that sentence. Derrida will lead this towards a distinction, later in the text, between a *decisive* arrest and a *suspensive* arrest: 'this is the pulse of the "word" *arrêt*, the arrhythmic pulsation of its syntax in the expression *arrêt de mort*. *Arrêter*, in the sense of suspending, is suspending the *arrêt*, in the sense of decision. *Arrêter*, in the sense of deciding, arrests the *arrêt*, in the sense of decision.'[16] The French word *arrêt*, then, has this double sense of verdict and suspension, the one annulling the other, the decision suspended, the suspension decided. But this is surely not solely the effect of a *double entendre*; the duality is already inherent in suspension as such, between suspension as the performative application of a judgement (I hereby suspend you from this institution) and suspension as an equally performative deferral of the execution of a decisive judgement, the temporary or permanent lifting of the effect of a law (I hereby suspend this sentence, the one I have just pronounced). This is because suspension is always already in a situation of pendency, of de-pendence and in-dependence, or inter-de-pendence, a situation that inheres with any *movement*, any interval, *any step whatever*. The step, the *pas* (as we know from Blanchot already both step and not – *Le Pas au-delà* –) lifts off, potentially leaving a trace, and comes back down, excepting levitation.[17]

The fact that in this instance the suspension at stake, and the sentence at stake, pertains to death draws evidently on the strong sense, the affective intensity, that surrounds the question of suspension here. The strongest, most poignant and ethically charged sense of suspension is perhaps where it relates to death and in particular to the death penalty, where death and the law come to touch each other. A suspended sentence, in the sense of a prison sentence to which one would be condemned if one infringed or transgressed certain conditions, gives us the sense of a threat which is hanging over, which overhangs, a sword of Damocles. In a weak sense this might be construed 'merely' as a delay or deferral. However, in a strong sense the suspension of the sentence refers to the power of sovereignty to decide on the state of exception. It tells us something which Derrida, after Kant, and Benjamin, but also and perhaps especially, Schmitt, never tire of reiterating – that the law is nothing without force, and without the force of something which is outside it. In Schmitt's murderous essay *The Concept of the Political*, we are told that the conceptual pair of friend and enemy, on which the very concept of the political depends, and without which it is nothing, is also wedded to the 'ever present possibility' (thus a possibility in suspense) of 'physical killing'.[18] Heeding Agamben, for whom sovereign power is conceptually intimate with the bare life that can be legally killed, but not sacrificed, this tells us also that the ultimate recourse of the law is the power, the potential to put to death, to kill and to isolate and produce the 'zone of indistinction' in which the state of emergency can attain concrete permanence.[19] Derrida also develops and explores this point in *Force of Law*, an extended meditation on Walter Benjamin's essay 'Critique of Violence', and originally addressed to a conference on 'Deconstruction and the Possibility of Justice' at Cardozo Law School.[20] We can note that a suspended sentence in the final instance refers to the delay but also to the imminent threat of the sword, the guillotine, the electric shock or the injection, through which the force of the law is finally and forcefully delivered. These are some of the concerns which programme Derrida's seminar on the death penalty at the Ecole des Hautes Etudes en Sciences Sociales in Paris between December 1999 and March 2001. The lexis of suspension does not enter into play to a great extent here, *explicitly*, except in cases where Derrida is dealing with the *suspension*, not the abolition, of the death penalty in some states of the United States in the latter years of the twentieth century, until ostensibly more 'humane', and less 'cruel' modes of execution were found. The apparatus of suspension does, however, programme Derrida's concerns in this seminar, since in one instance he addresses the question of forgiveness, of the pardon (the topic of the seminar for the previous two years, and the logic of the sovereign exception to the law). He writes of Schmitt's *Political Theology*, for example:

> In these pages, which I recommend you read, Schmitt analyzes all those states of exception in which the state has the right, the right to give itself the right to suspend right and law. Schmitt speaks of an 'unlimited authority' that consists in the power to 'suspend the entire existing order'. [. . .] Schmitt uses several times a very strong expression that defines both the exception and sovereignty: law *suspends itself*, law has the right or grants the right to suspend itself (this is the structure of the right to pardon: law above the laws, right above rights). One

has to start from the possibility of this self-suspension, of this interruption of itself by the law, in order to understand both the law and its foundation in the principle of sovereignty.[21]

The law suspends itself by virtue of a 'law above the laws', a lifting up of the law's imposition.[22] Derrida's foregrounding of the potential for self-suspension of the law in Schmitt's *Political Theology* resonates with other contemporary engagements with political sovereignty, including his own seminars on *The Beast and the Sovereign* at the EHESS in 2001–3, following the seminars on the death penalty, in which Derrida reflects on the indiscernibility or undecidability between these two modes of exception to the law and the institution of the human – the beast and the sovereign. Similarly, for Giorgio Agamben, the state of exception is conditioned by an indiscernibility between sovereignty and bare life, the life that may be killed but not sacrificed. And this state of exception is a 'state of emergency' in which the law is suspended or suspends itself.

Across this no doubt too-rapid overview of the motif of the suspended threat of the law's violence, and the suspension of the law involved in the institution of the law itself, what seems apparent is that decisiveness and decision depend upon a prior decision to suspend decisiveness. 'Sovereign is he who decides upon the exception.'[23] Moreover, the acute edge of this decisiveness and of this decisive suspension, this *arrêt*, falls down in the last instance upon the question of life and death, the threshold of life and death. Derrida's engagement with Schmitt and Agamben's Schmittian account of the dynamics of sovereign power and bare-life-that-can-be-killed isolate the body as living or dead as the threshold at or on which suspension acts, on which it decides. Death, then, is perhaps the (a) paradigmatic instance of decision; it is on this threshold that we can return to the question of the phenomenological register of suspension.

We can begin, again, with the corpse, as a phenomenon. Seeking to establish the suspended status of the image, Blanchot introduces, in the essay 'Two Versions of the Imaginary', a troubling proximity between the image and the cadaver.[24] The instance or topos of death (again one must question whether it can be assigned to a place or a topos), Blanchot makes very clear, radically suspends and disturbs the foundational clarity of the opposition of presence and absence; the corpse is both here and not here:

> Something is there before us which is not really the living person, nor is it any reality at all. It is neither the same as the person who was alive, nor is it another person, nor is it anything else. What is there, with the absolute calm of something that has found its place, does not, however, succeed in being convincingly here. Death suspends the relation to place, even though the deceased rests heavily in

his spot as if on the only basis that remains him. To be precise, the basis lacks, the place is missing, the corpse is not in its place.[25]

For Blanchot, the corpse introduces a disturbance in presence, an undecidability, or in a weaker sense a blurring of categories. In particular, it suspends the relation to place (*la mort suspend la relation au lieu*); this proposition, which plays on the polysemy of *lieu*, both place and moment (as in the French verbal form *avoir lieu*, consecrated in Mallarmé's proposition 'Rien n'aura lieu que le lieu', but also manifest in the legal term for the dismissal of a case: *non-lieu*[26]), invites us to imagine, to read, a temporal suspension, a terminus – the body *was* in its place but *is* now no longer – *and* a spatial suspension, in which case one might ask what else suspension is other than a disturbance of the relation to place and to placedness. Nevertheless, Blanchot's supplementary clause 'even though the deceased rests heavily in his spot (*s'y appuie pesamment*) as if on the only basis (*base*) that remains him' appeals to the law of gravity, to the force which pushes groundwards. Paradoxically, the suspension of placedness that the corpse in a strange sense 'embodies' or at least instantiates is manifest in the fact that it 'rests heavily on its spot', both immobile and horizontal, grounded, not in the sense of originated and centralized, but rather in the sense of pressing heavily on the ground. Death suspends a relation to place, then, but this suspension takes the form of a heavy material pressure on that place. The corpse, although suspending place, both here and not here, is still very much *on* its place, if not *in* it. What is suspended, then, is habitation, belonging, identity, occupation, territory and the suspension of these factors permits, or releases perhaps, the pressure of the material, its weight.[27]

Further on, Blanchot will propose a fairly abrasive critique of the idealism of art: if the grand images of classical art have no other 'guarantee' than the corpse, one might conclude that the formal purity of the image bears a fundamental connection to the 'elemental strangeness' and to 'the formless weight of being, present in absence' (*l'informe lourdeur de l'être présent dans l'absence*).[28] Setting aside for the moment the deceptively familiar collocation of the being that is present in its absence (which the comma separating the two clauses in the translation perhaps misleadingly attributes to being as such, rather than to the corpse), we should hesitate over 'formless weight', not only because of its oxymoronic force, but also because it calls us back to the corpse resting heavily on its spot; this weight or heaviness (*lourdeur*) is without form, not perhaps in the sense of without substance or materiality (it is now all and even *only* matter, *elemental* strangeness), but without formal identity, aesthetic form or categorical form. This is close to the sense given by Bataille to the word *informe*, which Blanchot may or may not be deliberately referencing here: *informe* is a word whose task is to desublimate, to bring things down – in the concluding expressions of Bataille's short entry for 'Informe' to the 'Critical Dictionary' of the late 1920s/early 1930s journal *Documents*, Bataille writes:

> In fact, for academic men to be happy, the universe would have to take shape. All of philosophy has no other goal: it is a matter of giving a frock coat to what is, a mathematical frockcoat. On the other hand, affirming that the universe resembles nothing and is only formless amounts to saying that the universe is something like a spider or spit.[29]

If what the spider and spit have in common, in Bataille's performative metaphor for the universe, is that they are ground-riven figures, condemned to a certain horizontality (spit insofar as it is spat out), like the big toe of the foot which in another contribution to *Documents* has a force of seduction inversely proportionate to the aesthetic beauty of the face of the body it supports.[30] Blanchot's 'informe lourdeur' is anything but light and inconsequential (*lourdeur* also suggests a serious issue, a *grave* issue), but it nevertheless draws something of its force from the echo of Bataille's concept and, by association, from Bataille's evaluation of the corpse as an instance of excess and eroticism.

Gravity has a role to play here, then. For Bataille, in early texts gathered posthumously under the title 'Dossier on the Pineal Eye', the human in its normative form is an instance of dynamic compromise between horizontality and verticality.[31] In what Rodolphe Gasché has called Bataille's 'phantasmatic mythology', the cosmic movement of the planet resembles the wheels of a locomotive which combine a rotational movement and a horizontal movement (of pistons and of the train itself); vegetation, Bataille suggests, is propelled vertically upwards by heliotropic energy, while animals move horizontally; humans in their evolution from apes 'stand up', and are 'erect', but nevertheless repress this vertical ascension through the normally horizontal orientation of vision.[32] The pineal eye, a corporeal (and phantasmatic) figure for the scream and the orgasm, in which the head is thrown back, figures the irrational but all too human propensity towards verticality. Throughout his work but particularly in these early texts, Bataille is obsessed, compulsively, with this impetus towards verticality; a poetics of erection and eruption punctuates his prose (witness, for example, the focus on the 'upright posture' of the military in the analysis of fascism, or the critique of the 'Icarian' tendency of Surrealism).[33] Such verticality, however, seems significant only insofar as it is correlated with an equally powerful tendency (and an equally powerful compulsion in Bataille's thought) towards collapse, castration, with the ground as the surface onto which things are prone to fall; it is as if, to return to the implicit dualism in Blanchot's account of the corpse which is not in its place, for Bataille things move between idealist ascension – the human tendency towards flight and verticality – and the weight of materiality, the entropic force of gravity which propels all things towards the grave.

Despite superficial appearances to the contrary, there is continuity between these early concerns of Bataille with cosmic dynamics and his later interest in experiences of ecstatic excess, resumed under the global terms of *inner experience* or *sovereignty*. Sovereignty, not unlike the informe, involves a suspension of existing paradigms. In the 1943 essay *Inner Experience*, Bataille sets out to question or to contest any authority, to set out on a 'voyage to the end of the possible of man', which will suppose 'the negation of the authorities and existing values which limit the possible'.[34] He adds that 'By virtue of the fact that it is negation of other values, other authorities, experience, having a positive existence, becomes itself positive value and authority'.[35] But how, Bataille asks, can experience be an authority in itself? Without other authorities or aims, would inner experience 'from that moment seem empty to me, henceforth impossible, without justification?'[36] Here he reports a conversation with Blanchot in which the latter responded thus: 'experience is authority, but that authority expiates itself [*que l'autorité s'expie*]'.[37] While expiation is not directly suspension, the same reflexive ungrounding is nevertheless at stake; the impetus behind it is a rigorous negation of authority and value and a concomitant ungrounding and removal of solid points of reference and anchorage. Bataille's subject, to the extent that he retains that word, is not the independent thinking subject of post-Cartesian philosophy, not the purposeful agent of Sartrean existentialism, but one for whom the ground is lacking, who lives in a state of suspension in mobile and shifting experience. Nevertheless, there is a reflexive authority, a basis for decision: authority expiates itself; it runs out to nothing. It is this that Bataille calls sovereignty, affirming in the unpublished third volume of the later project *The Accursed Share*, on 'Sovereignty', that 'Sovereignty is NOTHING'.[38]

These existential states of absolute contingency and improbability translate themselves intermittently in Bataille's writing into tropes of physical suspension.

I will point to a number of examples, the first from a 1931 text titled 'Sacrifices', written to accompany drawings by André Masson, which begins as follows: 'Me, I exist, suspended in a realized void – suspended from my own dread'.[39] What Bataille intends here is the absolute contingency of his existence, perhaps falling, and yet not falling, since the fall is arrested; there is a hook, the hook of contingency which has placed him here, existing, suspended. Elsewhere, in an anecdote or thought experiment which appears in *Guilty* (1944), Bataille refers to the hook, the chance of a hook, which retains him in existence, suspended in the arc of a fall. He writes: 'On a roof I saw large, sturdy hooks (crochets) placed halfway up. Suppose someone falls from a rooftop . . . couldn't he maybe *catch hold* of one of those hooks with an arm or a leg? If I fell from a rooftop, I'd plummet to the ground. But if a hook was there, I'd come to a stop halfway down!'[40] The fall, both in the physical and in the moral sense, is critically suspended. This arrest, however, depends on pure chance – that a hook is there and that one can catch hold of it; this eventuality does not arise from a decision but remains improbable and unpredictable.

This perverse phenomenology is also evident in a crucial scene in Bataille's novel *The Blue of Noon* (*Le Bleu du ciel*), written in 1935 but not published until 1957, my second example. Already in the dense and programmatic preface to the novel, Bataille writes: 'To a greater or lesser extent, everyone *depends* on stories . . .' (Tout homme est *suspendu* aux récits . . .).[41] This is a striking formulation which draws out the issue of suspense, narrative suspense, but also goes further than this, I think, and merits connection with what Bataille says later in the same preface where he talks of those books which are written out of a sense of rage, which are read in a feverish, trance-like state and which the reader feels their authors were constrained to write. There is an element of suspense but also of suspension in the relations between author, text and reader; it is as if the text suspends the usual and normative communicative relation, on the one hand, interrupting orthodox communication but also opening it out, with an affective breach. But Bataille's language also connotes the sense that the texts to which he refers suspend or put *on hold* the socially sanctioned and consensual rules and laws, discursive and experiential, which fix individuals as discontinuous entities. The texts hold their authors and readers over an affective abyss, which is threatening insofar as it offers no ground. This is what I think Bataille means when he talks about being 'suspended' by, from, through narratives; such narratives operate as hooks, from which we are suspended, in the absolute contingency of what is. It is significant also that among those books, Bataille mentions, which he feels the authors have been 'constrained' to write, one finds Blanchot's *Death Sentence*, as if the seam or the line – *le fil*, the wire – of suspension is running through these texts outside the intentionality of their authors.[42]

The scene to which I referred earlier occurs towards the end of the novel, when Troppmann and his lover Dirty, short for Dorothea, are in Trier, the birthplace of Karl Marx. Having walked out of the town to a ploughed field next to an escarpment overhanging the cemetery, on the day of the dead, the couple have sex, half-immersed in the earth of the field, but start to slip down towards the edge of the overhang. Troppmann manages to grab hold of something to arrest their fall, but since the graves of the cemetery below are each adorned with a candle (thus the distinction between starry sky and flickering ground becomes undecidable), he has the impression, he says, of falling into the void of the sky:

> At one turning in the path, an empty space opened beneath us. Curiously, this empty space, at our feet, was no less infinite than a starry sky over our heads. Flickering in the wind, a multitude of little lights was filling the night with silent, indecipherable celebration. Those stars, those candles – were flaming by the hundred on the ground; ground where ranks of lighted graves were massed. We were fascinated by this chasm of funereal stars. [. . .] Leaving the path across ploughed earth, we took the lovers' dozen steps. We still had the graves beneath us. [. . .] We were stunned making love over a starry graveyard. Each of the lights proclaimed a skeleton in its grave, and they thus formed a wavering sky, as unsteady as the motions of our mingled bodies. [. . .] She uttered a terrible scream. I clenched my teeth as hard as I could. At that moment we started sliding down the sloping ground. Father down, the rock formed an overhang. If I hadn't stopped our slide with my foot, we would have fallen into the night, and I might have wondered if we weren't falling into the void of the sky.[43]

Troppmann and Dirty are suspended, overhanging, at a threshold. But this suspension, and the dynamic of Troppmann's hallucinatory image, goes further than this in seeming to suspend the law of gravity, the direction of the fall. It is this suspension of referential normativity which Bataille finds integral to literature, its capacity, he says elsewhere of seeing the sea in the sky (here citing Rimbaud), *la mer allée avec le soleil.*[44] It is why literature in certain instances is an ally in the journey to the ends of the possible broached in *Inner Experience.*[45] Troppmann and Dirty do not fall, however, upwards or downwards; they are *on the edge*, *on the precipice*, and this state of suspension is the limit around which much of Bataille's thought revolves. The suspension takes places at or on the threshold, without tipping into the ether, or the other, without taking off for transcendence and without plummeting like Icarus. The subversive gestuality that runs across and through Bataille's writing is a suspension and an interruption of dialectical transformation, a suspension or interruption of the (grounding) idea of the subject and its subsequent alteration, without it having been decided what the result of that alteration might be.

This mood or mode of negative equivocation – neither one thing nor the other – is sustained across the novel, in the narrator Henri Troppmann's relations with the three female protagonists of the novel: Dirty, Lazare and Xénie, each of whom appears themselves ambivalently divided between sublimity and abjection. But it is also there in a looser sense in recurrent spatial images of in-betweenness, such as Troppmann's position on the beach at Barcelona, half immersed in the sea and somehow aware of his stance in relation to the surface of the earth:

> When I stood up, the water came to my stomach. I saw my legs, yellowish in the water, my two feet in the sand, and, out of the water, my torso, arms, and head. I felt an ironic curiosity in seeing myself – in seeing what this thing was [*de voir ce que c'était*] on the surface of the earth or sea [*à la surface de la terre (ou de la mer)*], this nearly naked character who was waiting for a plane to emerge several hours later from the depths of the sky.[46]

More crucially, perhaps, this troubling equivocation is also present in Troppmann's fascination, at the end of the novel, with the spectacle of a Nazi youth parade in Frankfurt, a vision he describes as obscene, and yet this 'rising tide of murder' is 'more incisive than life'. The novel ends in a mood of 'black irony' (*ironie noire*) provoked by this incisive or decisive commitment to catastrophe.

To return to the image of Troppmann and Dirty sliding down the slope above the precipice, but caught, hooked, at its edge, it is clear that this carefully constructed image has the effect, through its 'anti-phenomenological' postulation of a 'fall upwards', of underlining the contingency of upright posture, feet on the ground, of the ground as a stable foundation for the human foot and what it supports.[47] Nevertheless, there is a *hook*; Troppmann stops their slide with his foot; if he hadn't, they would have fallen. Bataille writes between this foundationless 'fall', and the 'hook' which stops the slide or the fall. In contrast to the (absent) ground and the foundation, the hook 'just happens to be there'; thus, Bataille hangs human existence and experience on a contingency, on the necessity of chance. Terrestrial supportedness, or having ones' feet on the ground, is recurrently relativized and dislocated as the basis not only of subjective certainty, but of morality and politics.[48] Bataille's critiques, in other areas of his work, of anthropomorphism and of restricted economies, have their starting point in a troublingly embodied consciousness of the contingency of terrestrial grounding, and the imminent sensation of a fall, whether upwards or downwards, provoked not only by the extreme lucidity of a sovereignty without content, but also by the contingency of *the hook*, of the *récit*, by which we are suspended, as in the opening proposition: '*Tout homme est suspendu aux récits.*'

To fall into the sky, to fall upwards, is evidently an anomaly in relation to the entropic tendency towards collapse that scans Bataille's work, and in relation to the law of gravity which is salient in the 'formless weight' of Blanchot's evocation of the materiality of the corpse. It installs an undecidability or a radical improbability through its phantasmatic vision of groundlessness. Nevertheless, there is a hook, which suspends Bataille's couple over the flickering graveyard, on the Day of the Dead. The hook of Troppmann's foot is the 'thetic' moment of arrest; the *arrêt* of Bataille's expression: 'if I hadn't stopped our slide with my foot' (*si je n'avais, d'un coup de pied, arrêté ce glissement*). The *arrêt*, both arrest and decree, is the contingent and improbable hook (not a base or a basis) from which reflection and decision become possible. The circumstance staged in *Blue of Noon* is both a decisive and a suspensive arrest; the hook interrupts an extreme situation of gravitational undecidability (upwards and downwards are made equivalent), but this decisive and suspensive arrest is radically improbable; chance decides – the event can only occur through the experience of the undecidable.

Notes

1 Jacques Derrida, 'Introduction', in John P. Leavey (trans.), *Parages* (Stanford: Stanford University Press, 2010), 6. Original French in *Parages* (Paris: Galilée, 1986), 15.

2 Ibid.

3 See Georges Bataille, 'Dossier hétérologie', in *Œuvres completes II* (Paris: Gallimard, 1970). Elements of this dossier of unpublished work, as well as critical articles upon it, are assembled in a special issue of *Theory, Culture, Society*, 35: 4–5 (July–September 2018).

4 See especially Maurice Merleau-Ponty, *The Structure of Behaviour*, trans. Alden Fisher (Pittsburgh: Duquesne University Press, 1983).

5 '"This Strange Institution Called LITERATURE": An Interview with Jacques Derrida', in *Acts of Literature* (London and New York: Routledge, 1992), 36.

6 Ibid., 41.

7 Ibid., 44.

8 Ibid., 45.

9 Ibid., 48.

10 Ibid., 49.

11 Ibid., 56.

12 Ibid.

13 Ibid.

14 The 'theme' (I hesitate over this qualification as it suggests that what is at stake is interior or secondary to the narrative itself, whereas – as suggested earlier – the radical undecidability or contingency from whence it arises is the very experience from which the narrative arises and which it allows) of the death sentence and of the suspension of the sentence is also powerfully 'present' (further hesitation) in Blanchot's text *L'Instant de ma mort* and in the text by Derrida which takes it as its starting point, *Demeure*. See the double volume which assembles these texts, translated by Elizabeth Rottenberg (Stanford: Stanford University Press, 2000).

15 Jacques Derrida, 'Living On (Borderlines)', trans. James Hulbert, in Harold Bloom (ed.), *Deconstruction and Criticism* (London: Routledge, 1979), 110.

16 Ibid., 114–15.

17 See Maurice Blanchot, *Le Pas au-delà* (Paris: Gallimard, 1973) translated as *The Step Not Beyond* (Albany: SUNY Press, 1992). See also Derrida's extended meditation on this and other texts by Blanchot in the essay 'Pas' in *Parages*, translated by John P. Leavey as 'Pace (Nots)' in *Parages*. The thematics of suspension and of the decision are also powerfully present throughout this work.

18 Carl Schmitt, *The Concept of the Political*, trans. George Schwab (Chicago: Chicago University Press, 2007), 32–3.

19 See Giorgio Agamben, *Homo Sacer: Sovereign Power and Bare Life*, trans. Daniel Heller-Roazen (Stanford: Stanford University Press, 1998).

20 See Jacques Derrida, 'Force of Law: The "Mystical Foundation of Authority"', trans. Mary Quaintance in Drucilla Cornell, Michel Rosenfeld and David Carlson (eds.), *Deconstruction and the Possibility of Justice* (London: Routledge, 1992).

21 Jacques Derrida, *The Death Penalty: Volume 1*, trans. Peggy Kamuf (Chicago: University of Chicago Press, 2014), 85.

22 See also Jacques Derrida, *The Beast and the Sovereign: Volume 1*, trans. Geoff Bennington (Chicago: Chicago University Press, 2011), in which Derrida discusses at length the suspension of the law inherent in the sovereign institution of law.

23 Carl Schmitt, *Political Theology: Four Chapters on the Concept of Sovereignty*, trans. George Schwab (Chicago: Chicago University Press, 2005), 5.

24 Maurice Blanchot, 'Two Versions of the Imaginary', trans. Ann Smock in *The Space of Literature* (Lincoln and London: University of Nebraska Press, 1982). For the French version, see 'Les deux versions de l'imaginaire', in *L'Espace littéraire* (Paris: Gallimard, 1955).

25 Ibid., 256.

26 The expression is drawn from Mallarmé's text 'Un coup de dès n'abolira jamais le hasard' (1897).

27 Jean-Luc Nancy, in the essay 'The Weight of a Thought', meditates on a semantic web he weaves around thought, weight and gravity. See Jean-Luc Nancy, *The Gravity of Thought* (Atlantic Highlands, NJ: Humanities Press, 1997).

28 Blanchot, 'Two Versions', 258.

29 Georges Bataille, 'Formless', in Allan Stoekl (trans. and ed.) with Carl R. Lovitt and Donald M. Leslie, *Visions of Excess: Selected Writings 1927-1939* (Minneapolis: University of Minnesota Press, 1986), 31.

30 See 'The Big Toe', in *Visions of Excess*, 20–3.

31 Georges Bataille, 'The Jesuve' and 'The Pineal Eye', in *Visions of Excess*. For the fuller French versions, see *Œuvres complètes II*.

32 Rodolphe Gasché, *Georges Bataille: Phenomenology and Phantasmology*, trans. Roland Végsö (Stanford: Stanford University Press, 2012).

33 See 'The Psychological Structure of Fascism' and 'The "Old Mole" and the prefix *sur* in the Words *Surhomme* and *Surrealist*', in *Visions of Excess*.

34 Georges Bataille, *Inner Experience*, trans. Leslie-Ann Boldt (Albany: SUNY Press, 1988), 7.

35 Ibid.

36 Ibid.

37 Ibid.

38 Georges Bataille, *The Accursed Share Volumes II & III* (New York: Zone Books, 1991), 256.

39 Georges Bataille, 'Sacrifices', in *Visions of Excess*, 130.

40 See Georges Bataille, *Guilty*, trans. Stuart Kendall (New York: SUNY Press, 2011), 74.

41 Georges Bataille, *Blue of Noon*, trans. Harry Mathews (London: Penguin, 2001), 105. French version in *Romans et récits* (Paris: Gallimard, 2004), 112.

42 Ibid.

43 Ibid., 99.

44 See Georges Bataille, 'Introduction', in Mary Dalwood (trans.), *Eroticism* (London: Marion Boyars, 1987), 25.

45 The gravitational suspension Bataille stages here resonates with a later moment in critical theory – in the work of Paul Virilio, whose focus on technologically induced speed and acceleration also suggests limits at which the fall can be upward, speed-overcoming gravity. See Paul Virilio, *Open Sky*, trans. Julie Rose (London: Verso, 1997), 68.

46 Bataille, *The Blue of Noon*, 82.

47 For an extensive account of Bataille's version of the 'fall', see Laurent Jenny, *L'Expérience de la chute: de Montaigne à Michaux* (Paris: Presses Universitaires de France, 1987).

48 See my essay 'Bataille's Nature: On (Not) Having One's Feet on the Ground', in Will Stronge (ed.), *Georges Bataille and Contemporary Thought* (London: Bloomsbury, 2017).

Works cited

Agamben, Giorgio, *Homo Sacer: Sovereign Power and Bare Life*, trans. Daniel Heller-Roazen. Stanford: Stanford University Press, 1998.

Bataille, Georges, 'Dossier hétérologie', in *Œuvres completes II*. Paris: Gallimard, 1970, 165–202.

Bataille, Georges, 'Formless', in Allan Stoekl (ed. and trans.), with Carl R. Lovitt and Donald M. Leslie, *Visions of Excess: Selected Writings 1927–1939*. Minneapolis: University of Minnesota Press, 1986, 31.

Bataille, Georges, 'Sacrifices', in Allan Stoekl (ed. and trans.), with Carl R. Lovitt and Donald M. Leslie, *Visions of Excess: Selected Writings 1927–1939*. Minneapolis: University of Minnesota Press, 1986, 130–6.

Bataille, Georges, 'The Big Toe', in Allan Stoekl (ed. and trans.), with Carl R. Lovitt and Donald M. Leslie, *Visions of Excess: Selected Writings 1927–1939*. Minneapolis: University of Minnesota Press, 1986, 20–3.

Bataille, Georges, 'The Jesuve', in Allan Stoekl (ed. and trans.), with Carl R. Lovitt and Donald M. Leslie, *Visions of Excess: Selected Writings 1927–1939*. Minneapolis: University of Minnesota Press, 1986, 73–8,

Bataille, Georges, 'The Pineal Eye', in Allan Stoekl (ed. and trans.), with Carl R. Lovitt and Donald M. Leslie, *Visions of Excess: Selected Writings 1927–1939*. Minneapolis: University of Minnesota Press, 1986, 79–90.

Bataille, Georges, 'The Psychological Structure of Fascism', Allan Stoekl (ed. and trans.), with Carl R. Lovitt and Donald M. Leslie, *Visions of Excess*: *Selected Writings 1927–1939*. Minneapolis: University of Minnesota Press, 1986, 137–60.

Bataille, Georges, 'The "Old Mole" and the Prefix *sur* in the Words *Surhomme* and *Surrealist*', in Allan Stoekl (ed. and trans.), with Carl R. Lovitt and Donald M. Leslie, *Visions of Excess: Selected Writings 1927–1939*. Minneapolis: University of Minnesota Press, 1986, 32–44.

Bataille, Georges, *Eroticism*, trans. Mary Dalwood. London: Marion Boyars, 1987.

Bataille, Georges, *Inner Experience*, trans. Leslie-Ann Boldt. Albany, SUNY Press, 1988.

Bataille, Georges, *The Accursed Share Volumes II & III*. New York: Zone Books, 1991.

Bataille, Georges, *Blue of Noon*, trans. Harry Mathews. London: Penguin, 2001.

Bataille, Georges, *Romans et récits*. Paris: Gallimard, 2004.

Bataille, Georges, *Guilty*, trans. Stuart Kendall. New York: SUNY Press, 2011.

'Bataille and Heterology', *Theory, Culture, Society*, 35 (July–September 2018): 4–5.

Blanchot, Maurice, 'Les deux versions de l'imaginaire', in *L'Espace littéraire*. Paris: Gallimard, 1955, 345–59.

Blanchot, Maurice, 'Two Versions of the Imaginary', trans. Ann Smock in *The Space of Literature*. Lincoln and London: University of Nebraska Press, 1982, 254–63.

Blanchot, Maurice, *The Step Not Beyond*. Albany, SUNY Press, 1992.

Blanchot, Maurice, and Jacques Derrida, *The Instant of My Death/Demeure*, trans. Elizabeth Rottenberg. Stanford: Stanford University Press, 2000.

Derrida, Jacques, 'Living On (Borderlines)', trans. James Hulbert, in Harold Bloom (ed.), *Deconstruction and Criticism*. London: Routledge, 1979, 75–176.

Derrida, Jacques, 'Introduction', in *Parages*. Paris: Galilée, 1986, 9–17.

Derrida, Jacques, 'Pas', in *Parages*. Paris: Galilée, 1986, 21–116.

Derrida, Jacques, 'Force of Law: The "Mystical Foundation of Authority"', trans. Mary Quaintance in Drucilla Cornell, Michel Rosenfeld and David Carlson (eds.), *Deconstruction and the Possibility of Justice*. London: Routledge, 1992, 3–67.

Derrida, Jacques, '"This Strange Institution called Literature": An Interview with Jacques Derrida', in *Acts of Literature*. London and New York: Routledge, 1992, 33–75.

Derrida, Jacques, 'Introduction', in John P. Leavey (trans.), *Parages*. Stanford: Stanford University Press, 2010, 1–8.

Derrida, Jacques, 'Pace (Nots)', trans. John. P Leavey, in *Parages*. Stanford: Stanford University Press, 2010, 11–102.

Derrida, Jacques, *The Beast and the Sovereign: Volume 1*, trans. Geoff Bennington. Chicago: Chicago University Press, 2011.

Derrida, Jacques, *The Death Penalty: Volume 1*, trans. Peggy Kamuf. Chicago: University of Chicago Press, 2014.

ffrench, Patrick, 'Bataille's Nature: On (Not) Having One's Feet on the Ground', in Will Stronge (ed.), *Georges Bataille and Contemporary Thought*. London: Bloomsbury, 2017, 33–50.

Gasché, Rodolphe, *Georges Bataille: Phenomenology and Phantasmology*, trans. Roland Végsö. Stanford: Stanford University Press, 2012.

Jenny, Laurent, *L'Expérience de la chute: de Montaigne à Michaux*. Paris: Presses Universitaires de France, 1987.

Merleau-Ponty, Maurice, *The Structure of Behaviour*, trans. Alden Fisher. Pittsburgh: Duquesne University Press, 1983.

Nancy, Jean-Luc, 'The Weight of Thought', in *The Gravity of Thought*. Atlantic Highlands, NJ: Humanities Press, 1997, 75–84.

Schmitt, Carl, *Political Theology: Four Chapters on the Concept of Sovereignty*, trans. George Schwab. Chicago: Chicago University Press, 2005.

Schmitt, Carl, *The Concept of the Political*, trans. George Schwab. Chicago: Chicago University Press, 2007, 32–3.

Virilio, Paul, *Open Sky*, trans. Julie Rose. London: Verso, 1997.

3

Poetry, formalism and undecidability
Some verse explorations
Christopher Norris

Introduction

These poems – perhaps better called verse-essays – are part of a much larger project that I have been pursuing over the past ten years.[1] The project is unusual in literary terms since it seeks to revive a generic conception that has been distinctly marginalized in the wake of movements like Romanticism and Modernism.[2] This is the idea of poetry as a mode of discourse continuous with – rather than existing quite separately from – the discourses of subject areas or disciplines like history, philosophy, politics or science. Whereas poets during the 'long' eighteenth century found it perfectly appropriate to discuss such matters, poets and critics from the early nineteenth century on have tended to think it an intrusion into poetry's sealed-off domain by extraneous interests and concerns.

That belief goes along with a raft of other precepts, such as poetry's non-propositional character, its emotive or attitudinal rather than cognitive content, its belonging to a realm of inwrought paradoxical meanings without assignable truth-values and its offering 'pseudo-statements' to meet our existential needs in place of science's knowledge-productive though soulless hypotheses.[3] It is also reflected in, and partly responsible for, the predominance of lyric in present-day poetic practice, a feature that again has a proximate source in German and English Romanticism.[4] At its most extreme, this produces an intensely subjective, self-preoccupied focus on mind-states maximally remote from any wider currency of thought or debate. My own verse-essays, taking a lead from the poet-critic William Empson, work on precisely the contrary set of precepts. That is, they propose that poems can and should engage with issues beyond those sacrosanct 'words on the page'; that such issues include the truth (or otherwise) of poetic statements, however complex, qualified or oblique; that the physical sciences and philosophy do indeed fall very much within its remit; and that poetry may therefore have creative-exploratory potential when it concerns itself with unresolved questions in philosophy of science.[5]

Here the main topics are uncertainty and undecidability (a distinction worth noting!) as they affect quantum physics, mathematics and logic. These are poems in the formal, that is, rhymed and metrical mode that in various ways foreground, instance or thematize the issues involved. My aim is to specify – or at any rate get clearer about – the character of such debates when transposed from a broadly scientific or logico-mathematical context to that of literature, the arts or humanities. Should 'uncertainty' then best be thought of as a theme, a concept, a suggestive analogy, a metaphor or simply a substitute for more familiar literary notions like ambiguity, paradox or aporia? Central here is Jacques Derrida's frequent yet just as frequently ignored insistence that deconstruction, properly so-called, has to do with undecidability as concerns the logical syntax and not (or not primarily) the over/under-determined semantics of texts.[6] This is the relevance of Gödel's Theorem in those few but crucially load-bearing passages where it is invoked by way of more-than-analogical support for Derrida's deconstructive readings.

On the other hand, there are clearly legitimate, non-abusive extrapolations from the *topos* of undecidability that don't purport to meet any such rigorous logico-mathematical standard and which instead earn their keep by various, more or less complex analogical ways around. It is in the latter – decidedly not the former – context that my poems seek to show how such a claim might (or of course might not!) work out. Undecidability functions here both as a theme and as an operative strategy involving elements – such as rhyme and metre – that exhibit a constant interplay of chance and necessity, freedom and constraint, creativity and certain structural limits on invention. Those antinomies have been foregrounded in Derrida's writing from the outset and have large implications for the topic of this volume, as likewise for the claim that formal verse may act as an intermediary discourse or point of conceptual linkage/leverage between science, philosophy and literature. Of course, the terms 'formal' and 'formalism' have very different senses and applications in logic, mathematics and the formal sciences on the one hand and poetry, fiction and literary theory on the other hand. Nevertheless, I am proposing that one thing they share is the metalinguistic capacity to explore the kinds of paradox, Derridean aporia or performative contradiction that arise at the limits of classical thought. I should add that the Gödel limerick sequence makes no such elevated claim but is there as a light-touch interlude in what has to count, by contemporary lights, as some pretty demanding poetic fare.

I won't go into detail on more specific matters of form, style and genre except to say – a bit of fighting talk here! – that free-verse practitioners and their critical cheerleaders get it badly wrong when they suppose rhyme and metre to act as inhibitors of creativity or blocks to verbal inventiveness. Rhyme has come in for some particularly tin-eared and obtuse polemics from commentators in the contemporary mainstream who adopt this line. On the contrary, when put to creative-exploratory use, as intended here, it can push language and thought into regions of semantic-intellectual discovery beyond anything likely to transpire in the course of (say) an academic article or book-chapter where word choice and argumentative drift are more thoroughly worked out in advance. Insofar as 'free verse' lives up to its own prescription – when the term becomes oxymoronic since the result would not be 'verse' at all – it suffers from the same prosaic restriction of following preconceived thought patterns and thus being non-responsive to language in all its manifold affordances of sound and sense. One advantage of formal poetry for my purposes is that it allows verse-music to coexist on equal and intimate terms with complexities of thought and intellectual content. This interaction, with rhyme as a principal driver, may enable poetry to achieve insights not only into its own workings or those of language more generally but also into topics – like uncertainty and undecidability – that lend themselves to treatment in a performative (verse-poetic) rather than a purely constative (prosaic-discursive) mode.

Hence, for instance, my choice of the extended villanelle with its three-line stanzas and alternating double refrain as a verse-form that challenges the rhymester to avoid any effect of redundancy by constant shifts of perspective, implication or qualifying tone. The headnotes and epigraphs that preface each poem are there as a courtesy to readers who might not have come across the relevant sources while also giving them something to hold on to while the prosody and verse-music do their work. I suppose they can be thought of as undecidably integral and/or non-integral to the poem, that is, conceived – like Derrida's aporetic key terms 'supplement', 'pharmakon', 'parergon' and so forth – as shuttling endlessly back and forth between those destabilized poles.[7] Thus, when he shows how Kant is unable to make good his claims about the non-intrinsic status of the parergon – whether the 'literal' frame around a painting or the role of framing/distinguishing concepts in the discourse of aesthetics – we can read his demonstration as applying likewise to the supposed categorical distinction between poems and their parergonal ('extraneous') outworks such as epigraphs and headnotes. Moreover, it is at the level of syntax or logical grammar, not that of semantics, that those key terms turn out to generate chains of deviant, non-bivalent, paraconsistent or (in Derrida's idiom) 'supplementary' reasoning.

The same applies to these poems with their often fairly complex syntactic structures, their frequent use of enjambment and their programmatic eschewal of anything like the high-Modernist stress on image, metaphor and symbol over other, inherently more sociable since down-to-earth tropes such as metonymy and allegory. Indeed, they could be read as so many attempts to seize back resources which poetry has lately seemed keen to renounce, chief among them rhyme, metre and syntax in its more logically probing or speculative uses.

Six villanelles on quantum themes

Ultraviolet

The amount of radiation emitted in a given frequency range should be proportional to the number of modes in that range. The best of classical physics suggested that all modes had an equal chance of being produced, and that the number of modes went up proportionally to the square of the frequency. But the predicted continual increase in radiated energy with frequency (dubbed the 'ultraviolet catastrophe') did not happen. Nature knew better.

Hyperphysics

Things can't go on like this, you must agree.
Unless the scale proves discrete it's a case
Of ultraviolet catastrophe.

Good news: the black box comes with guarantee
That things change stepwise, limits stay in place.
We can't go on like this, you must agree.

It's quantum physics that provides the key;
Discreteness rules so we'll not have to face
Some ultraviolet catastrophe.

Start infra-red, shift wavelengths, then we'll see
Just how we fare as things heat up apace:
They can't go on like this, you must agree.

Discrete or not, discretion bids that we
Grow warmer step by step lest it take place,
That ultraviolet catastrophe.

That's why, despite Planck's limit-point decree,
The comfort's one we're hard-put to embrace.
Things can't go on like this, you must agree;
Fear ultraviolet catastrophe!

The Copenhagen view

Bohr: 'Heisenberg, I have to say – if people are to be measured strictly in terms of observable quantities . . . '

Heisenberg: 'Then we should need a strange new quantum ethics.'

Bohr: You've never been able to understand the suggestiveness of paradox and contradiction. That's your problem. You live and breathe paradox and contradiction, but you can no more see the beauty of them than the fish can see the beauty of the water.

Michael Frayn, *Copenhagen*

The Copenhagen view: take both on board,
Wave/particle; let contradiction thrive!
It's logic's either/or we can't afford.

Both/and brings hope of harmony restored
So our twin paradigms may co-survive.
The Copenhagen view: take both on board.

Let those logicians henceforth be ignored
When for strict bivalence they vainly strive:
It's logic's either/or we can't afford.

Else their demand would have us lovers floored,
Along with half the physicists alive!
The Copenhagen view: take both on board.

So long as all appearances accord
With our best theory, give it a high five!
It's logic's either/or we can't afford.

Why emulate those realists who deplored
Our line till their pet theories took a dive?
The Copenhagen view: take both on board.

Then logic's apt to seem a mouse that roared
And pipe down once anomalies arrive.
It's logic's either/or we can't afford.

Yet still they tell us 'truth's its own reward'
And say it's with unreason we connive.
The Copenhagen view: take both on board.

Could be it's why their case strikes such a chord
With us who'd some good middle way contrive.
It's logic's either/or we can't afford

To recognise, but there's a touch of fraud
About the consolations we derive.
The Copenhagen view: take both on board.

Let's face it, these are cat-box thoughts we've shored
Against truth's quantum-state-reducing drive.
It's logic's either/or we can't afford.
The Copenhagen view: take both on board.

Hidden variables

Theoretical physicists live in a classical world, looking out into a quantum-mechanical world. The latter we describe only subjectively, in terms of procedures and results in our classical domain.

It can be argued that in trying to see behind the formal predictions of quantum theory we are just making trouble for ourselves. Was not precisely this the lesson that had to be learned before quantum mechanics could be constructed, that it is futile to try to see behind the observed phenomena.

J.S. Bell, *Speakable and Unspeakable in Quantum Mechanics*

'No hidden variables', the rule-book goes.
They'd take the weirdness out and set things straight.
Why the equations work nobody knows.

No in-the-source spin-values to disclose:
They'd fix beforehand every change of state.
'No hidden variables', the rule-book goes.

Those realist-friendly theories fail to pose
Such questions as our mystic times dictate.
Why the equations work nobody knows.

New-agers jump at anything that throws
A spanner in the works; at any rate
'No hidden variables', the rule-book goes.

It's any realist questioning of those
Remote entangled particles they hate.
Why the equations work nobody knows.

Again, the fear's not hard to diagnose:
Love works so long as it stays part blind-date.
'No hidden variables', the rule-book goes.

Or rather: as the intimacy grows
So must our light-year distances dilate.
Why the equations work nobody knows.

Maybe that's why Bohr/Heisenberg first chose
This way-out view of things to propagate:
'No hidden variables', the rule-book goes.

Quantum entanglement: the ratios
Mean we're in touch though messages must wait.
Why the equations work nobody knows,

But then, why worry? All the data shows
They come out right where values commutate.
'No hidden variables', the rule-book goes.

Though Einstein kept the Bohr crowd on their toes
With thought-experiments, they'd just re-state
'Why the equations work nobody knows'.

And us, let's not forget what closeness owes
To distance and not share in Echo's fate.
'No hidden variables', the rule-book goes;
Why the equations work nobody knows.

Decoherence

The nonevent in question is due to a 'Quantum Oblivion' effect, where a very brief virtual interaction undergoes 'unhappening'. Oblivion underlies quantum erasure and several other peculiar effects. [Some have proposed] a retrocausal evolution that accounts for such self-cancellation, involving exchange of negative physical values between earlier and later events.

Elitzur, Cohen and Shushi, 'The Too-Late-Choice Experiment'

No point our asking how it ended here.
Wave-functions cancel; antecedents fade.
It's our twinned histories that disappear.

Some word, some gesture came to interfere
And so produced an outcome long delayed:
No point our asking how it ended here.

First irony: though things now show up clear
The past turns secretive, anterograde.
It's our twinned histories that disappear.

And second: why then presuppose that we're
The 'we' that launched this temporal glissade?
No point our asking how it ended here.

This eigenstate's our only souvenir
Of states once superposed but now decayed.
It's our twinned histories that disappear.

Bit wasted, all that swish measurement gear,
With outcomes macroscopically displayed;
No point our asking how it ended here.

Says Feynman: it's when path-integrals smear
That order quells the quantum-state cascade.
It's our twinned histories that disappear.

Says Bohm: allow a pilot-wave to steer
The particle and then you've got it made.
Still no point asking how it ended here.

Says Bohr: agreed, this quantum stuff is queer,
But that's how the new physics game is played.
It's our twinned histories that disappear.

I say: small solace from the quantum-sphere
For us old lags who've looked to it for aid.
No point our asking how it ended here;
It's our twinned histories that disappear.

Many Worlds

The Many-Worlds Interpretation of quantum mechanics holds that there
are many worlds which exist in parallel at the same space and time as
our own. The existence of the other worlds makes it possible to remove
randomness and action at a distance from quantum theory and thus from
all physics.

Lev Vaidman

All these different worlds and every arrangement of configurations are all
there just like our arrangement of configurations, we just happen to be
sitting in this one. It's possible, but I'm not very happy with it.

Richard Feynman

The access problem, but let's not despair.
Let's give that Many-Worlds idea a shot.
Things might go otherwise in worlds elsewhere.

We like to dream them up in our armchair
Though robust types insist we'd better not.
The access problem, but let's not despair.

Though wave-collapse precludes our being there
It lets our counterfactuals hit the spot:
Things might go otherwise in worlds elsewhere.

Why rule them out if life gets hard to bear
And they're the only Shangri-Las you've got?
The access problem, but let's not despair.

Why not hypothesize another pair
Like us, our doubles in an upbeat plot?
Things might go otherwise in worlds elsewhere.

Still we and they, our counterparts, could share
No trans-world intimations of what's what:
The access problem, but let's not despair.

Some make-believe such happenings are rare
Though possible, but they're the pop-sci lot.
Things might go otherwise in worlds elsewhere.

It's that word 'might' that's set the hoper's snare
Since wavicles first passed the double slot:
The access problem, but let's not despair.

'We bring no this-world answer to your prayer',
The experts say, 'no means to tie the knot:
Things might go otherwise in worlds elsewhere'.

Still hold-out hopers may elect to err
Since they've no expert's copy-book to blot.
The access problem, but let's not despair;
Things might go otherwise in worlds elsewhere.

Many Minds

The Many Minds interpretation examines the consequences of the Everett
Many-Worlds interpretation from the perspective of the mind. Rather than
many worlds branching at each quantum decision point, it is the observer's
mind that is branching.

Yoav Aviram

Let's see if Many Minds can do the trick.
It's Many Worlds plus minds to sift and sort.
Just one wave-function, so we two might click.

Those other quantum theories (take your pick)
All have their points but finally fall short:
Let's see if Many Minds can do the trick.

It says: if those world-versions seem to flick
Past endlessly, let's put it down to thought.
Just one wave-function, so we two might click.

It uses all the same arithmetic
And all same equations we've been taught:
Let's see if Many Minds can do the trick.

The difference is, this theory doesn't stick
At disjunct worlds where mind-states go for naught:
Just one wave-function, so we two might click.

It counts them both within its bailiwick
Since minds decide for worlds: launch or abort!
Let's see if Many Minds can do the trick.

Then maybe us two loners, if we're quick,
Might co-perceive a world of first resort.
Just one wave-function, so we two might click;
Let's see if Many Minds can do the trick.

Tykhe's share

*Yet even for those who strive, Tykhe (Fortune) maybe conceals her light, ere
yet their steps attain the furthest goal; for her gifts render both of good and
ill. And often does the craft of lesser souls outstrip and bring to naught the
strength of better men.*

Pindar, *Isthmian Ode* IV

*But soon time (khronos) that accomplishes all will pass the portals of our house,
and then all pollution will be expelled from the hearth by cleansing rites that
drive out calamity. The dice of fortune (tykhai) will turn as they fall and lie with
faces all lovely to behold, favourably disposed to whomever stays in our house.*

Aeschylus, *The Libation Bearers*

1

No credit where no share of willed intent.
When things go well it's rarely down to your
Shrewd grasp of acts and consequences, nor,
As poems go, just saying what you meant.

Reflect a little and you'll see it's more
How things fall out than willed or heaven-sent,
The deed or word fulfilling all that went
To motivate its choice from Tykhe's store.

Let's say it shows at most a certain bent,
A yen for certain trade-routes to explore
As chance affords, and from that point ignore
All tales of what-if's sunken continent.

Always the sense of some unopened door
That might have opened had occasion lent
You grounds enough, yet always the event
That closed it seconds, hours or years before.

Tant pis: no major cause of discontent
So long as you've that wishful thought to shore
Against the thought-worm nestling at its core
That shows your wish-account far over-spent.

2

That's what the poets and folk-heroes do
To help us out: play up to the idea
Of demiurgic powers that tell us we're,
Like them, all set to make the world anew.

The cannier types found ways to make it clear:
'Don't let us put this thing across on you;
Our pleasure-dome's a house of cards, it's true,
Our noble deeds not quite what they appear'.

For every metaphor entails a slew
Of jostling crass metonymies that veer
Off-course till timeless Symbol gets a steer
From time-bound allegory and joins the queue.

So likewise in the man-of-action sphere
Where it's the oarsmen of Odysseus' crew
That bring the mast-strapped hero safely through,
Plus wind, ship, Circe's words, and steering gear.

Let's all get high on these out-of-the-blue
Prophetic revelations, yet adhere
To prosier standards when our ship sails near
The siren reefs or caves of Xanadu.

Then our best guide to that high-risk frontier
Where visions loom is a shrewd scholar who,
Like J. Livingston Lowes, accords their due
To facts that strike the earthbound eye or ear.

3

Not quite the spirit-downer it might seem,
This proto-deconstructive will to show
What checks impede the action-man's get-go
Or humdrum details pack the poet's dream.

If it's from mundane metonyms they grow,

Those metaphors, then we've the language-scheme
Of Jakobson to level our esteem
For lyric heights and what goes on below.

Besides, as Yeats reminds us, the regime
Of metaphor and symbol may bestow
Its blessing on regimes possessed of no
Such saving grace as lets his verse redeem,

For some, the violent images that owe
Their power to sundry variants on the theme
Of how it fades, the visionary gleam,
Once *Demos* gets to shake the status quo.

A stone, he says, to vex the living stream,
Though more, I'd say, to turbulate the flow
Of Yeats's wild imagining and throw
Some metonymic shades across the beam

Of his desire that nothing spoil the show,
That words conspire to tout the fascist meme,
That syntax yield as symbol reigns supreme,
And force gives form the zealot's old heave-ho.

Note: J. Livingston Lowes was a US literary critic whose 1927 book *The Road to Xanadu* is a remarkably detailed and erudite study of the memories, materials and verbal associations that went into the making of Coleridge's visionary poem 'Kubla Khan'. Roman Jakobson was a Czech structural linguist who first showed that the master-tropes metaphor and metonymy were central to all human language and could be used as the basis for a poetics and a typology of literary genres. Paul de Man was a highly controversial literary theorist who pressed Jakobson's distinction in a radically deconstructive direction.

Truth, love and number: A colloquy

The appropriateness of the language of mathematics for the formulation of the laws of physics is a wonderful gift which we neither understand nor deserve. We should be grateful for it and hope that it will remain valid in future research.

Eugene Wigner, 'The Unreasonable Effectiveness of
Mathematics in the Natural Sciences'

Being true is different from being taken as true . . . . I understand by 'laws of logic' not psychological laws of takings-to-be-true, but laws of truth. The laws of truth . . . are boundary stones set in an eternal foundation.

Gottlob Frege, *The Foundations of Arithmetic*

The viewpoint of the formalist must lead to the conviction that if other symbolic formulas should be substituted for the ones that now represent the mathematical-logical laws, the absence of the sensation of delight, called 'consciousness of legitimacy', which might be the result of such substitution would not in the least invalidate its mathematical exactness.

L.E.J. Brouwer, *Intuitionism and Formalism*

Numbers are not objects at all, because in giving the properties . . . of numbers you merely characterize an abstract structure – and the distinction lies in the fact that the 'elements' of the structure have no properties other than those relating them to other 'elements' of the same structure.

Paul Benacerraf, 'What Numbers Could Not Be'

A Dilemma (Wigner)

It works, but why it works we can't explain.
A mystery: ask any physicist.
We seek an answer, but we seek in vain.

How can we think it's real-world truths they gain
With all the math-based axioms they enlist?
It works, but why it works we can't explain.

Echt-Platonists, at home in ghost-domain,
Yet find the Forms reluctant to assist.
We seek an answer, but we seek in vain.

That's the real problem: doctrines too arcane,
Like that, can yield the physics-mill no grist.
It works, but why it works we can't explain.

Some say: keep maths empirical, abstain
From abstract talk; but there's a lot they've missed!
We seek an answer, but we seek in vain.

A flat dilemma, the logician's bane:
'Objective truth or knowledge', that's the gist.
It works, but why it works we can't explain.

No wonder puzzlers find the thing a strain,
Whether empiricist or rationalist:
We seek an answer, but we seek in vain.

Small hope we might yet reconcile the twain
Where each try warns the trier: please desist!
It works, but why it works we can't explain.

Cease hoping, and you'll go against the grain
Of all that whispers: try another twist!
We seek an answer, but we seek in vain.

For mathematics may afford the brain
A glimpse of truths that clash yet coexist.
It works, though why it works we can't explain;
We seek an answer, but we seek in vain.

An Option (J.S. Mill)

Stay earthbound, make geometry your guide.
No lift from wings that beat in empty space;
No problem measurement can't take in stride.

Count, add, subtract, then multiply, divide:
The sums work out, they tell us what's the case.
Stay earthbound, make geometry your guide.

The physics pay-off proves they're bona-fide,
Though it comes down to simple stuff at base:
No problem measurement can't take in stride.

Those bother-heads need Plato to provide
A shadow-realm of Forms that they can chase.
Stay earthbound, make geometry your guide.

The rule holds good for maths pure and applied:
Look hard, you'll find a maths/world interface.
No problem measurement can't take in stride.

That's why you've physics breakthroughs alongside
The maths discoveries: it's a relay race!
Stay earthbound, make geometry your guide.

It's also why the mystery-mongers slide
From Plato's to the sceptic's tight embrace.
No problem measurement can't take in stride.

A simple point: if abstract qualms collide
With what we know then knowledge holds the ace:
Stay earthbound, make geometry your guide.

'Where things add up': please tell the swivel-eyed
Math-sceptics that's where knowledge has its place.
No problem measurement can't take in stride.

Why think our mortal reckonings serve to hide
Platonic forms of which we find no trace?
Stay earthbound, make geometry your guide.

It's here below that numbers must reside
With fractions, multiples, or lengths you pace.
No problem measurement can't take in stride;
Stay earthbound, make geometry your guide.

Another Option (Gottlob Frege)

No truths unless objective and ideal.
By formal proofs alone we know what's true.
Let sense withdraw, let thought display the real.

Why trust empiricists like Mill whose zeal
For Ockham's Razor sends their thoughts askew?
No truths unless objective and ideal.

Then those there are, like Brouwer, who say 'feel,
Intuit, live your proofs!' – a motley crew.
Let sense withdraw, let thought display the real.

I say: unless truth set its timeless seal
On all our thoughts we've not the faintest clue:
No truths unless objective and ideal.

Empiricists make sense their biggest deal,
'Facts of experience', but it just won't do:
Let sense withdraw, let thought display the real.

It's why they always reinvent the wheel,
Shun formal proofs, tout common-sense in lieu:
No truths unless objective and ideal.

Myself, I've long since silenced that appeal
To any sense-reports that might leak through:
Let sense withdraw, let thought display the real.

You tell me not to make a mystic meal
Of my Platonic doctrine: I'll tell you
'No truths unless objective and ideal'.

Those sceptics: all their sophistries reveal
Is just how deep in their own juice they stew.
Let sense withdraw, let thought display the real.

Grant them their faulty premises, and we'll
Be brought around to share that crazy view.
No truths unless objective and ideal.

That's why we Platonists need nerves of steel
To pay objective truth the homage due.
Let sense withdraw, let thought display the real.

For else those ersatz creeds would rush to heal
The truth-shaped rift in all we thought we knew.
No truths unless objective and ideal;
Let sense withdraw, let thought display the real.

Intuitionism (Brouwer)

Why opt for truth when proof's the best you'll get?
Drop truth-talk, Brouwer says, and feel your way.
No point just piling up an unpaid debt.

Objectivists have goals that can't be met;
They pitch the stakes sky-high but never pay.
Why opt for truth when proof's the best you'll get?

The trouble is, you place an outsize bet
With naught to lose whatever odds you lay.
No point just piling up an unpaid debt.

Our option leaves you Platonists to fret
While we say Plato's led you lot astray!
Why opt for truth when proof's the best you'll get?

That's their big counter-thesis: 'once you let
Truth go the logic falls out as it may'.
No point just piling up an unpaid debt.

So what? say intuitionists: no sweat!
Let your best hunch decide the state of play.
Why opt for truth when proof's the best you'll get?

Besides, how else allow for those as yet
Unproven theorems in our dossier?
No point just piling up an unpaid debt.

Though Fregeans think our methods pose a threat
To bivalence, to logic's yea-or-nay,
Why opt for truth when proof's the best you'll get?

That either/or knits far too coarse a net
To catch the nuances our proofs convey:
No point just piling up an unpaid debt.

Rather it's our intuitive mind-set
That has, here as in love, the final say.
Why opt for truth when proof's the best you'll get?
No point just piling up an unpaid debt.

Love and/of Truth

Where love comes into it's the question here.
Love-objects range across the widest scale.
Most holdings-true involve some holding-dear.

It's love of truth that makes the truths show clear,
Though sometimes (think of Frege) it may fail.
Where love comes into it's the question here.

Trust intuition and you'll likely veer
Too far off logic's course to glimpse the grail:
Most holdings-true resist some holding-dear.

Take truth ideal and absolute to steer
By and you'll be a cautionary tale.
Where love comes into it's the question here.

For love long disciplined at truth's frontier
May find a dead-end to the logic-trail:
Most holdings-true involve some holding-dear.

Though Frege's case should tell us just how near
To full-scale paranoia this can sail,
Where love comes into it's the question here.

Still let's not treat his case as one of mere
Psychic disorder in the threatened male:
Most holdings-true resist some holding-dear.

For there's no room in truth's exalted sphere
For feelings he decreed beyond the pale.
Where love comes into it's the question here;

Also the tricky question whether we're
Well placed to say where logic's wheels derail:
Most holdings-true involve some holding-dear.

One thing's for sure: no judgment more severe
Than his relentless quest that truth prevail.
Where love comes into it's the question here;
Most holdings-true resist some holding-dear.

Plato's Shade

Make love your guide to truth, says Plato's shade.
'Perfection of the life or work', Yeats said,
Yet should love die, what truths shall make the grade?

It's numbers, sets, and measures all arrayed
In due proportion that should fill your head:
Make love your guide to truth, says Plato's shade.

Yet though that math-fixation surely played
A leading role, so too did love purebred:
If love should die, what truths shall make the grade?

By shared participation it's conveyed,
That highest Form of Good to which we're led.
Make love your guide to truth, says Plato's shade.

Yet Frege's case suggests that we've mislaid
The key-word somewhere, lost the vital thread:
If love should die, what truths shall make the grade?

That zeal for truth, in him, at last forbade
All thoughts by human-kindlier passions fed.
Make love your guide to truth, says Plato's shade.

The intuitionist replies: be swayed
By inklings, hunches, feeling-cues instead:
If love should die, what truths shall make the grade?

Bring love's fine touch to mathematics' aid,
Spare no regret for old illusions shed.
'Yet what of truth, love's guide?', says Plato's shade.

'Let feeling judge and all the Forms must fade
To simulacra, like my painted bed;
If truth should die, how shall love make the grade?'

How keep them clear if love should serenade
Our thoughts until their content goes unread?
Make truth your guide to love, says Plato's shade,
Yet should love die, what truths shall make the grade?

Ten limericks after Kurt Gödel

*I wish to designate the following as the most important question which can
be asked with regard to the axioms: to prove that they are not contradictory,
that a definite number of logical steps based upon them can never lead to
contradictory results.*

David Hilbert

Any consistent formal system F *within which a certain amount of elementary
arithmetic can be carried out is incomplete; that is, there are statements of the
language of* F *that can neither be proved nor disproved in* F.

Panu Raatikainen, 'Gödel's Incompleteness Theorems'

*For in reality Cantor's conjecture must be either true or false, and its
undecidability from the axioms as known today can only mean that these
axioms do not contain a complete description of reality.*

Kurt Gödel

The mathematician Kurt Gödel
Found a proof that made colleagues' blood curdle,
For it left them in shock
When he proved you could knock
A big hole in all proofs – quite a hurdle!

That his theorem held good all the same
Brought a shift in the rules of the game
Since reliance on formal
Procedures as normal
Showed you stuck in that Banksy-like frame.

That some axioms can't be decided
True/false was a thought that collided
With the cardinal rule
That they'd learned back in school
And by which they routinely abided.

So it was that they'd once bet their shirts
On the checklist of Hilbert dead-certs
Which they thought would soon yield
Every prize in the field
But now reeled at this stunner of Kurt's.

For it's tough luck (what luck could be tougher?)
If your thought-train runs into the buffer
So it's quickly derailed
And your paper's marked 'failed':
Such a blow for high-hopers to suffer!

Follow Wittgenstein, dump Bertrand Russell,
Or you'll find all this logical fuss'll
Just get in the way
Of what plain words can say
Without flexing an analyst's muscle.

Still it died hard, the logicist dream
Of a bivalent truth-value scheme
Where a gap in your proof
Meant you'd managed to goof,
Not subvert the whole logic-regime.

As for Gödel, he chose to construe it
As a proof we could grasp or intuit
By some power of the mind
Wholly different in kind
From the way that rule-followers do it.

Thus he thought we'd do better to seek
Fresh assurance in Plato's mystique

Of a transcendent realm
Where, with *nous* at the helm,
They could steer themselves down Problem Creek.

Yet it must be cold comfort for those
Still appalled at the spanner it throws
Into every last hope
To explore the full scope
Of what logic alone might disclose.

Note

'Banksy-like frame': a reference to the street-artist's instantly famous self-destroying/self-consuming work 'Girl with a Balloon'. This stencil auto-shredded as it was being auctioned at Sotheby's for just over £1 million. It was subsequently retitled 'Love In a Bin'.

Rules

One follows the rule mechanically. Hence one compares it with a mechanism. 'Mechanical' – that means: without thinking. But entirely *without thinking? Without reflecting?*

This was our paradox: no course of action could be determined by a rule, because every course of action can be made to accord with the rule.

Ludwig Wittgenstein, *Philosophical Investigations*

When I respond in one way rather than another to such a problem as '68 + 57', I can have no justification for one response rather than another. . . . Indeed, there is no fact about me that distinguishes between my meaning a definite function by 'plus' (which determines my responses in new cases) and my meaning nothing at all.

How can I justify my present application of such a rule, when a sceptic could easily interpret it so as to yield any of an indefinite number of other results? It seems that my application of it is an unjustified stab in the dark. I apply the rule blindly.

Saul Kripke, *Wittgenstein on Rules and Private Language*

1

No simple matter, following a rule.
You say 'rule n+2, no scope to stray,
Just follow teacher, as you did in school'.

Yet maybe someone wants to play the fool,
Or starts a new game, or declines to play.
No simple matter, following a rule.

Why lay it down that 'n+2' unspool
Exactly as the rule-enforcers say?
'Just follow teacher, as you did at school':

No doubt wise counsel, but the sort that you'll
Find otiose come rule-recension day.
No simple matter, following a rule.

Maybe there's some smart kid who thinks it cool
To take instruction in a different way;
Just 'follows teacher', as you did at school,

But sees it as his big chance to re-tool
The whole +2 numerical array.
No simple matter, following a rule.

Just look at those big-breakthrough guys like Boole;
Hardly the kind of precept they'd obey,
'Just follow teacher, as you did at school'.

They're more the types who'd turn your ridicule
Right round, leave you with demon doubts to slay:
No simple matter, following a rule.

All pedagogues can do is join the pool
Of communal math-wisdom, come what may:
Just follow teacher, as you did at school.

Not getting far beyond the vestibule
Of Hilbert's grand hotel's the price you pay.
No simple matter, following a rule;
Just follow teacher, as you did at school.

2

Some rules there are that ought to see us through.
Can't all change constantly as time goes by.
Things don't add up? It must be down to you.

How cope if five's the sum of two plus two?
Arithmetic's one place where rules apply!
Count on, and count on it the rails run true.

How think at all if thinking's apt to slew
Off momentarily on some blue-sky
Diversion so that logic goes askew?

Blame it on Wittgenstein; it's he who drew
The crazy inference: no reason why
All those rule-followers reason as they do.

Maybe a thing that loner never knew
Was just how far such sceptic doctrines try
The faith of trusting types like me and you,

Those who depend on promises or who,
If the signs point that way, opt to rely
On love's shared indices as they accrue.

Let's not pretend we'll never misconstrue
The signs, or have a motive to deny,
In light of some unlooked-for après-coup,

The pertinence of rules that self-renew
Or stay in force however far a cry
Time present seems from that set-fair debut.

Yet, equally, let's give the credit due
To players by the book who'd still fight shy
Of saying 'rules are there to break', or sue

For breach of trust if promises outgrew
The context of their making, or defy
The sceptic's rule of constant rule-review.

For as with maths, so here: there's cause to rue
That quick-shift way with rules that has them fly
The very thought of outcomes bang on cue

Or thrill to think that somewhere in the queue
Of numbers, out of sight to the mind's eye,
There lies in wait an unknown Waterloo.

The task of heading off that rendezvous
With destiny must be what keeps them spry,
Those rule-deniers keen to bid adieu

To any system where the fixed taboo
On innovation tends to cut-and-dry
Live thoughts into a robot retinue.

Still there's another side of it: take too
Relaxed a line on rules and you'll untie
Too many bonds and leave yourself with few

Real chances for the sorts of *jamais-vu*
Yet rule-based inference that no wise guy,
Like Wittgenstein's rule-bender, should eschew
Lest numbers, words and lives all go awry.

3

That rules change constantly some rule decrees,
Some meta-rule that changes with the rest.
Still let's not think we change them as we please.

Forget the maths case; he was out to tease,
That wise-guy kid, not out to pass the test,
Though rules change constantly, some rule decrees.

If Wittgenstein picked up that number-wheeze
And ran with it, let's not be too impressed,
Nor think to change the rules just as we please.

He merely deals in null hypotheses,
In claims devoid of consequence at best,
Though rules change constantly, some rule decrees.

For it's elsewhere, not in the realm of these
Conundrums, that the upset's manifest,
For us who can't change rules just as we please.

That they *could* change must leave us ill at ease,
Or anxious that this knowledge be suppressed,
That rules change constantly; some rule decrees

It must be so, though still the thought may seize
Us unawares at times, no longer blest
By that good thought: can't change rules as we please!

Rules are like locks to which we've lost the keys
Yet think they'll close or spring at our behest.
The rules change constantly, some rule decrees.

Partly they feed our hopes, partly appease
Our darkest fears; yet never on request
Since we can't change the rules just as we please.

Still it's the thought of rule-change tends to freeze
Our waking thoughts and leave us dream-distressed:
The rules change constantly, some rule decrees.

That thought's the one that brings us to our knees
In the small hours, by rule-change fears obsessed,
Since we can't change the rules just as we please.

But that's the thing: no depth of expertise
In rule-change method helps us hopers wrest
Control back; constant change, some rule decrees.

Best policy: I'll back the rule that she's
Now backing, one in which we joint-invest
Since we can't change the rules just as we please.

Won't have them say I can't see wood for trees;
It's woods of ours these termite doubts infest.
The rules change constantly, some rule decrees.

A handy rule: 'misfortunes come in threes',
They say, though 'count to three' seems risky lest
We think to change the rules just as we please.

Now thoughts of rule-change re-exert their squeeze
On hopes sprung lately in the human breast
Where rules change constantly, some rule decrees.

So here we are, all ready to reprise
The repertoire by which we second-guessed
This truth: no changing rules just as we please.

Rather they shift unnoticed, by degrees,
As rights and wrongs are over time redressed.
The rules change constantly, some rule decrees;
Still let's not think we change them as we please.

Notes

1   See, for instance, Christopher Norris, *The Winnowing Fan: Verse-Essays in Creative
    Criticism* (London: Bloomsbury, 2017); *For the Tempus-Fugitives: Poems and Verse-*

Essays (Eastbourne: Sussex Academic Press, 2017); *The Matter of Rhyme: Verse-Music and the Ring of Ideas* (Brighton: Sussex University Press, 2018).

2   See especially Frank Kermode, *Romantic Image* (London and New York: Routledge & Kegan Paul, 1957).

3   See among others Cleanth Brooks, *The Well Wrought Urn: Studies in Poetic Structure* (New York: Harcourt Brace, 1947); W.K Wimsatt, *The Verbal Icon: Studies in the Meaning of Poems* (Kentucky: University of Kentucky Press, 1954).

4   For some acute commentary, see Jonathan Culler, *Theory of the Lyric* (Cambridge, MA: Harvard University Press, 2015).

5   See especially William Empson, *The Structure of Complex Words* (London: Chatto & Windus, 1951) and *Argufying: Essays on Literature and Culture* (London: Oxford University Press, 1987); also Christopher Norris, *William Empson and the Philosophy of Literary Criticism* (London: Athlone, 1978).

6   Thus, Derrida: 'An undecidable proposition, as Gödel demonstrated in 1931, is a proposition which, given a system of axioms governing a multiplicity, is neither an analytical nor deductive consequence of those axioms, nor in contradiction with them, neither true nor false with respect to those axioms. Tertium datur, without synthesis.' See Jacques Derrida, 'The Double Session', in Barbara Johnson (trans.), *Dissemination* (Chicago: University of Chicago Press, 1981), 219.

7   See Derrida, *Dissemination* (op. cit.); also *Of Grammatology*, trans. Gayatri Spivak (Baltimore: Johns Hopkins University Press, 1976), *Margins of Philosophy*, trans. Alan Bass (Chicago: Chicago University Press, 1982), and 'The Parergon', in Geoff Bennington and Ian McLeod (trans.), *The Truth in Painting* (Chicago: University of Chicago Press, 1987), 15–147.

Works cited

Brooks, Cleanth, *The Well Wrought Urn: Studies in Poetic Structure*. New York: Harcourt Brace, 1947.

Culler, Jonathan, *Theory of the Lyric*. Cambridge, MA: Harvard University Press, 2015.

Derrida, Jacques, *Of Grammatology*, trans. Gayatri Spivak. Baltimore: Johns Hopkins University Press, 1976.

Derrida, Jacques, 'The Double Session', in Barbara Johnson (ed.), *Dissemination*. Chicago: University of Chicago Press, 1981.

Derrida, Jacques, *Margins of Philosophy*, trans. Alan Bass. Chicago: Chicago University Press, 1982.

Derrida, Jacques, 'The Parergon', in *The Truth in Painting*, trans. Geoff Bennington and Ian McLeod. Chicago: University of Chicago Press, 1987, 15–147.

Empson, William, *The Structure of Complex Words*. London: Chatto & Windus, 1951.

Empson, William, *Argufying: Essays on Literature and Culture*. London: Oxford University Press, 1987.

Kermode, Frank, *Romantic Image*. London and New York: Routledge & Kegan Paul, 1957.

Norris, Christopher, *William Empson and the Philosophy of Literary Criticism*. London: Athlone, 1978.

Norris, Christopher, *For the Tempus-Fugitives: Poems and Verse-Essays*. Eastbourne: Sussex Academic Press, 2017.

Norris, Christopher, *The Winnowing Fan: Verse-Essays in Creative Criticism*. London: Bloomsbury, 2017.

Norris, Christopher, *The Matter of Rhyme: Verse-Music and the Ring of Ideas*. Brighton: Sussex University Press, 2018.

Wimsatt, W. K., *The Verbal Icon: Studies in the Meaning of Poems*. Lexington, KY: University of Kentucky Press, 1954.

Part II

Life-writing and uncertainty

4

In an undecidable

An ethical and literary right

Christopher Fynsk

On 21 June 1945, Robert Antelme addressed a letter to Dionys Mascolo whose effects on Mascolo's subsequent life were immeasurable – all the more so, we might say, for the fact that the existence of the letter was 'forgotten' for four decades. I offer a translation of it here in its entirety in order to prepare the space for the commentary to follow:

> I am going to try to write a few lines to you, by which I mean accomplish my first act as a 'solidified' living being – because I've already accomplished numerous acts as a living being: I've cried, for instance, and tears are as far as possible from death – ; it is to you that I write first, because I want you to be able to maintain within yourself, perhaps for a little while longer, the wondrous feeling of having saved a man. I say 'a while' because to the same degree the one 'saved' holds eternally before him the image of the saviour, to the same extent the saviour has a tendency to see the image of his act grow indistinct and even to render common the subject he tore from evil. Thus, my dear D., we are in some sense now completely separate; our consciences, from one to the other, no longer weigh the same; there will always be some immodesty in my eyes, in my words; you will try not to see.
>
> I'd like to tell you other things on this subject that seem important to me, but I perceive that I run a fairly grave danger: D., I think I no longer know what is said and what is not said. In hell one says everything, and it must be for this that we recognize it; for my part it is certainly in this way that it was revealed to me. In our world, on the contrary, one is accustomed to choosing and I believe I no longer know how to choose. Well, in what represented hell for me in others – 'saying everything' – was where I lived my paradise; for this is something you must know D., that during the first days when I was in my bed and I spoke to you, to you and Marguerite above all, I was not a man of this earth. I stress this fact that haunts me retrospectively.

To have been able to give freedom to words that were barely formed and in any case were without years, without age, but took shape only from my breath, this, you see, this happiness wounded me definitively, and at this moment, I who believed myself so far from death by some affliction – typhus, fever, and so forth – I could think of dying only from this very happiness. And now, I have begun again to give a form to things: at least my spirit and my body try to, but I repeat, I think I no longer know how to choose. So there are surely tremendous vulgarities in what I am saying, and what you call in your laughter an incredible 'tyranny.' Am I therefore going to have to 'retool' myself, scrape myself down, so that one sees only a smooth envelope once more? You'll tell me that my language is ill-fitting and the best oil is one that reveals a thousand rough spots without ceasing to be oil. In reality, I believe that the problem I'm posing is nonetheless a moral one. I have the feeling, which perhaps not all of my comrades have, of being a new living being, not in Wells' sense of the word, in the fantastic sense, but on the contrary in the most hidden sense. So that my true sickness, which began so tenderly just a few weeks ago now – and at that time it was still bearable – now reaches its maturity and becomes very intractable. Here is an appendage that grows, a spirit without channels or compartments, in sum a freedom perhaps ready to grasp itself, perhaps ready to annihilate other freedoms, either to kill them or better to embrace them.

So if one wanted to see a man take form, one might observe me up close, taking into the account the morbid character of the formative process.

Forgive me for insisting; it must be unbearable, for you who 'gets on' to hear an individual speak of his original indeterminacy; I think there is even something boorish in all this and that you will be right in answering that in a few months I will have ceased being reborn, that I too will get on and no doubt even along that abandoned path that I left a year ago. You'll tell me this, D., or not, you'll think it or not, depending on whether you will or will not have some faith in man.

You are certainly one of the few beings in whom I most fear fatigue, I mean despair. There are many whom I have loved a great deal and whose despair left me indifferent – and I refer there to a kind of definitive state. I left them in their state, or I revelled or struggled in bringing them back. For you D., whose despair must constantly mix with joy, flights, and unfathomable pauses, I could not bear that this despair fix itself and become established, now above all. I told you that I was not afraid and that such was my sole fear. If you laugh, if you tease me a little in saying that you have never seen so much future, I will tell you that I recognized for myself the right to have this fear.

I stopped there because my hand was hurting; I take up again this Wednesday morning. There was a superb storm last night and the park is fresh. You came for dinner last night; I would have liked you to stay a little longer with us. But I believe that I am holding on to you a little too much; I no longer have the right now – the mirage has passed, I begin to resemble myself. And moreover I have a fear, I'd almost say a horror of going back into that shell; I didn't think that the infernal or marvelous voyage would ever end (I speak of these last weeks). All my friends shower me with a satisfaction that is full of goodness regarding my resemblance with myself, and it seems to me that I am living 'The Picture of Dorian Grey' in reverse. I've undergone the extraordinary adventure of being able to prefer myself other.

My dear D., those moments when I could tell you so many things buried for over a year, things so rich and so solitary for having been kept from the enemy and inflated against him, will never return. I told you this already when I was sick and I repeat it several times now, because all of this is quite dead and if I tried to reawaken these things, I'd be nothing but a dirty whore.

I'm not far from being one, in fact, but I don't think it's my fault, and every person who has lived something extraordinary runs this risk. In reality, I don't care and I don't think about it. The sole truth is that a certain hardness, I'd say even a cruelty, gains a hold in me; each day I see sympathies die, and almost affections, and this without disquiet. None of it will have been useless and I go forward peacefully in a firm solitude. There still remains in me at times a feeling of horror that is a bit too sharp, but soon, no doubt, all of this will have smoothed out and become neutralized. Then, perhaps, I will accept the resemblance with myself because I will know that it doesn't exist; I will accept the portrait: there will no longer be a portrait.

Alice is going to Paris; I'm passing these sheets on to her. I haven't entirely reread them; forgive me. I'll continue, no doubt, because in addressing them to you, I don't have too strong an impression of losing my time.

Try if you can to find a bit more objectivity in this, I had hoped to put more into it; unfortunately it would surprise me if you could.

The best to you,

Robert

Thursday, 21 June 1945

I hope it will be apparent why this letter came to my mind as I approached the question of the pertinence of the term 'undecidable' in the context of the use of language. It is true that the term does not appear in the letter, and the letter does not immediately evoke some truth value in the experience with language to which it refers that would exceed the bounds of determinable meaning in a given linguistic framework. The letter addresses, rather, the bounds of linguistic freedom in social usage and, thus, the laws of propriety, which come to appear uncertain under the pressure of an imperious need to speak and, more precisely, to say all. 'Undecidable' touches inevitably on the meaning of this 'all' for those to whom such speech is addressed, but for Antelme, it involves most immediately what can and cannot be said. What can and cannot be said in any social relation, on the one hand, and over against this, what must be said for the preservation of an exceptional relation he seeks to protect and where the being of those who share this relation is at stake. I call the relation exceptional, and it certainly is in many respects, but I think we should also recognize its general import in that the act of speech that presents an undecidable character in this case engages something of the linguistic event that Levinas evoked when he referred to a trauma that is brought by the saying of the other in the ethical relation, and to the decision to speak or kill that also presents itself there. The undecidable in this instance, as we will see, inheres in the ethical relation as such. Antelme will address it as a 'moral' problem, in light of the nascent freedom he has experienced, and the difficulty it poses is inseparable from what Antelme does not hesitate to name, despite the doubt and ambivalence that resonates in all his statements, a *right* with respect to the other. The possible conditions for addressing this other, this friend, have become profoundly unsure. But a right presents itself in this relation that is not in question.

The striking surety of Antelme's appeal to a right in this address goes unremarked in the seventy-odd pages of Dionys Mascolo's response, which takes the form of an attempted anamnesis, forty years after the fact, devoted to the meaning of the letter and its repercussions in Mascolo's life. This response, *Autour d'un effort de mémoire*, is a remarkable and admirable text.[1] But somehow Mascolo does not register this appeal, even if he seeks to respond to the concern that lies behind it.

There is a notable silence here that prompts me to juxtapose Mascolo's commentary on this letter with another text by Maurice Blanchot, published six years later, that may actually have been composed in remembrance of this same letter.[2] There are no definitive grounds for establishing the shared reference, or for detecting more than an indirect response on Blanchot's part, which would also have been informed by long study of Antelme's post-war testimony and long friendship. It could very well be that Blanchot simply knew or heard something in that way of speaking, that characteristic address to the other that Mascolo sought to characterize as '*inconsolé*', that required his own response.[3] Let me therefore limit myself to suggesting, even as I note the arresting proximity, that we are dealing with two divergent responses to the same undecidable, the same infinite in the human relation to speech that Antelme brought to his words in his exchanges with those intimate with him. I will be very allusive here, but let me note that Antelme once defined friendship as the multiplication of death (and difference).[4] In the responses of Mascolo and Blanchot to the speech of Antelme, we witness something of this kind in a profoundly affirmative form.

Let me now turn first to Antelme's letter and underscore some of its most relevant traits for this discussion. To do this at all properly, I must touch very briefly upon its circumstances (from the spring of 1945), which are offered to us by Mascolo's memoire. Mascolo's account of these circumstances, as it happens, bear marks of his awareness of an essay by Blanchot (originally from 1962) that addressed Antelme's experience with language in the time of his internment.[5] This introduces a curious fold into the pairing of texts that I am undertaking. But the crucial point for us, to which Mascolo and Blanchot both attend, is that in the period of his detention, Antelme had withheld an essential form of speech from his captors, even as he approached the impossibility of refusal itself. His deliverance, recounted in extraordinary pages by Mascolo, then proved to be a deliverance of speech, an unchecked flow that was received by the two who were closest to Antelme at this time, Mascolo and then Marguerite Duras. This is the speaking to which Mascolo refers when he evokes the intense joy he knew in liberating 'words without age' that were formed in and with what must have been the most weak and precious breath. This is the speaking in which he presumably experienced what it meant to say everything, and before which he hesitates, now that he has begun to regain a sense of physical and mental propriety, a sense of self that conforms to the presentation of self required in the most basic social decorum.

We will notice that Antelme expresses considerable unease about this initial experience of deliverance. He is 'haunted' by it, he says, describing this kind of effusion as something he had previously known as 'hellish' (presumably in pre-war social contexts[6]), but had now been experienced as 'paradisiacal', bringing a joy, a *jouissance* so great that he thought it would bring his death (and let us note from what Mascolo reports of the opinions of the doctors that it could well have). The deliverance from a deathly oppression and a state very near to death, known in and as a liberation of speech, is something like a rebirth and the experience of a new infancy, from which the recovering Antelme now begins to emerge with a new capacity to grasp the 'form' of things. But something else 'tenderly' emerged in that wounding joy, a 'freedom' Antelme cannot separate from a kind of sickness for the way it resists all containment in the forms of a proper '*bien-être*' as it matures.

Thus, the crisis in which Antelme writes during what was presumably the night of June 20 – a crisis marked in writing that is profoundly indeterminate and ambivalent – is based not only in his sense that the aperture for a speaking of the kind he has enjoyed (in which he said 'all') is closing, but also a growing exigency of this faculty or this unruly spirit of freedom that demands to embrace all from the non-ground of 'all', thereby destabilizing his relation both to language and to the other (relations that cannot be thought apart from one another in this moment). After the storm on that night, which will bring a kind of catharsis and a renunciation, some form of calming of that imperious freedom, Antelme will pronounce the end of what he calls the 'infernal, or marvellous' passage in which he underwent 'the extraordinary adventure of being able to prefer himself other'.

Mascolo's commentary, what I have called an anamnesis since it draws from sources that exceed recollection or reflective thought to approach something at least partially repressed, represents an effort to regain access to the origins of the experience to which Antelme testifies in his letter. It is an experience that Mascolo understands as an experience with language, which in its 'untouchable and inexhaustible signifying reality', as he puts it, constitutes that 'thanks to which our presence to the world took on meaning and continues to be founded'.[7] This is, once again, an event that sent into a form of ongoing exile those who experienced it, most immediately Mascolo and Duras, and Antelme himself with them – a form of exile that was also the ground of a singular form of community. 'Robert', Mascolo writes, 'remained bound [to what he says in the letter] all his life, and we with him. He threw us into the place from which he speaks and we never came back from it. [. . .] Through his return, he had deported us with him'.[8] To approach what I have been tempted to term somewhat loosely the 'undecidable' in Antelme's experience, we have to approach that site of speech (which becomes a space of writing), in relation to which Mascolo and Duras suffered a displacement so profound, according to Mascolo, that it produced a 'communization' of the soul[9] that drove them and those who joined their company (including Blanchot) towards new forms of sociality.

But regaining that site of enunciation where the exigency of saying remained at stake was hardly easy even for Antelme himself (by the time he wrote his letter), because saying all, as Mascolo recounts, involved both joy and extreme trepidation. Mascolo reports that Antelme's first words were urgent, even desperate; he wanted to communicate every detail of his experience in the camp, knowing that his death could be imminent. Mascolo captured these faint words in an obscure fashion, claiming on one page that he would be unable to recall them, while noting on the succeeding page that he registered them in such a way as to be capable of restoring the essential, should Antelme die. Saying all in this respect meant communicating the experience of detention, in all its dimensions. But it also meant communicating a fear – a fear linked to the most profound message he was delivering and a fear for the possibility of its reception. Mascolo broaches this topic in the following way:

> Even though he is not assured of survival, everything he says to me, still punctuated at moments by visions, people, or places, says above all the fear, or the difficulty, even the impossibility, of living again after having willed to survive.[10]

Mascolo understands the difficulty voiced here to be deriving from the self-imposition of a terrible responsibility. To choose to live, as he has understood from Antelme, is to remove from oneself every alibi with respect to what one does with this life. The burden is infinite. To say 'all' in this sense is to confront and say something like the meaning of human meaning, which one must assume fully, despite – or because of – its abyssal grounds. I condense crudely here, pushing a bit past Mascolo's 'existential' formulation in light of what Antelme appears to have discovered of the human, but without casting doubt on what Mascolo claims to have understood of the fear that makes Antelme pull back, even in his first days of return.

The awkward phrase I have just offered regarding 'the human' derives from what Mascolo goes on to add with respect to Antelme's experience. The choice of life, we read, is made by one who has truly passed from life, experiencing not death as such (*la mort sans phrases,* as Mascolo puts it[11]) in the passage to the other side, but rather that which can be reported of such a dying, which involves a *death to oneself* that brings an opening to the other or *autrui,* and thus an opening unto what Antelme will name the 'unity' of the human species, or human kind. The core of the speech that Antelme would finally have reserved from his oppressors, but to which he was exposed by that oppression, and which was then brought forward in the exigency to say all, was the saying of this relation. What Antelme affirms is not simply a right to be recognized as human after the terrible dehumanization practised by the Nazis. It is rather the recognition that the oppressed and the oppressor are the same in the essence of their being – that they share the same condition of being human, an 'indestructible', as Blanchot puts it, that only emerges all the more as it provokes the Nazi disavowal and fury. Antelme thus affirms an irreducible relation to the oppressor. To will to survive will entail assuming this difficult knowledge.

Mascolo, in a very Christian formulation that is characteristic of this memoire, calls this message the 'news' ('*la nouvelle*'[12]) with which he returns. What drives Antelme at the time of his return, in Mascolo's view, is the imperative of delivering this news. But it was in fact terrifying for him, as Mascolo recognizes, and perhaps even more frightening than Mascolo allows, though he describes this fear openly. Writing of the first night in the presence of Antelme's unarrested speech, Mascolo declares that 'being lost to oneself in this way means, and there is the overwhelming revelation that opens a future in a sense more forbidding than death itself, becoming for oneself something sacred'.[13]

The turn taken here by Mascolo with respect to the sacralization of the human will lead to the heart of Mascolo's interpretation of the news communicated by Antelme. I will return to this shortly. Let me first continue with my very brief consideration of the knowledge Antelme brings from 'the other side' concerning the unity of the species and the trepidation it inspires. In what measure can such knowledge be said, or provide the foundation for the institutions that sustain human usage? In what measure can such knowledge be shared in society? It was certainly received by Mascolo in the first days of Antelme's return, a time of such transgressive and exceptional intimacy that Mascolo himself is uneasy about acknowledging it. But this transmission was perhaps only possible in this time of Antelme's precarious weakness and a shared vulnerability. Could the freedom it implies (which seems to take on almost a life of its own in the time of Antelme's recovery) ever be sustained? Antelme recognizes, by the time of the composition of his letter, that it cannot; the 'new being' it animates actually cannot survive.

Antelme writes of his desire to save in Mascolo, as we have heard, the sense of having saved another. For Antelme, this task is apparently inseparable from preserving in Mascolo a capacity for something other than the 'despair' that is proper to mature reason in its judgement of the possible (that of which the human being is capable). He wants to preserve, for Mascolo, relation to something he knows to be 'impossible' and which inheres in the grounds of their friendship, something almost infantile in his nature that Antelme links to hope. Undoubtedly, he senses that something of his own being, as one newly reborn, is actually at stake in this.

Jean-Francois Lyotard has taught us to grasp in the notion of infancy something that quite surpasses the standard opposition of the infantile and the mature. Despite Antelme's constant recourse to such oppositions in his letter, it is clear that he is quite sensitive to the promise of this 'exceptional' dimension in human experience, even as he faces its terrors. The freedom Antelme has known in exposure to the other (from the ground of an experience of a form of death) certainly has an ungoverned and abyssal character. But this experience of an 'impossible' informs the 'moral' claim made in relation to the friend.

I have tried to underscore Antelme's extreme ambivalence regarding the knowledge he relays concerning his experience in the camp and the meaning of what it is to return to the world. He is afraid it is something he cannot assume, so afraid that he actually hesitates in his own decision to return. The knowledge of the unity of the species and the responsibility it imposes has something terrible in it. He is no less afraid of losing what has brought this knowledge, which is an exposure to the other. He has undergone the 'extraordinary adventure' of *preferring* himself other by reason of the opening to the world and to the other human being it affords. With respect to that other, it permits an intimacy and a form of communication that exceeds the law (a relay of that intimacy, in other words a speech). But doubt, fear and an awareness that Mascolo suitably terms 'tragic' also suffuse what Antelme seeks to affirm in this experience.

Mascolo himself must have known something of the fear and some form of doubt. The mere fact that he could have forgotten the existence of such a letter for forty years suggests that something in it threatened him, something more than the avowed impropriety of the address. Of course, the sentiments it bore may have been so profoundly familiar to Mascolo in the time of its composition that it could not stand forth in his mind from the broader circumstances of the moment (Antelme, as he tells us, was effusive and surely quite repetitive). Nonetheless, there was something unresolved for him with respect to this letter, something obliging. There is no question that there is real courage in Mascolo's attempt at anamnesis after those forty years, in his own confrontation with the question of what can be said or cannot be said, and in his effort to decipher the meaning of the letter, for himself and for his friends. Yet there is something of Antelme's fear that Mascolo does not reproduce in his attempt to answer Antelme's words regarding the despair that could easily overtake him.

That answer comes in his account of the effect Antelme's return had on the lives of Mascolo and his friends, its profoundly *deporting* effect. Becoming-Jewish, and becoming-communist, with Antelme, in the wake of the event of his return, is offered as an obscure assumption of the import of this event, the working of a spirit that was less than conscious in its feverish stirring and pursuits, but which, for Mascolo, assured a continuity with this event (and thus the possibility of the anamnesis he undertakes). By the work of this spirit, Mascolo claims, he and his friends did not succumb to despair in the way Antelme had feared.[14]

But Mascolo also seems to be defending himself from the possibility of despair, and his construction of the event of return bears marks of that defence. Here, I must return to Mascolo's tendency to sacralize the very presence of Antelme and the message he bore. A full analysis of the pertinent scene would carry us far afield, but let me note that in the pages following the ones from which I have quoted regarding Antelme's extreme ambivalence with respect to his own decision to return to the world after his experience in the camps, Mascolo provides an account of an incident in which he claims to 'see' in Antelme's person the communication of '*la nouvelle*' with which Antelme returns.

The scene, which Antelme names an '*Ecce Homo*', involves Antelme's assisted entry into a brasserie in Verdun in the course of his return to Paris. His appearance, his 'image', as Mascolo refers to it, provokes what Mascolo names a 'common passion of thought' in the stunned witnesses, which is first an admiration of what is initially recognized as 'the perseverance of a refusal opposed to what could be no more than an ungraspable neutrality of evil'.[15] Mascolo then qualifies this presence as one of a 'second innocence', a source of truth that gives an innocence in knowledge. The legible silence of this presentation, Mascolo continues, was an 'event of speech': 'the avowal, on the part of one who knows, that there is no issue from the condition of being human, martyrdom itself not serving this end; that such an absence of escape cuts off also the retreat of despair.' So, in the face of Antelme's presence, subsisting in an 'effacement or uselessness of time', a 'positive and stable indeterminacy, between what is from here and what is from elsewhere, from now and from all time', despair is not possible.

Mascolo's response to the fear addressed to him by Antelme thus takes the form of a reassurance (to himself and to the reader) that the link to the moment of their greatest intimacy is secure and that he cannot lose sight of the epiphany in which the ground of the intimacy he knew, in and by Antelme's effusive speech on the first days, was given to him. Whatever contingencies might intervene, the despair Antelme feared would never take hold.

It is quite a claim, and I again respectfully hesitate to question it, even though it is not at all clear to me that it can be made consistent with what Mascolo evokes of the fear, the difficulty, even the impossibility of living again, experienced by Antelme. Without doubting anything of the importance and fundamental fidelity of Mascolo's testimony regarding the deportation and formation of a new understanding of community, it is perhaps still necessary to consider in greater depth the meaning of 'survival'.

I suggested at the outset of my remarks that it is perhaps possible to hear in a brief text by Maurice Blanchot a second response to the address contained in Robert Antelme's letter to Dionys Mascolo. This second response diverges profoundly from Mascolo's and is of a quite different tonality from that of the letter itself; but this very divergence is part of what prompts me to suggest that we deal with something perhaps rightly called 'undecidable' in Antelme's experience of what saying all to the other from the state of 'indeterminacy' he knew implied.

Let me now cite this brief text by Blanchot, entitled 'In the Night that is Watched Over':

> It is slowly, in those nights when I sleep without sleeping, that I became conscious (this word is inappropriate) of your proximity, which is distant nonetheless. I persuaded myself that you were here: not you, but this repeated phrase: 'I am going far away, I am going far away.'
>
> I immediately understood that Robert, so generous, so little concerned about himself, was not speaking to me about or for himself, but of all the places of extermination, of which (if it was him speaking) he listed a few: 'Listen to them, listen to the names: Treblinka, Chelmno, Belzec, Majdanek, Auschwitz, Sobibor, Birkenau, Ravensbruck, Dachau.'
>
> 'But', I say, speaking, not speaking, 'do we forget?' – 'Yes, you forget, you forget all the more for remembering. Your memory does not impede you from living, from surviving, nor even from loving me. But one does not love a dead person, because then the meaning escapes you, the impossibility of meaning, the nonbeing and impossibility of non-being.'
>
> When I reread these lines, I know that I have already lost sight of Robert Antelme, the incomparable friend I knew. He was so simple, and at the same time so rich, with a knowledge that the greatest minds lacked. In the experience of servitude that was his, even if he shared it with others, he kept the human truth from which he knew not to exclude even those who oppressed him.
>
> But he went even further: not recognizing a companion (K.) he had come to see in the infirmary, who was still alive, he understood that there is a nothingness in life itself, an unfathomable void against which one has to defend oneself, even while acknowledging its approach. We must learn to live with this void. We will maintain plenitude even in nothingness.
>
> This is why, Robert, I still have my place next to you. And this 'night watched over' in which you come to see me is not an illusion where everything would disappear but my right to make you live, even in the void I feel approaching.

I trust one will recognize why I think I hear in this text an echo from Antelme's letter, perhaps even a response. The link, once again, is probably not direct (at least no documentation suggests this). All we can assume is that Blanchot was familiar with the letter by reason of the fact that Mascolo consulted with a number of friends before publishing it, and was already well prepared to receive what it communicates from the basis of long experience with Antelme and the community that formed around him.[16] But it is striking that Blanchot appears to return to one of the most acute moments in Antelme's address to Mascolo – that moment where its urgency was most critical. Here, again, is the last sentence written that first night of Antelme's first act of writing: 'If you laugh, if, teasing me a little, you respond that you've never seen so much future ahead, I'll tell you that I recognised my right to this fear.' And here again is Blanchot's sentence: 'And this "night watched over" in which you came to see me is not an "illusion" where everything would disappear, but my right to make you live, even in the void I feel approaching.' In either case, the word 'right' stands forth quite powerfully, even though it is spoken from one side, and then the other, of Antelme's passing.

To establish properly the bridging and the transformation that occurs when Blanchot takes over the term 'right' (which can be established, I believe, irregardless of whether there is direct citation or reference), I would need to undertake a quite extensive commentary on Blanchot's understanding of Antelme's experience in the camps and in the ensuing days (as presented in 'The Indestructible') and I would need to pause at some length over what Blanchot understands with the term 'effacement' – a term that plays a very significant and insistent role in Blanchot's post-war writing.[17] It would also be necessary to attend to his singular attention to the notion of 'right' throughout this same period. Here, I must rely on previously published work. Essentially, but all too briefly, Blanchot understands Antelme's experience to be one of extreme exposure, to the point, as Mascolo notes, quoting Blanchot, that he became other to himself (*autrui pour soi-même*), or, as Blanchot also puts it a bit more radically in his essay of 1962, host to the other. When Antelme returned to the world and sought to say 'all', he attempted to say what this exposure had afforded to him of a knowledge of the human condition and the grounds of human sociality – something fundamentally prior to 'individual' experience and something for which the word 'unity' does not finally suffice. What he would have *communicated* in this manner, particularly in the first days of a 'free association', was something like the pure experience of relation to the other. In his speech and his person, he would therefore have presented not the simple, full presence of a human being, which served as the ground for the identification that Mascolo thought he witnessed that evening in Verdun, but the presence/absence of a human being exposed to effacement and actually capable of 'preferring', for a brief time, being other. Saying 'all' would have included saying effacement, which is what Blanchot hears that night without sleep in which Antelme came to him; it would also entail saying the fear that attends this passage – a fear upon which Blanchot meditated at considerable length in his volume from 1973, *Le pas au-delà*.[18] The affirmative tone of Blanchot's brief text can prompt us to look away from the 'nothingness' to which he refers. But Blanchot is uncompromising in his understanding of that void, and this makes the claim he advances to what I propose to call a *literary* act all the more immense.

In Antelme's letter to Mascolo, the 'right' claimed by Antelme surely inheres in what he knows of Mascolo and what he knows of their friendship. In this sense it has a singular, personal character. But it would also inhere in the knowledge he has gained in his experience of a kind of rebirth and deliverance, a re-traversal of a kind of infancy and a new awareness of the conditions of its vulnerability and just exigencies. I emphasize, too, that it is a right to a certain fear. This is again partially of a personal character: fear is most immediately for the intimacy he has known with Mascolo in the time of his return (a time of deliverance for both of them) and Mascolo's own well-being. He fears an injury he could bring to this relation through some form of offense, and he fears the normal passing of this relation that comes with the process of recovery: the passage from intimacy to an 'understanding' from the friend that aids an accruing self-conformity or 'self-resemblance' solidified by all the accompanying alienations of an internalized decorum and mature social usage. But there is also something more fundamental at stake, a 'moral' problem, as Antelme puts it. What was communicated freely in those first weeks had to be honoured, starting with the form of communication itself and the freedom of the relation it entails, in all its fearful meaning.

A decade after Antelme's actual passing, and haunted by a claim like the one addressed to Mascolo (which might be translated with the words 'do not forget'), Blanchot returns to Antelme's teaching to grasp the conditions of a different, but not unrelated, form of accompaniment from the one envisioned by Mascolo – a different form of being- or dying-with. Answering Antelme's teaching (via recollection of Antelme's narrative in *L'espèce humaine*) gives Blanchot the capacity to recognize in that haunting solicitation of 'the night watched over' something quite real. The condition in which effacement is communicated, he specifies, is not a state of simple dissolution 'where everything would disappear'. Thus, a state that opens upon what Blanchot once named *'l'espace littéraire'* (something engaged in the performance of this very text) is opposed to a common understanding of the illusory condition of dream or fantasy. It is 'real' in the sense that it confers the right to a 'watch' over the living speech of the other – a right, we might say, to this literary act.

Mascolo knew the exigency of a new form of community from the grounds of what he received of Antelme's presence, in speech and act. Blanchot would join this very community (which formed around Antelme, who was both guide and participant). But he also received something else in that presence, another exigency he would have to learn and assume. In its very extravagance with respect to social usage, Antelme's 'free' speech and what remained of the knowledge communicated there, provided the 'moral' grounds for what Blanchot would call another form of relation, another form of being in community. Blanchot gave these grounds a singular historical meaning, as we see in the text I have cited (I refer to the references to the camps). We will also find something comparable in the astonishing words he devotes to what he hesitantly calls 'the presence of the people' in his reflections on the 'communitary exigency' and the events of 1968 in *The Unavowable Community*.[19] Undoubtedly, we must learn to read in Antelme's experience of an 'undecidable' something of Blanchot's 'unavowable', 'an impossibility of meaning' which is linked to effacement. And we must push further in grasping how Blanchot's immense claim to a *right* to the literary act he describes and performs in his commemorative statement ('my right to make you live') might also be heard in a spontaneous assemblage in the street, when death calls for testimony on the part of what may be at least momentarily called a community, or even a 'people'. Today, our attention to that claim is more imperative than ever.

Notes

1 Dionys Mascolo, *Autour d'un effort de mémoire* (Paris: Maurice Nadeau, 1987).

2 I refer to a brief piece published in the journal *Lignes* (1994). It was collected in *Robert Antelme: Textes inédits sur L'espèce humaine, Essais et témoignages*, ed. Daniel Dobbels (Paris: Gallimard, 1996), 71–6. The text is presented in translation in Zakir Paul (ed.), *Maurice Blanchot: Political Writings* (New York: Fordham University Press, 2010), 133–4.

3 The essay concludes with a return to this leitmotif of Antelme's 'disconsolate' state (p. 89).

4 From a letter to Mascolo cited in *Autour d'un effort de mémoire*, p. 23 (dated by Moscolo as being from 1949 to 1950): 'Dionys, I would like to tell you that I do not think of friendship as a positive thing, I mean as a value, but much rather, I mean to say, as a state, an identification, thus a multiplication of death, a multiplication of interrogation, the site that is miraculously the most neutral from which one can perceive and feel the constant of an unknown, the place where difference in its sharpest sense lives – as one would understand this at "the end of history", – flourishes only at the heart of its contrary – death's proximity.'

5 'L'indestructible' was first published in 1962 in the *NRF*, no. 112, pp. 671–80, and then collected in *L'entretien infini* (Gallimard, 1969), The Infinite Conversation, trans., Susan Hanson (Minneapolis: University of Minnesota Press, 1993), 123–35.

6 The following sentence, beginning with the words, 'In our world, on the contrary',
   might suggest that the 'hell' to which he refers was in the camps, in which case
   Antelme could be referring to an early experience in his incarceration—that is, an
   experience with other prisoners.
7 *Autour d'un effort de mémoire*, 19.
8 Ibid., 22.
9 Ibid.
10 Ibid., 52.
11 Ibid., 53. As I have noted elsewhere (*Last Steps: Maurice Blanchot's Exilic Writing*
   [New York: Fordham University Press, 2013], 46), this simple idiom puts the lie to
   Giorgio Agamben's very speculative construction of the figure of the Muselmann in
   Remnants of Auschwitz: The Witness and the Archive. In labelling Agamben's analysis
   'speculative', I am referring to his entire construction of the Muselmann's experience
   and the one who claims to speak for it. This problematic position ('exceptional', in
   its pretended sovereignty) is profoundly foreign to the stances taken by Antelme,
   Mascolo and Blanchot.
12 Ibid., 53.
13 Mascolo appends to these words the following note:
   'In the camp, he will say, the man of faith himself is led to substitute the creature
   for God: *"Negated as man by the SS, the man in the Christian comes to take on in
   importance the place of God." (L'espèce humaine.)*'
        The translation of both '*l'homme*' and '*l'espèce*' presents significant difficulties.
   I translate the first literally as it appears in Mascolo's citation, though I would
   be inclined to render it a bit more freely with 'human'. For '*espèce*', in relation to
   Antelme's text, I have always preferred 'kind'.
        Let me add here that I think we must be very careful in the use of the term
   'sacred'. In *The Infinite Conversation*, Blanchot draws upon words of Jacob to his
   brother Esau that point in the direction I am following here. The phrase 'I see you
   as one sees God' ('The Indestructible', 129) does not exalt the other or profane God;
   rather, it has a profoundly defamiliarizing effect with respect to our understanding
   of the presence of that human other. I do not read Antelme's challenging sentence
   as pointing necessarily to a 'sacralization' of the human in the standard sense of this
   term; what is involved is rather, first, a displacement of both God and humankind,
   which is perhaps not without relation to the effective conversion to which Antelme,
   Mascolo and Duras are impelled. As Mascolo will insist in his memoire, the 'news'
   brought by Antelme, in his words and person, will produce a kind of *deportation*
   in their existence by which they are rendered Jewish and Communist. Blanchot,
   it might be argued, will have known the same effect. (Though he never made the
   step of conversation, his opening to Jewish thought, following the teaching of
   Levinas, is profound; one may consult, in this respect, the opening section of 'The
   Indestructible', entitled 'Being Jewish' [123–9].) For Blanchot, particularly, there is

no place for a 'sacralization' of the human, even as the human opens upon that place that must remain vacant. There is effectively a kind of humanism here, but one that exceeds any metaphysical or theological construction.

Following Blanchot, we might hear in 'sacred,' a 'separation'. The human, understood in relation (in the exposure to *autrui*, and thus an originary being-together) is 'apart', transcending every sociopolitical determination. The experience of this separation and the 'freedom' it entails is what Antelme will suffer at the time of his return, not knowing what can be said and what cannot.

14 See pages 19 and 20 of *Autour d'un effort de mémoire* for Mascolo's discussion of this secondary consciousness or knowledge that takes form in 'receiving the event in what is unprecedented in it, even before having grasped its disconcerting import'.

15 I cite, in this paragraph, from pages 56 and 57 of *Autour d'un effort de mémoire*.

16 I want to take the opportunity here to remember, and thank, Monique Antelme for what she was able to tell me about this community and the warmth of Maurice Blanchot himself.

17 Here I must refer to my reading of 'The Indestructible', in *Last Steps: Maurice Blanchot's Exilic Writing*, 34–54. I have also discussed the topic of effacement in an essay entitled 'The Place of Friendship: Maurice Blanchot and Robert Antelme' (in the Danish Yearbook of Philosophy, Vol. 48–49 [2013–2014], 21–36), an essay in which I offer an analysis of 'In the Night Watched Over'. I pause in this last essay over Blanchot's famous commemorative statement for Georges Bataille, in which Blanchot addresses the problem of 'commemoration' itself and the necessity of facing 'the impossibility of meaning' presented by the death of the other. In the opening paragraph of his piece on Bataille, which carries of the title of the volume in which it was collected, *L'amitié*, we read a striking statement on effacement that anticipates the later text for Antelme but does not offer the affirmation which that later piece will pursue in its performance of assuming the watch to which its title refers. Here are the last sentences of this paragraph: 'Vainly do we try to maintain, with our words, with our writings, what is absent; vainly do we offer it the appeal of our memories and a sort of figure, the joy of remaining with the day, life prolonged by a truthful appearance. We are only looking to fill a void, we cannot bear the pain: the affirmation of this void. Who could agree to receive its insignificance, an insignificance so enormous that we do not have a memory capable of containing it and such that we ourselves must already slip into oblivion in order to sustain it, for the time of this slippage, into the very enigma this insignificance represents? Everything we say tends to veil the one affirmation: that all must fade [*que tout doit s'effacer*] and that we can remain loyal only so long as we watch over this movement that fades [*qui s'efface*], to which something in us that rejects all memory already belongs.' *L'amitié* (Paris: Gallimard, 1971), 326; *Friendship*, trans. Elizabeth Rottenberg (Stanford: Stanford University Press, 1997), 289.

As for the notion of right, we should recall the title of Blanchot's monumental essay,
'Literature and the Right to Death', and then the important use of the term at the
time of his return to politics in the late 1950s, where he argued for a right to refusal.

18   Maurice Blanchot, *Le pas au-delà* (Paris: Gallimard, 1973); *The Step Not Beyond*,
     trans. Lycette Nelson (Albany: SUNY Press, 1986).

19   Maurice Blanchot, *La communauté inavouable* (Paris: Les Éditions de Minuit,
     1983), 52–7; *The Unavowable Community*, trans. Pierre Joris (Barrytown: Station
     Hill Press, 1985).

Works cited

Antelme, Robert, *L'espece humaine*. Paris: Gallimard, 1957.

Blanchot, Maurice, *L'entretien infini*. Paris: Gallimard, 1969.

Blanchot, Maurice, *L'amitie*. Paris: Gallimard, 1971.

Blanchot, Maurice, *Le pas au-dela*. Paris: Gallimard, 1973.

Blanchot, Maurice, *La communaute inavouable*. Paris: Editions de Minuit, 1983.

Blanchot, Maurice, *The Unavowable Community*, trans. Pierre Joris. Barrytown: Station
Hill Press, 1985.

Blanchot, Maurice, *The Step Not Beyond*, trans. Lycette Nelson. Albany: SUNY Press,
1986.

Blanchot, Maurice, *The Infinite Conversation*, trans. Susan Hanson. Minneapolis:
University of Minnesota Press, 1993.

Blanchot, Maurice, *Friendship*, trans. Elizabeth Rottenberg. Stanford: Stanford
University Press, 1997.

Blanchot, Maurice, *Political Writings*, ed. Zakir Paul. New York: Fordham University
Press, 2010.

Dobbels, Daniel (ed.), *Robert Antelme: Textes inedits sur L'espece humaine*. Paris:
Gallimard, 1996.

Fynsk, Christopher, *Last Steps: Maurice Blanchot's Exilic Writing*. New York: Fordham
U. Press, 2013.

Fynsk, Christopher, 'The Place of Friendship: Maurice Blanchot and Robert Antelme',
Danish Yearbook of Philosophy, nos. 48–9, 21–36.

Mascolo, Dionys, *Autour d'un effort de memoire*. Paris: Maurice Nadeau, 1987.

5

Temporal undecidability

In retrospect and prospect

Max Saunders

At first the idea was that I was to write about a particular form of undecidability that was the subject of my book *Self Impression*: when readers, or sometimes even writers, cannot decide whether what they're reading, or writing, is autobiography or fiction. Autobiography is often thought of, as systematized in the work of one of its leading theorists, Philippe Lejeune, as invoking some form of contractual relation to verifiable fact or at least personal authenticity.[1] An autobiographer may select, heighten, establish patterns and imply meanings arising from them. But the episodes in the narrative are understood to represent real occurrences, relationships, feelings. Whereas a fiction, such as a novel, may draw on autobiographical experience – perhaps has so to draw to at least some extent. But what matters most is not the truth to the author's life, but the story; the invention and imagination; and the feeling it gives us that it's 'true to life' in a more general sense, true to anyone's life, or everyone's.

Of course the idea that any clear distinction like this between autobiography and fiction can be upheld has been challenged by both creative writers and critics. That is precisely the subject of *Self Impression*, which takes as its starting point an ingenious essay by the writer Stephen Reynolds from what may seem the surprisingly early date of 1906, with a title sounding surprisingly postmodern in its portmanteau undecidedness: 'Autobiografiction'.[2]

Reynolds's argument was that in the two or three decades around the turn of the century, a new variety of writing had sprung up poised precisely between these categories. He thought it was a relatively minor subgenre; and the works he picks out as examples, by writers like Mark Rutherford, A.C. Benson and George Gissing, do indeed seem limited in scope as well as dated, fustily Edwardian to our tastes now, though they were all bestsellers in their day. What he is describing is different from the autobiographical novel, which usually narrates the author's first-person experience in third-person omniscient form. Autobiografiction is written in first-person autobiographical form. It's just that its story isn't the author's. Or not exactly. Or we can't be sure: it's a genuine undecidability. It's that undecidability that separates it from fictional autobiography – as, for example, *Gulliver's Travels*. Or even *Jane Eyre: An Autobiography*.

But it seems to me that the new form which Reynolds had spotted emerging was to prove central to much of the interesting writing to come not only in Modernism, but especially in postmodern and contemporary fiction. As he was writing the essay, figures like Joyce and Proust were beginning to reimagine autobiographical fiction and fictional autobiography completely. Modernists like Ford, Woolf or Stein were to continue in that vein. Then the postmodern version was named as autofiction, a clear descendant of autobiografiction. If autofiction seems a more elegant term for it, it's at the expense of the attention to formal autobiography. That is, autofiction sounds like it could be any autobiographical novel, not necessarily a fiction in the form of an autobiography.

But then I was – how shall I say? – undecided. I wasn't sure I had enough new ideas about autobiografiction to take it up again; and anyway, I had moved onto a very different subject: futurology in the interwar book series *To-Day and To-Morrow*.[3] In many ways it is hard to imagine a more different subject. Instead of the retrospect of autobiography or fictional narrative, the prospect of prediction. Instead of the poignant, often anxious tone of much *fin-de-siècle* autobiografiction, the carefree, exhilarating utopianism or witty cynicism (or, bizarrely, in an unusual version of undecidability, both) of writers and thinkers teasing out among post-war ruins possibilities for a better world.

In *To-Day and To-Morrow*, as its title foretells, writers chose a subject, described its contemporary developments and imagined its future. The series was edited by C. K. Ogden, the collaborator of I.A. Richards, from 1923 to 1931 – very much the period of high Modernism; and it included a number of modern writers: Vernon Lee, Robert Graves, Vera Brittain, Winifred Holtby, Hugh MacDiarmid, Lewis Grassic Gibbon, Andre Maurois and so on. The futurological experiment was what was distinctive about *To-Day and To-Morrow*; and it attracted many of the best minds of the period: scientists like J.B.S. Haldane, James Jeans and J.D. Bernal; philosophers like Bertrand Russell and Sarvepalli Radhakrishnan (who was later president of India); public intellectuals like Sylvia Pankhurst and C.E.M. Joad and nearly a hundred others.

Such a project is shot through with thinking about time. Many of the volumes reflect the ideas of the new Einsteinian physics of space–time, for example. Part of the fascination though is seeing writers trying to find new ways of writing about time; and especially of writing about the future. Most of the volumes are committed to a progressive, rationalist, enlightenment view of science as offering a better basis for prediction than traditional modes such as magic or religion or prophecy. Yet they know that their predictions can only be provisional, speculative, in a word undecidable.

H.G. Wells – who really should have written for *To-Day and To-Morrow* but didn't – perhaps he was too old, too *passé* by then! – was certainly the figure the authors in the series looked up to, or back to. One of his pioneering books speculating about the future had been *Anticipations*, of 1902, or, to give it its full title: *Anticipations of the Reactions of Mechanical and Scientific Progress upon Human Life and Thought*:

> It is proposed in this book to present in as orderly an arrangement as the necessarily diffused nature of the subject admits, certain speculations about the trend of present forces, speculations which, taken all together, will build up an imperfect and very hypothetical, but sincerely intended forecast of the way things will probably go in this new century. Necessarily diffidence will be one of the graces of the performance. Hitherto such forecasts have been presented almost invariably in the form of fiction, and commonly the provocation of the satirical opportunity has been too much for the writer; the narrative form becomes more and more of a nuisance as the speculative inductions become sincerer, and here it will be abandoned altogether in favour of a texture of frank inquiries and arranged considerations.[4]

When we juxtapose these two apparently incommensurable kinds of writing together – on the one hand, autobiography and its hybrid, autobiografictional forms; on the other hand, futurology – what might the contrast be able to add to our consideration of undecidablility? A contrast, that is, between undecidabilities of retrospect on the one hand, when autobiographical writing looks back and summons up the past. And on the other hand, undecidabilities of looking forwards, of prospect.

They're undecidable in different ways, certainly. Writing about a past, which has already happened, seems an easier proposition, at least at first sight. People are more likely to write their memoirs than to turn prophets. We know something has happened to us; and we know, or think we know, what it was that happened. We know what we think of it.

On the other hand, the future will almost certainly surprise us. Writing about a future that hasn't yet happened poses a particular set of problems to do with how to write about it, how to represent it; specifically problems about authority; the authority of who decides what is decidable or undecidable.

Nietzsche alone among philosophers seems undaunted by the future. No classical stoicism or Asian mystical self-abnegation for him! No diffidence to grace his performance. Unlike the rest of us all too humans, he feels as sure of his future as of his past; because he is confident he is 'a destiny':

> On this perfect day, when everything has become ripe and not only the grapes are growing brown, a ray of sunlight has fallen on my life: I looked behind me, I looked before me, never have I seen so many and such good things together. Not in vain have I buried my forty-fourth year today, I was entitled to bury it – what there was of life in it is rescued, is immortal. The first book of the *Revaluation of all Values*, the *Songs of Zarathustra*, the *Twilight of the Idols*, my attempt to philosophize with a hammer – all of them gifts of this year, of its last quarter even! *How should I not be grateful to my whole life? –* And so I tell myself my life.[5]

And yet from another – perhaps the opposite – point of view, to approach autobiography from the perspective of futurology is to heighten our awareness of the speculativeness of that enterprise too. Do we really know what happened to us and what we think about it?

In a brilliant passage from the *Confessions of an English Opium Eater*, Thomas De Quincey explains how this question has both epistemological and moral aspects:

> In fact, every intricate and untried path in life, where it was from the first a matter of arbitrary choice to enter upon it or avoid it, is effectually a path through a vast Hercynian forest, unexplored and unmapped, where each several turn in your advance leaves you open to new anticipations of what is next to be expected, and consequently open to altered valuations of all that has been already traversed. Even the character of your own absolute experience, past and gone, which (if anything in this world) you might surely answer for as sealed and settled for ever – even this you must submit to hold in suspense, as a thing conditional and contingent upon what is yet to come – liable to have its provisional character affirmed or reversed, according to the new combinations into which it may enter with elements only yet perhaps in the earliest stages of development.[6]

Now you may say that this realization was open to De Quincey in the nineteenth century, and that therefore he didn't need modernism and scientific futurology to arrive at it. Indeed, that vision of experience as always provisional and continually exfoliating like a living thing is a quintessentially Romantic one. But Romantic autobiography's exaltation of memory – of what Wordsworth termed 'emotion recollected in tranquillity' – is too easily characterized as an investment in the past. Approaching it from the perspective of futurology sharpens our attention to the importance of the future in such visions. Recollection is retrospective; but the emotion being recollected includes the exhilaration of future possibilities, whether in the stirrings of a new spirit in society or in the stirrings of a youthful mind. 'Bliss was it in that dawn to be alive, / But to be young was very heaven!'[7] Why? Because it was the sense of a beginning (of a revolution, of a life), with all its promise and excitement. Notice De Quincey's terms: 'each several turn in your advance leaves you open to new anticipations of what is next to be expected.' That of course is what the future felt like for Wells too: each new advance gave rise to anticipations of things to come.

Memory for De Quincey is thus saturated with past anticipations of possible futures. But he is saying something else as well. That the character of our experience – what it is like, what it feels like, what it means to us – can be 'affirmed or reversed' – can be changed – by what is still to come. When the ancient Greeks said that call no man happy till he was dead, they were thinking of a person's fate. You might live a long life you thought was happy, but if you're betrayed at the end and die tragically, you'd no longer be an exemplar of the happy life. The happiness of the happy episodes isn't compromised; it's the overall judgement that changes. True, if someone comes along and reveals that you've killed your father and married your mother, you might feel differently about what you thought of as your marital bliss. But that's not really the point. It's a shift from one fixed interpretation – happiness – to another – disaster, terror, tragedy and so on. You had a fate. You just didn't know what it was, or the form it would take. Whereas what De Quincey is talking about is something different. It's not so much that the future shifts your sense of your experience from one decision to another; rather, it makes it undecidable. Because anything you decide, or revalue, can still go on shifting its shape.

The writers of *To-Day and To-Morrow* have several strategies for addressing the provisionality of speculations about the future. One is to be diffident, only projecting one generation or lifetime ahead. Most of them don't venture beyond fifty years or so into the future, on the grounds that extrapolating current trends for a few decades is a safe bet. Though one of the most audacious of the writers, J. B. S. Haldane, in a later essay called 'The Last Judgement: A Scientist Turns to Prophecy', was prepared to project much further ahead than that. Most of his text is given in the form of an account written by the descendants of humans living on Venus forty million years in the future. Yet even this was diffidence by Haldane's standard. He was a biologist, and his argument is that such timespans are slight in evolutionary terms. Haldane says he can imagine a future that far ahead because that long ago our ancestors were already mammals and probably monkeys, whereas he finds it impossible to project his imagination forwards by ten times as much, since 400 million years ago our ancestors were fishlike, and 'a corresponding change in our descendants' is too alien to imagine.[8]

Another strategy is to be aware of how predictions are not neutral, but can affect the outcome. We talk of 'self-fulfilling prophecies'. But F. C. S. Schiller, in an ingenious volume called *Cassandra, or the Future of the British Empire* (1926) was more interested in self-defeating ones. He begins with this paradox. If prophets are believed, people take evasive action. So only those who aren't believed turn out to be true prophets – like Cassandra. Schiller sees the Versailles 'settlement' as promoting, rather, 'a general unsettlement' of European affairs, 'of which the consequences, economic and political, will endure until the next convulsion, which they are admirably calculated to precipitate and aggravate'.[9] Another world war had come to him to seem inevitable because no one wanted to believe it would happen.

One of the modes several of the writers use is what I term 'future *history*'.[10] Rather than writing the future as prophecy from the point of view of today, they imagine a historian in the distant future looking back, to a point somewhere between now and then; and writing our future as their history.

From one point of view, this makes the future seem less undecidable; in that it imagines it as having taken a particular course. Vera Brittain, for example, in her brilliant volume *Halcyon, or the Future of Monogamy* for the series, imagines a feminist future historian writing the history of the developments in women's rights still unachieved at the time Brittain was writing – 1929. True, the Representation of the People (Equal Franchise) Act of 1928 had just lowered the voting age for women from thirty to twenty-one, equalizing it with that for men. But the further emancipation Brittain could then only hope for is presented as achieved fact. Her fictional future historian describes 'The Period of Sexual Reform', which includes the passing of the 'Sexual Instruction (Schools and Welfare Centres) Act' of 1948, and the 'Matrimonial Causes Act' of 1959, which broadened the possible grounds for divorce, and made consensual divorce legal.[11] Such a strategy not only short-circuits embarrassment about sounding like a deranged prophet. It also serves her progressive cause by presenting a world in which such battles have been won, showing them as achievable, and as nothing any sensible person need worry about.

Yet from another point of view, what the trope gives us is something odd, certainly very paradoxical. A history, but of something that has not happened, or at least not yet. So while on the one hand it makes for decidablility – yes, this could actually happen; you can choose this future – on the other hand, it invites scepticism about history itself. If the history of the future can be fabricated thus, how can we be sure the history of the past isn't equally fabricated? Not fake news, but fake ancient history?

Brittain suggests humorously that future history has been transformed by psychical research. Her future historian says: 'Only one or two examples are needed to illustrate this period', 'now so well known owing to the recent research work of the Historio-Telepathic Institute' (p. 18). The joke is nicely turned. The idea of a 'Historio-Telepathic Institute' suggests that generalized narratives about past feelings, thoughts and experiences, despite attempts to ground them in the rigorous accumulation of evidence, can never shed their speculative aspect either. It's a view that makes history seem as undecidable as prophecy.

Robert Graves wrote two volumes for the series, on the future of humour and the future of swearing. In both he too draws on this future history trope, and again in ways which make us sceptical about history (as we might expect from a writer who, in the *I, Claudius* series, was to excel in fake ancient history). He argues that both humour and swearing are so context-dependent that today's practices will be unintelligible to our descendants. Not least because, where they involve taboo, as with swearing, the crucial evidence will be asterisked out of the record, so future historians will have no chance of recovering what it was.

Finally, in this group of examples, though it was actually the first: Haldane again, in the volume *Daedalus; or, Science and the Future*, which inspired the series, does future history for part of it, which he writes in the form of: 'some extracts from an essay on the influence of biology on history during the 20th century which will (it is hoped) be read by a rather stupid undergraduate member of this university to his supervisor during his first term 150 years hence.'[12] Here too the device has the effect of making radical new inventions seem familiar, especially the prediction that was to arouse most interest in *Daedalus*, of what Haldane called 'ectogenesis', or gestation of children outside the mother's body, in an artificial womb. It was the vision that was to inspire his friend Aldous Huxley's *Brave New World*, with its 'hatcheries' in which citizens are mass-produced through a kind of cloning. (It was Haldane, again, who coined the term 'clone'.) But Haldane's future history trope again undermines the notion of history, through his parody of the garbled and lazy version of historiography cobbled together by his future student.

Autobiography, then, by pulling the self back to its past, simultaneously seeks to pull the *past* into the present; though, as we saw with De Quincey, that past is everywhere open to the anticipations and revaluations of the future. Futurology, by contrast, as it seeks to project the present into the future, by the same token tries to pull the *future* into the present; though it frequently does so in the mode of future historiography. What they share is thus a form of temporal dislocation or relocation or time-shifting, perplexing conjunctions of times which disturb our sense of when we are.

It is easier to see with futurology, *because* we have no direct experience yet of the future, so there's something immediately odd and counter-intuitive about thinking about it, or being shown it. Conversely, the very fact that we do have direct experience of the past is, I think, what prevents us from seeing what a strange thing is happening when we recreate it now, whether in memory or in writing. The memory, or the representation, is in the wrong time. Not then, but now. And its proximity to us enables us to inspect it and question it in ways we perhaps couldn't or didn't at the time. This may seem an obvious or even a trivial distinction. Of course, the original experience and the moment of remembering it and writing about it occur at different times. Of course, as we get older, the distance in time between the remembering self and the self remembered increases. But the crucial point, which follows from those obvious ones, is that those differences mean that our relationship to the experience, and our understanding of it, has changed, and is changing, and will continue to change. It has become undecidable.

To get a purchase on what effects writers can produce using these forms of temporal dislocation, consider Proust. I start with William Empson's wonderfully irreverent response:

> you remember how Proust, at the end of that great novel, having convinced the reader with the full sophistication of his genius that he is going to produce an apocalypse, brings out with pathetic faith, as a fact of absolute value, that sometimes when you are living in one place you are reminded of living in another place, and this, since you are now apparently living in two places, means that you are outside time, in the only state of beatitude he can imagine. In any one place (atmosphere, mental climate) life is intolerable; in any two it is an ecstasy. Is it the number two, one is forced to speculate, which is of this encouraging character?[13]

This is funny about Proust's social satire. If the milieux he describes were so petty and frustrating, surely being in more than one at a time would just make things worse, not better. Those words 'apocalypse' and 'ecstasy' there suggest that Empson's resistance to Proust's assertion of the redemptive nature of involuntary memory was his usual resistance to anything religious or quasi-religious. For what is really at stake here is immortality. If a chance circumstance – a madeleine dipped in tea, an uneven paving stone – can trigger a memory of the past to flood back in all its plenitude, then that moment, that had been over and forgotten, is revealed as not having been lost after all, but still present. If our experience can be re-experienced as exactly the same years later, then it exists out of time; immune from the transformations of voluntary memory. And that thought seems to offer a hope that if our experience exists outside time, it might be able to exist outside our lifetime too. I don't know how far Proust believed in anything quite so mystical, but he certainly believed that it could exist outside his lifetime in a work of art, a work of literature. The reason the distinction between voluntary and involuntary memory is so important to him is that involuntary memory offers him a way of contesting the idea that memories change experiences. Yes, willed memories may do that; but in his account of the involuntary ones, the original is somehow preserved intact, with all the aura of an original work of art.

Fine if you're having a cup of tea, or stumbling on a stone. But if you're writing an immense novel, aren't you doing something different from simply re-experiencing the past? Indeed, while Proust's argument claims the timeless persistence of the past, his hyper-aesthetic hyper-elaboration of his memories opens up the gap between the remembered past and its present re-creation. Indeed, *A La Recherche* famously opens on such an abyss – the description of the subject on the borderline between sleeping and waking, and losing his sense of temporal and spatial co-ordinates, being conscious of being perplexed about where and when he is and what time it is. Then this undecidability is subordinated to the opening sentence: 'Longtemps je me suis couché de bonne heure' (For a long time I used to go to bed early). The discord between the adverb of long continuity and the perfect tense suggesting a completed, so discontinuous, action immediately disorients us in relation to time. So the memory of temporal disorientation is itself disorientated; it doesn't so much refer to a single memory of a single moment, but any one in a long series of such moments, or all of them together.

That's all straightforward enough, or, at least, a complex instance of a straightforward situation. It's all in the past tense, referring to the narrator's history before the act of writing about it. But that elaborate *description* imagining the sleeper clutching at orientating straws as his sleep is disturbed didn't exist before he started writing about it. Its time is the present of the narration. The novel is research because it is finding out something new; a memory the self did not know it had till it imagined it.

The affect produced by these mirroring forms of temporal dislocation is of interest too. Whether you bring the past or the future back into the present, you make it strange, defamiliarize it. It floats free of its normal chronological and narrative contexts. It looks different. It is open to new possibilities of apprehension and judgement, as De Quincey says. Decisions we have made in the past about what our lives have been, and how we want to live, need to be reconsidered. That seems to me an important version of undecidability.

This kind of autobiographical undecidablility, then, is undecidable in two ways, or along two axes. It is a hermeneutic undecidability; about what an experience means and how we understand it. But it is also an undecidability about time: about when the experience really is, and when it can be said to exist. But the practice of autobiography is founded on a disattention to that difference, on getting us to accept the substitution of the later memory for the earlier experience.

But when you do attend to the difference, then the abyss of the temporal kind of undecidability opens up. One way of thinking about this existential dislocation is to see it as an aspect of what performativity theory has brought to autobiography theory: the sense that an autobiographical subject doesn't pre-exist the narration, but is brought into being by it.[14] But what I want to add to that account is a clearer sense of the temporal dislocation involved: in writing the memory, reconstructing it in words, it comes into being in that form at the moment of writing. So the memory is *of* the past, but it is also *of* the present – the moment of writing or reading. Its temporal location is thus genuinely undecidable.

It is perhaps worth noting that this account tallies with recent research on the neuroscience of memory, which suggests that our common metaphor for seeing memory as a kind of recording apparatus is wrong. Rather than a memory being recorded and archived, and then retrieved later on, it is more a case of the memory needing to be recreated with each remembering. This accounts for its susceptibility to being modified or falsified, for autobiography to turn into autobiografiction. If it isn't the original master tape, then the memory cannot be located unequivocally in the past. The strangeness of autobiography – the way it defamiliarizes our experience – is precisely in the way it disturbs its temporal location, making the past seem present and the present seem past.

This dislocation is more evident with futurology, because we cannot summon up our future in the same way that memory allows us to summon up our past. Our vision of the future has not been part of an actual future that we can imagine as being back to our time. It can only be a product of our mental processes. Neuroscience, again, is finding these processes of future-envisioning closely related to the production of memories, and that memory impairment also compromises our ability to think ahead.[15]

The philosopher F. H. Bradley (on whom T. S. Eliot wrote the dissertation for his uncompleted doctorate) asked an intriguing question: 'why do we remember forwards and not backwards?'[16] This complicates the argument, suggesting how the characteristic 'feel' of memory is not just a matter of jumping around in time, but is to do with the direction in which we move from one memory to another. (That is why the analogy between memory and cinema is so seductive: we rewind back to the past, but play memories forward.) In fact, Bradley thinks that though in general the time-direction in which we think our memories matches the time-direction in which we live, it is nonetheless possible in certain circumstances – when our emotional investment in the past is greater than in the present – for memory's time-direction to be reversed:

> Our thoughts seem really to go back when the exclusive object of interest is placed far behind us, and we retrace towards it every unwilling advance that has carried us away. Each event adds a link, but our mind moves from each later link back to the earlier; we are interested in each solely as a thing to be passed by, in the order which carries our thoughts home. And, I apprehend, memory may here travel back from the later to the former, because for our interest the earliest is the end. Thus, when we steam against the sea from our native shore, if we thought of our selves we should go forward against the waves. But as our hearts are left behind, we follow each wave that sweeps backwards and seems to lengthen the interval. And, in remembering objects passed by upon the waters, I think, contrary to our main habit, our memory might take the road that leads to our desire.[17]

Bradley's question enables us to pose an equivalent one about the time-direction of our future thinking. If thinking about the future were the mirror image of remembering the past, we might expect its direction of travel to be reversed in the mirror. In memory we usually jump back to a point in the past and then follow in our own footsteps in the same direction we original trod them. If future thinking reversed this pattern, we would jump to a point in the future, then work back step by step till we returned to the present. Yet generally we do not. Instead, we start from the present, and keep to our familiar time-direction. Whether we are predicting, or writing 'future history', we narrate first one event, then what happens after it. The only difference is whether we imagine the future from our familiar vantage point in the present, and use the future tense, or imagine ourselves looking back on the events of the imagined future from the perspective of an even-more distant future, and narrate them in the past tense as if they had already taken place.

Bradley starts his essay by saying, 'To the reader who is new to this question it may wear the appearance of a paradox. He may reply that to go forwards is obvious and natural.' The real paradox seems to me to lie elsewhere, in the structure of memory. We look backwards, but think forwards. What distinguishes future thinking from memory, according to this view, is precisely that it is *not* the mirror image of memory. When we imagine the future, we look forwards *and* think forwards. In other words, futurology feels so different from memory not only because its events are fictional, and not only because they are on the other end of our timeline from our past, but because this *relation* between the direction of looking and the direction of thinking is also different.

Though not to De Quincey, perhaps; since to him, recalling the past was bound up with anticipating the future. In another classic moment from the *Confessions*, about the Whispering Gallery in St Paul's Cathedral, he remembers his almost-seventeen-year-old self recalling his fifteen-year-old self there, recalling the ancient Roman proverb that 'a word once uttered is irrevocable'. It had been an earlier anxiety for him: 'Long before that fifteenth year of mine, I had noticed, as a worm lying at the heart of life and fretting its security, the fact that innumerable acts of choice change countenance and are variously appraised at varying stages of life – shift with the shifting hours.'[18] The reverberating echo of his friend's whisper feels like fate, but paradoxically also enacts the worry that a moment of decision can never be put behind one, but keeps coming back. His moments of decision are fraught with the anticipations that later memories will speak with that stern Roman voice.

> Already, at fifteen, I had become deeply ashamed of judgments which I had once pronounced, of idle hopes that I had once encouraged, false admirations or contempts with which once I had sympathised. And, as to acts which I surveyed with any doubts at all, I never felt sure that after some succession of years I might not feel withering doubts about them, both as to principle and as to inevitable results.[19]

For a writer, the idea that 'a word once uttered is irrevocable' is doubly dreadful: it comprehends not only the words one speaks, but the words one writes. Yet there is a deeply paradoxical aspect to this episode and De Quincey's attitude towards it. The Roman proverb implies that utterances are for all time. What writer does not aspire to immortality and posterity through their words? De Quincey is more concerned that his feelings about the words will change, that self-criticism will force him to regret uttering them. Yet this concedes that though the words may remain, their signification changes. You may not be able to unsay them but you can unmean them. The views they express can be abjured.

No wonder then that he revised his autobiography – from the first appearance of the *Confessions* in the *London Magazine* in 1821 to book in 1822 to expanded edition in 1856 (and then in further autobiographical works like the *Suspiria De Profundis*). Indeed, this passage about St Paul's was one of the 1856 additions. He was always revising his memories even before the events they recorded. De Quincey wrote: 'Far more of our deepest thoughts and feelings pass to us through perplexed combinations of *concrete* objects, pass to us as *involutes* . . . in compound experiences incapable of being disentangled than ever reach us directly, and in their own abstract shapes.'[20] This is rightly taken as anticipating Freud's *Interpretation of Dreams*, and its discussion of the displacement of affects and their condensation around dream symbols. But the involution of De Quincey's feelings is a matter of time as much as anything else. It is an extreme form of temporal undecidability.

For less involuted people though, I have been arguing that the temporal dislocations of futurology are normally more disconcerting than those of memory. This is not because the mental process of positing a future moment differs from that of positing a past one; and certainly not because remembering is more common than anticipating. We clearly do both constantly. It must be because we are less used to narrating our futures than our past, whether to ourselves or to others, less used to placing the events in our mind's eye in relation to each other, in a sequence. Though remembering also feels less undecidable, of course, in the sense that we know where all those memories lead to. We are the terminus of our own memories; at least for the moment. With hindsight, there is no doubt about where the choices made have led. They have led to us, to now. But that is not how it felt at the time, when we could not know the consequences of all our choices and actions. One great danger of autobiography is what might be termed the 'teleological fallacy', in which past experiences are understood purely in terms of their subsequent results. Sartre gives a wonderful example in his childhood memoir *Les Mots*, of a children's book he was given about the childhoods of famous men. Each is given only his first name, but knowing adults are able to identify the adult genius from the prophetic childhood vignette. For example, young 'Rafaello' is taken to see the Pope, and when asked about him afterwards, replies: 'What Holy father? All I saw was colours!'[21]

Gary Saul Morson labels this teleological determinism as 'foreshadowing': the advancing of a narrative under the shadow of the knowledge of what is to come.[22] He distinguishes it from what he calls 'sideshadowing', which denotes a mode of narration which tries to keep open a sense of the other possible paths that might have been taken at any one moment: 'sideshadowing restores *the possibility of possibility*', he argues: 'It teaches a fundamental lesson: to understand a moment is to grasp not only what did happen but also what might have happened.'[23] He is writing of Russian realist fiction, but the distinction is equally telling applied to autobiography. It is the effect De Quincey aims at in the *Confessions*. He wants to recapture his sense of the risks and anxieties attendant on each choice and each action. It is a sense of fatefulness, but the opposite of a foreshadowed fatalism, inexorably grinding towards the prophesied destiny, the fate known in advance. Instead, the anxieties arise from the feeling that what you are doing now is constructing your fate but precisely without your knowing what it will turn out to be.

We can imagine possible futures for ourselves. But because they might be illusory, and because they are not ones we have lived yet, they feel necessarily provisional, a garden or Hercynian forest of forking paths. Will I choose this kind of life, or that? In the past, the choices of action or decision have been made. But – as De Quincey says – the choices of interpretation keep coming back. Was I this kind of person, or that kind? Was my life like this, or like that?

This distinction between contemplating decisions to be taken in the future, and those already taken in the past, brings out an important temporal ambiguity in the very term 'undecidability'. From the perspective of foresight, a choice is undecidable because you simply cannot choose between the forking paths. With hindsight, you made your choice, but may feel it was the wrong decision. You would no longer decide it thus. In this sense, a decision can seem undecidable in retrospect, because you have 'un-decided' it. But from this point of view, undecidability also makes us think about the nature of decisions. What is a decision? The metaphor of forking paths is perhaps misleading; or, at least, an impression in retrospect. Sometimes, to be sure, we reach points in a life which seem genuine cases of either/or. To pick a course to study; to take a job; to buy something; to take a trip. Or not. But in other cases, we have found directions through a landscape in which paths as such were not visible. Our lives, that is, may sometimes take a shape as much as a result of drift or circumstances as of an act of will on our part. Sometimes what seem even the more momentous steps – to move house, to marry, to have children, to emigrate – though we talk about them as the result of decisions, may come about incrementally, as a result of many small encounters, accidents, surprises, zig-zags. They may not feel quite like 'decisions' at all at the time. Undecidability in literature is perhaps an attempt to recapture this aspect of the texture of experience. Sometimes it is less a matter of hesitating between distinct alternatives, and more that existence doesn't always present itself with such logical clarity. That, after all, is one of the great themes of tragedy: that a person may end up having created their own fate without making that choice, but inadvertently, either through unwitting actions (as in Greek tragedy) or through what Hardy called a 'concatenation of events'.[24]

Another way of putting this would be to say that sideshadowed autobiography tries to represent the past as being still undecided, as fluid and mercurial, as still having as much to play for, as the future. Such autobiography can be fictional. Indeed, it shows how autobiography can only be fictional, even when it is true: one narrative alongside other possible narratives that we imagine to explain ourselves to others or to ourselves. Take John Dowell, the narrator of Ford's novel *The Good Soldier*, in one of fiction's great articulations of radical undecidability, trying to convey his perplexity that his memory of his and his wife's friendship with the Ashburnhams feels like one kind of idyllic life, whereas what he has learned since reveals it as treacherous and catastrophic:

> We were, if you will, one of those tall ships with the white sails upon a blue sea, one of those things that seem the proudest and the safest of all the beautiful and safe things that God has permitted the mind of men to frame. Where better could one take refuge? Where better?
>
> Permanence? Stability! I can't believe it's gone. I can't believe that that long, tranquil life, which was just stepping a minuet, vanished in four crashing days at the end of nine years and six weeks...
>
> No, by God, it is false! It wasn't a minuet that we stepped; it was a prison—a prison full of screaming hysterics, tied down so that they might not outsound the rolling of our carriage wheels as we went along the shaded avenues of the Taunus Wald.[25]

For De Quincey, there is something sublime about the imagination's power to reinvent its past. For Dowell, it is something tragic that leaves him feeling he doesn't know his past, his own experience, his own decisions. Dowell is living between two incompatible times, and the predicament is an agony for him rather than an ecstasy. Because most of his experience for the previous nine years has suddenly become radically undecidable. But not in a good way.

Notes

1   P. Lejeune, 'The Autobiographical Pact', in Lejeune, *On Autobiography*, ed. Paul John Eakin, trans. Katherine Leary (Minneapolis: University of Minnesota Press, 1989).

2 Stephen Reynolds, 'Autobiografiction', *Speaker*, new series, 15, no. 366 (6 October 1906): 28, 30. Max Saunders, *Self-Impression: Life-Writing, Autobiografiction and the Forms of Modern Literature* (Oxford: Oxford University Press, 2010).

3 See Max Saunders, *Imagined Futures: Writing, Science, and Modernity in the To-Day and To-Morrow Book Series, 1923–31* (Oxford: Oxford University Press, 2019).

4 H. Wells, *Anticipations of the Reactions of Mechanical and Scientific Progress upon Human Life and Thought*, fourth edition (London: Chapman and Hall, 1902), 1–2.

5 F. Nietzsche, *Ecce Homo*, trans. R. J. Hollingdale (London: Penguin, 1992), on Destiny. Epigraph to *Ecce Homo*, 37.

6 T. De Quincey, *Confessions of an English Opium Eater* (London: Penguin, 1986), 181–2.

7 W. Wordsworth, 'The French Revolution as It Appeared to Enthusiasts at Its Commencement', (1809); also *The Prelude* (1850) bk. 9, l. 108.

8 J. Haldane, 'The Last Judgement', *Possible Worlds* (London: Chatto & Windus, 1927), 287–312, 292.

9 F. Schiller, *Cassandra, or the Future of the British Empire* (London: Kegan Paul Trench and Trübner, 1926), 50.

10 See Saunders, *Imagined Futures*, 134–52.

11 V. Brittain, *Halcyon, or the Future of Monogamy* (London: Kegan Paul Trench and Trübner, 1929), 81, 85.

12 J. Haldane, *Daedalus; or, Science and the Future* (London: Kegan Paul Trench and Trübner, 1923), 56–7.

13 William Empson, *Seven Types of Ambiguity* [1930; third edition, 1961] (Harmondsworth: Pelican, 1977), 158.

14 See, for example, Sidonie Smith, 'Performativity, Autobiographical Practice, Resistance', in Sidonie Smith and Julia Watson (eds), *Women, Autobiography, Theory: A Reader* (Madison: University of Wisconsin Press, 1998), 108–15.

15 See, for example, https://www.technologynetworks.com/neuroscience/news/how-the-brains-gps-switches-between-different-possible-futures-330140.

16 F. H. Bradley, 'Why Do We Remember Forwards and Not Backwards?' *Mind*, 12: 48 (October, 1887): 579–82.

17 Ibid., 582.

18 T. De Quincey, *Confessions* (London: Oxford World's Classics, 1902), 88.

19 Ibid.

20 De Quincey, 'Autobiography', in David Masson (ed.), *The Collected Writings of Thomas De Quincey*, 14 vols (Edinburgh: A & C Black, 1889–90); vol. 1, 39; 43.

21 J.-P. Sartre, *Words*, trans. Irene Clephane (Harmondsworth: Penguin, 1967), 127–8.

22 See Gary Saul Morson, *Narrative and Freedom: The Shadows of Time* (New Haven: Yale University Press, 1994).

23 Ibid., 119.
24 'Henchard, like all his kind, was superstitious, and he could not help thinking that the concatenation of events this evening had produced was the scheme of some sinister intelligence bent on punishing him.' *The Mayor of Casterbridge* (London: Macmillan, 1902), 151.
25 F. Ford, *The Good Soldier*, ed. Max Saunders (Oxford: Oxford University Press, 2012), 12–13.

Works cited

Bradley, F., 'Why Do We Remember Forwards and Not Backwards?' *Mind*, 12, no. 48 (1887): 579–82.
Brittain, V., *Halcyon, or the Future of Monogamy*. London: Kegan Paul Trench and Trübner, 1929.
De Quincey, T., *Confessions of an English Opium Eater*. London: Penguin, 1986.
De Quincey, T., 'Autobiography', in David Masson (ed.), *The Collected Writings of Thomas De Quincey*. 14 vols. Edinburgh: A & C Black, 1889–9000.
Empson, W., *Seven Types of Ambiguity* (1930), third edition. Harmondsworth: Pelican, 1961.
Ford, F., *The Good Soldier*, ed. Max Saunders. Oxford: Oxford University Press, 2012.
Haldane, J., *Daedalus; or, Science and the Future*. London: Kegan Paul Trench and Trübner, 1923.
Haldane, J., 'The Last Judgement', in *Possible Worlds*. London: Chatto & Windus, 1927.
Hardy, T., *The Mayor of Casterbridge*. London: Macmillan, 1902.
Lejeune, P., 'The Autobiographical Pact', in Paul John Eakin (ed.) and Katherine Leary (trans.), Lejeune, *On Autobiography*. Minneapolis: University of Minnesota Press, 1989.
Morson, G., *Narrative and Freedom: The Shadows of Time*. New Haven: Yale University Press, 1994.
Nietzsche, F., *Ecce Homo*, trans. R. J. Hollingdale. London: Penguin, 1992.
Reynolds, S., 'Autobiografiction', *Speaker*, new series, 15, no. 366 (6 October 1906): 28, 30.
Sartre, J.-P., *Words*, trans. Irene Clephane. Harmondsworth: Penguin, 1967.
Saunders, M., *Self-Impression: Life-Writing, Autobiografiction and the Forms of Modern Literature*. Oxford: Oxford University Press, 2010.
Saunders, M., *Imagined Futures: Writing, Science, and Modernity in the To-Day and To-Morrow Book Series, 1923–31*. Oxford: Oxford University Press, 2019.
Schiller, F., *Cassandra, or the Future of the British Empire*. London: Kegan Paul Trench and Trübner, 1926.

Smith, S., 'Performativity, Autobiographical Practice, Resistance', in Sidonie Smith and Julia Watson (eds), *Women, Autobiography, Theory: A Reader*, Madison: University of Wisconsin Press, 1998.

Wells, H., *Anticipations of the Reactions of Mechanical and Scientific Progress upon Human Life and Thought*, fourth edition. London: Chapman and Hall, 1902.

Wordsworth, W., 'The French Revolution as It Appeared to Enthusiasts at Its Commencement'; see also *The Prelude* (1850) bk. 9, l. 108 (1809).

6

Ghosts of dead authors

Mieke Bal

Preamble: 'Is that you?'

A painting by American artist Ken Aptekar shows the (self-?) portrait of Walter Shirlaw. The figure looks the viewer straight in the eye. Over the painting is a glass plate with visible bolds, on which sand-blasted lettering reads:

> 'Is that you?' the art student asks.
> I tell him it's a self-portrait
> by Walter Shirlaw from around 1880.
> The art student tells me
> to forget about the Shirlaw.
> 'Boring', he says.

I understand the student's question, 'Is that you?' Knowing the artist, I'd say, minus the exuberant nineteenth-century moustache, the likeness is striking. Another face that hovers above these two – Shirlaw's and Aptekar's – is Vincent van Gogh's. Many people have asked about the resemblance between Van Gogh and Aptekar, regardless of this particular painting. But that is not the point. It is the look, the eyes, that make the merging, the confusion. Painted eyes looking at us: the viewer feels addressed. A painted face: the idea of likeness comes up, inevitably. But then, there is that glass plate: transparent, hence, not covering the face; yet, making the priority between the face and the letters an undecidable dilemma. It is like the Wittgensteinian Rabbit/Duck, or the caricature of Freud's face with an old woman versus a naked young woman.

But the art student is not here, now, when I see this painting. Nor is the artist, and the model even less. The glass plate does not *show* but *tells* about a brief conversation between the artist (Aptekar) and a student. The text is a narrative. The story is told in the present tense, either a historical present or a seriously present-present, which foregrounds the act of looking as necessarily taking place now. The art student feels confronted with a doubling of the man standing in front of him. But he hesitates. Is it a self-portrait of his teacher? In fact, the portrait *is* a self-portrait, and for an art student, the question of *self*-portraiture in contrast to *allo*-portraiture is relevant. But it is not a self-portrait of the teacher, nor of the artist Ken Aptekar. It is of someone else, long gone, irrelevant for the aspiring artist. Or is he/it? The teacher, with whom he is talking, who lives here-now, made this painting. But he made it with the glass plate over it, and the entire discussion with the absent student has become part of it, in its typical Aptekarian succinctness that turns it into a poem, or a 'micro-narrative'[1] (Figure 6.1).

This artwork inspired me for the present chapter, additionally because the letters on the glass plate leave their shadows. It is impossible to see the painting behind the glass without seeing the glass, the letters and the letters' shadows.

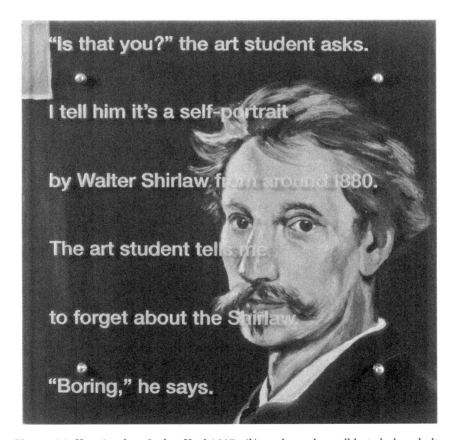

Figure 6.1 Ken Aptekar, *Is that You?* 1997 oil/wood panel, sandblasted glass, bolts, 24" × 24" (61cm × 61 cm), after Walter Shirlaw, Self-portrait (undated).

And yet, in spite of that triple layering, the face looks straight at us. 'Is that you?' is a question of identity, likeness and representation, but embedded in the 'I'/'you' exchange of the here and now. Shirlaw's alleged self remains, lingering as a shadow of the now-dead artist, whom the living artist has both brought to life and definitely killed off; the art student's judgement 'boring' goes to prove it. Nevertheless, by 'repainting' the original self-portrait, enforcing the direct facial confrontation, the contemporary artist compels an awareness that once upon a time a painter called Walter Shirlaw lived and worked, and looked people in the eye, in the then-present. Aptekar has achieved a very striking 'aliveness' of the dead artist's eyes, as if 'he' or 'it' was seriously interested in a dialogue with 'us'. But who is 'us'? The art student? The viewer of the work as it currently hangs on the wall? The lack of specific expression in the eyes, yet an intensity of looking: How can a black circular blot with a small white dot inside it, have such a strong effect?

If we are quick, thinking on our feet, we can still hold on to that past person, and step on board of the ship led by that other Walter, surname Benjamin, who left with us the following cautionary 'thought-image' in his fifth thesis on the philosophy of history: '[E]very image of the past that is not recognized by the present as one of its own concerns threatens to disappear irretrievably.' It seems difficult to do what Benjamin recommends: to take the past seriously not as something 'out there' in time, but as 'one of our own concerns'. Whenever we talk about past disasters, with the Holocaust as a prime example, we say, or think, 'never again'. Yet, the assumption of pastness of that past makes us blind to the reiterative aspects of it, and to the way in which the past, unable to stand still in historians' reconstructions, keeps roaring its head, precisely because we rest too assured in that warm bath of 'never again'. Benjamin's condition for the possibility of history is that the past remains the present's own concern, not something we would like to disavow ('never again') but that we should recognize as relevant today. The difference, or the undecidability, between the 'historical present' which is a past made livelier, and the present-present, remains stubbornly present.[2]

This statement by Benjamin has always inspired, activated me, whenever I was thinking or writing about the past, and accused by historians of being 'ahistorical' – a judgement that has made me devote a book to the question of history, *and, in, for*, the present. Benjamin follows me around, compelling me to articulate how what I see, describe, or even, sometimes (re-)make, is relevant for the present, even if, or precisely because, it 'belongs' to the past. Aptekar's artistic project as a 'repainter' makes a similar point, which is why I open this chapter with his work. Without reiterating my position, which I have termed, with a wink, 'preposterous history', in the wake of Benjamin's caution, in what follows, the constant presence of this intellectual 'ghost' must be taken on board, precisely because its pastness remains undecidable. This prelude through Aptekar's repainting as narrative is meant to focus the discussion of undecidability on issues that are, in the end invariably, of narrative.[3]

Is there an author in this text?

For people who know my work, this heading may sound bizarre. I have a long history of denying authors the voice they don't have, in other words, the right to decide how to read their work – a position against authorial intention I maintain. Yet, restless and anti-dogmatic as I am, I feel compelled by the issue of undecidability to complicate the potential presence of authorship nevertheless. Not, as a deterministic dictation of what the text means, according to our projection onto the alleged authorial intention. The concept of 'implied author', then, in 1961, usefully, but ultimately detrimentally introduced by Wayne Booth and sixty years later, still alleged by many, has given literary scholars the license to say that what they think the author to have meant the text to mean, according to what those scholars come up with as the text's meaning. The intricate sentence I just wrote reflects the kind of meandering argumentation such projections need. It serves to abolish both 'authorial intention' and 'implied author'.

I have argued against this desperate attempt of alleging the 'implied author' in order to salvage the New Criticism's warning against projection through the very act of projecting. But to 'see' something authorial in the text is not by definition an erroneous projection. As it happens, sometimes, I see the author, dimly, as a ghostly presence that makes readers think beyond the obvious of the narrative plot as a (linear) series of events (only). This appearance of the author's 'ghost' occurs when narrative itself falters. Paradoxically, those ghostly authors may salvage, yet undermine in productive ways, what seems undecidable. Instead of expressions of authorial intentions, disguised as 'implied author', I will argue that these appearances do the opposite. Undecidability is necessary for literature to keep its readers on their thinking toes. I will juxtapose – not oppose – two very different instances of novelistic undecidability, not with the purpose of deciding about authorial presence, but to keep the undecidable truly undecidable. In the one, the undecidability is primarily a narratological issue of focalization; in the other, primarily one of fictionality.[4]

Given my aversion to the appeal to authorial intention, I only read biographies when there is a real need. For example, when I felt compelled to contradict a reputation that is both highly influential and totally wrong (Descartes). Or when the literary text seemed so contradictory to what I knew of the author's personality that I wondered if I was misreading (Flaubert). In both cases, I undertook to read the biographies only after having thoroughly studied the texts without knowing anything about the author. Conversely, it was inevitable when a part of the novel 'sounded' autobiographical, so that I had to check out if this was the right diagnosis, which brought the dilemma of fiction and history up (Cervantes).

On Descartes, I could not bear the constantly reiterated judgements about his mind–body split and excessive rationalism, and phrases such as 'post-Cartesian'. I learned from biographies what I already intuited when reading not only the obvious textbook text *Discourse on Method*, but also the late book *The Passions of the Soul*. The former is closer to an autobiography than the genre of a treatise on method would admit. And of the latter, one only needs to give the title the chance to speak to see how the ingrained idea of the mind–body split is untenable, since 'Passion' stands in-between, as a connector. Flaubert has a pretty bad reputation in view of his relationship to women. However, an instance of undecidability compelled me to read the excellent biography by Pierre-Marc de Biasi. I call this book 'excellent' because it is not judgemental, and the information it provides is often really relevant for the literature, as such. So, instead of projecting a meaning on the literary texts, it highlights, enhances textual aspects that are striking and exciting, but seem 'undecidable'. For example, I found meaningful how De Biasi points out tendencies in Flaubert that converge with my intuition that the well-known cinematic quality of his writing is indeed so in very precise ways, harbouring a theory of cinema.[5]

Having studied the biography of Miguel de Cervantes, in connection with the chapters 39–41 of the first part of his novel *Don Quixote*, the first (post-?) modern one in the history of Western literature, I want to experiment with a connection that acknowledges and learns from the author's biography, and its impact on the experimental novel he wrote, while avoiding the risk of projection and maintaining a sensitivity to fictionality. This work could almost be considered the essential demonstration of fictionality. For such a fanciful book, an autobiographical grounding would be highly unlikely. I will focus on the combination of horror story and fairy tale that results in those three chapters from a merging of fiction and memory. Instead of claiming a causal relation between the two, I argue for the ghostly presence of the author in the text, guarding and grounding the undecidability. With 'ghost' I mean a spectral after-effect that has an impact on the literary text, its form and its content, indistinguishably. The ghost, as a shadow, will not depart from its referent, relentlessly sticking to it. It is invisible, yet compelling. But no intention can be projected on it.[6]

In a video installation I have recently made and am currently showing, I stage the traumatized subjectivity that makes linearity impossible, compels constantly reiterated action, cannot escape violence and precludes conclusive endings. The experience of making that work enables me to write an essay that adds to the undecidability of the author's ghost two other undecidabilities: that between linguistic and visual imaginative thinking, and that between showing and invoking trauma. These are intertwined. Intermediality, thus, facilitates an understanding of the form of intersubjectivity that is the artistic presence of trauma without representing the traumatizing event. To answer the question of this section's heading: there is, of course, an author 'in' the text, to the extent that he or she wrote it, leaving their traces. But that totally obvious fact is no help when we read it. It is, rather, a hindrance to bring someone in who is not here, not now. Long gone, in most cases. Aptekar's triple layering counters such invocation. Instead, I want to consider how it is in the most undecidable textual moments that we can assume – no more than that! – the authors show their hands. It matters to the extent that such undecidabilities, when slowing the reading down, may become mirrors of the text as a whole, as mise en abyme. And, to extend that argument: if the moments of undecidability are the most important ones for reading literature, they may be as close as we can get to what matters in the texts.[7]

On the topic of Descartes's madness, I must be very brief. Descartes did not write fiction, had no literary pretensions and was never shy about his authorship; so, bringing him up here can only serve laterally. I refer to him because he was systematically misread. When I made a film and video installation on Descartes, I had not yet read the amazing book by Kyoo Lee, which completely justified my intuitive sense that Descartes's writings show enough irrationality, let's say 'madness', to vindicate his work from the wishful-thinking idea that we are, today, 'post-Cartesian'. The persistent deceptive and arrogant progressivism in our thinking is fond of the qualifier 'post-Cartesian' as something we have happily left behind. What it is we need so eagerly to disavow is worth examining: today's world could use a little more rationality, for starters. But it is that 'post-' thinking itself that betrays us as, I'd say, *pre*-Cartesian, as failing to integrate doubt in reason. Caught in a world where dogma ruled and disbelieving it was severely punishable, Descartes spent his life doubting dualism and attempting to overcome it, rationally as well as in his capricious behaviour. Had we really listened to him, that vexed preposition 'post-' itself would be used with more (Cartesian) doubt. Using audiovisual images to put this on the table was my attempt to bring thought and images together in mutual support.[8]

Once he started showing his writings to others, the philosopher was constantly under ecclesiastic surveillance – or thought he was (Freud: being paranoid doesn't mean people aren't out to get you). He moved around, mainly in the United Provinces (today's Netherlands), refusing to leave forwarding addresses, which was quite a deed for someone who was writing and publishing in that pre-email era. He was also considered a great man. One can see the ambivalence coming. Because glory is never enough for the fundamentally insecure, he managed to fall out with quite some friends. The mathematician Beeckman is the best-known example. This master of rationalism did his thinking often in the turmoil of extreme emotions. He was a good-enough Catholic, yet dangerously close to heresy.

He led the life of both a nomad and what the French call(ed) an *honnête homme*: someone of good breeding and education, whose talents and skills could not be captured by isolated disciplines. Let's keep the nuance of 'honnête' as honest, decent, within purview. However, the wide knowledge across disciplines is the most typical feature of such an *honnête homme*. From biology to philosophy, astrology and medicine, Descartes shone in them all. But also, he was an expert in what we would now call 'mental illness'. This is less known, less widely discussed. One may wonder why. Yet it is very clear, when he comforted his pen-pal Elisabeth, who was suffering from a bout of it, that he knew what he was talking about, and he was effectively able to help her overcome what we would now call, her trauma. Where did that skill come from? My guess is, to cite Eve Kossofsky Sedgwick in the context of homosexuality: it takes one to know one. This is why I credit him with the 'invention' of psychoanalysis – his conception of the subject making its later explicit invention possible, but more precisely than that, he acted towards Elisabeth as a (successful) clinical analyst.[9]

This statement comes from my proposal, already developed much earlier, to consider prognostic interpretation. This idea is not of my own invention. In my academic memory, it was art historian Michael Ann Holly's making of a strong and persuasive argument about the way artworks predict later interpretations of them, which would enact the back-and-forth movement of time as I have later elaborated and proposed to consider it. A bit after my launching of the concept of 'preposterous history', Georges Didi-Huberman reduced the idea of such temporal turbulence to the simpler one of 'anachronism', something he had gleaned from earlier work of Hubert Damisch. Here, however, I limit myself to the idea of Descartes as the precursor, even 'inventor' or, to use his own ambiguous term, 'soul' of psychoanalysis. There are several earlier intimations of this idea. In order to cordon off the projection impulse, I studied Descartes in parallel with his friend-by-correspondence Queen Kristina of Sweden. She beckoned him, and impelled by vanity no doubt, he went, aware that his fragile health advised against it. He lived – as the saying has it, he lived to regret it – for only a brief six weeks. Once they met, they were clumsy together[10] (Figure 6.2).

I imagine both Descartes and Kristina, at whose court he died, suffered from the symptoms of the neurosis *abandonment complex* – a tendency to reject affective bonds while constantly seeking them. Out of fear to be abandoned, they prefer to be the first to do the abandoning. This is what underpinned their passionate attachments to, then rejections, of others. Always craving, but feigning indifference out of fear that parental abandonment would repeat itself. And since these things tend to be reciprocal, they were seen as alternatingly attractive and repulsive. It also explains why the queen insisted on the meeting, but then didn't do much to take intellectual advantage of Descartes's presence. It also explains their brilliance, and the suffering it took to achieve it. Yes, there

Figure 6.2 Thomas Germaine plays Descartes. Photo: Przemo Wojciechowski.

is an author in Descartes's texts, not 'implied' but explicit, not biographical but ghostly, and, sometimes, not linguistically readable but through the imagination and the senses. And he is not the one he has been made out to be. But enough on Descartes for now; let's look at Flaubert, his ghost and the undecidability it serves.[11]

Flaubert's realism[12]

The issue in this section is that of a sense-based aspect of literature mostly addressed for poetry, yet relevant for novels as well: sound. Just as, when reading, we cannot help but 'see' images, we also hear sounds. Both are the products of focalization, the showing of what the narrative voice declares to be there as the content of the text. This is not limited to the sounds described and to those of the words when read out loud. As the narrative prose, appealing to the reader's imagination, creates visual 'imagings', it has the same kind of multiple appeal to the auditive imagination.[13]

The deployment of the audio image is an example of the paradox of anachronistic (preposterous) loyalty and the way it can counter Flaubertian 'stupid' repetition through risking it. The sounds – murmuring, bells tolling, sheep bleating and cows mooing, Emma pleading, love-talking and screaming – constitute one of the cinematic features of this pre-cinema novel: a network of sounds characterized by *indistinction* like Dolby sound. They are reiterative, durable and routine, thus joining in the army of 'stupidities' Flaubert was so keenly interested in. Here, I limit myself to the use of *direct discourse* to create an image that, itself, as an audio image, is in Free Indirect Discourse, to 'un-repeat' a narrative sentence, making its undecidability prominent, irresolvable and intensely realistic in a critical sense.

Of the thousands of narrative sentences, some stand out as unforgettable. We (Michelle Williams Gamaker and myself) have taken some of these up in our film project MADAME B (see note 5), as starting points for a different kind of narration – one that, paradoxically, thrives on undecidability to make its point. Most of the film's dialogues are literal quotations from the novel, reframed to become for the present its 'own concern' (Benjamin). But in spite of its unfilmable length, the novel is sparse in direct discourse. Sometimes, therefore, we have given our actors not a quotation to utter but a sentence to run with – a phrase, an expression, a thought – asking them for actorial improvisation. Sonic images result; these developments are important through the way they constitute a sense-based repetition of narrative content that, subsequently, finds its place in a story without having a textual location. This is exactly how Flaubert muddles the waters on 'who speaks?' as he deploys Free Indirect Discourse to eliminate direct discourse; but he goes beyond that form of ambiguity and dis-attributes even FID, making it undecidable. The narratological concepts of narrator and focalizer as the 'senders' of discourse and vision, respectively, cannot be to assigned to particular subjects.[14]

My example is a transmutation or 'imaging' of the famous sentence: 'Sa conversation était plate comme un trottoir de rue' (His conversation was flat like a side walk, I, 7). This sentence occurs in a description of Emma's disillusionment after her wedding, when married life turns out quite boring. It is devastating for Charles in Emma's eyes – if we consider the sentence a case of Free Indirect Discourse – but nothing is less definite than that free-floating discourse. According to Culler, *unmooring discourse*, and thus precluding facile judgemental attitudes, is precisely Flaubert's project of having his 'stupidity' cake and eating it, too. Hence, to be 'loyal' to Flaubert, we must deploy that floating discourse as the utter form of realism. His realism is anchored in a critique of his own time, which will only work today if it is as severe on our own time. This was our filmmakers' dilemma. But attributing the focalization of that sentence to Emma would be deciding on the undecidable. The unanswerability of narratological questions can be just as revealing as their more usual and comfortable answerability – or more. This negativity is part of the point of narratology.[15]

The short sentence is a prime instance of the economy of words, Flaubert's narrative aesthetic. The usage of the generic noun 'conversation' is accompanied by a verb in the past tense called imperfect, which, here, has nothing of Flaubert's experimental aberrant use of that tense. It simply expresses the reiteration of routine, and implies, precisely, many words, that end up, like a load of stones, bludgeoning one to death. This sentence needed including not only as a narrative expression of a non-event, but also as a representation of the boredom that will kill Emma. It causes, in other words, a reversal in the narrative economy and its dynamic between narration and description; for us as filmmakers, between literary and cinematic: a reversal that is necessary in order to be 'loyal' to the novel by betraying it.[16]

The iterative, hence, stupid character of the flat conversation implies that the sentence, Emma's perception of its contents and the slide towards the adventure that follows: all that cannot easily be audiovisualized, and especially not with Flaubertian concision, for which one comparison sufficed. It is when they try hardest to do that that so many films based on novels fail to engage. Film is a laboratory where we explore what storytelling is and can do rather than repeat what (we think) Flaubert did. We only talked with the actors, then took the camera without rehearsal. For the quality of improvised acting is in the spontaneous, the first time – the freshness that is the opposite of the utter stupidity the sentence conveys, with a comparison that is so far-fetched that one wonders why Flaubert brought it in. This must remain precisely that: undecidable.

Our goal was to turn the short narrative sentence as well as the repetitive, boring direct discourse that it replaced into an audio image in a Flaubertian, free-floating, undecidable Free Indirect Discourse. This allows the immersive spectator to experience, on an intuitive, sensate level, a double, conflicted perception instead of an unmarked repetition. The transformation of narrative discourse, via direct discourse into an audiovisual Free Indirect Discourse was called for, also, to implicate another short narrative sentence that resonates with the comparison: 'C'était surtout aux heures des repas qu'elle n'en pouvait plus' (especially during meals she couldn't stand it anymore). A narrative summing up follows this sentence: 'toute l'amertume de son existence lui semblait servie sur son assiette' (it seemed to her that the entire bitterness of her existence was served to her on her plate). The former sentence can be considered narrative since it tells more or less of an event: Emma's exhaustion. The latter, by means of 'seemed to her', renders Emma's focalization. But narratologically speaking, the comparison of the flat sidewalk remains floating, undecidable. Conflating the short passages into an extensive audio(-visual) image does justice to the failed 'dialogic' nature of Charles's monologic conversations and saves them from simple stupidity.

The actor playing Charles, French Thomas Germaine, had simply announced that he wanted to hold these iterative conversations on four subjects, spread out over four evening dinners, marked by different outfits: the weather, the project to build a shed in the garden, one of his patients and the tasteless quality of the raspberries this year. One can see the clichés of stupidity, and its corollary, the boredom inflicted on its addressee, coming. The actress playing Emma, Finnish Marja Skaffari, only needed to sit tight, showing in her face the visual echo of Charles discourse. Between the two characters, the sonic image, thus, functioned much like the visual performative images in which the film abounds. An example is the first visual confrontation, which we staged in an alternation of a voyeuristic Charles, who spies on the young woman without showing himself, and Emma, once she sees him or imagines him, looking flirtatiously. Both modes of looking tend to be subject to social censoring, or judgementalism. The two repetitive images, ready for judgement, cross, and thereby become performative; the result is the next scene, the wedding. Here, the audio image touches the visual image of Emma's silent boredom, so that dialogism (across the senses) annuls the sheer repetition that would have opened the discourse to facile judgement.

We filmed the scene with two stable cameras, each focusing on one of the two faces. We edited it almost exclusively with Emma's face visible. That is where the boredom inscribed itself with increasing exasperation. It is thus that an intermedial Free Indirect Discourse can take shape, even if, or precisely because, Charles is the one who talks exclusively. Yet, the two characters produce the boredom, ending in horror, *together*. But it had to be Emma who was the prisoner of the stupid conversation – flat, like a sidewalk, hence crushing. Flat equals heavy (Figure 6.3).

But again, the connection between 'flat' and 'heavy', hence 'crushing', is not outspoken, and the comparison is so incongruous that its point seems to be precisely that: unclear, undecidable. Surely, Emma would neither speak nor even think in such terms. 'Flat like a sidewalk': it makes as little sense as the things Charles says. According to the performative conception of the look, in the audiovisual image it is the spectator who enables Emma to show her boredom, and, at the end, when boredom transforms into horror, to scream, producing her own audio image. For, it is the spectator who, seeing and feeling the horror, reads the face and grants the boredom visibility. The reader-spectator must decide on the undecidable. The homework the novel assigns

Figure 6.3 Scene 'Boredom Sets In': Marja Skaffari enacting Emma's boredom; video still.

is not to decide but to be flabbergasted by the undecidability. This prevents a facile judgement. This is Flaubertian FID, against an automatic judgement, an assumption and attribution of stupidity. Could this be Flaubert's ghostly presence in the novel?

At the same time, we wanted to withdraw ('save') Charles from the sphere of contempt with which criticism surrounds him, a reception that makes his character ineffective because it shields the readers from their own routine clichés, whereas the 'contamination' of inanity as a social illness is the point of the undecidability, and of Flaubert's social critique, aka. 'realism'. Once the actor says pleadingly: 'say something!' Thus, he gives shape to the anxiety of the character who is also a prisoner of this hopeless marriage. Flat, or stupid as his conversation is, as a character he is powerless to escape them. He suffers from his own clichés, and, in the same move, incites us to interrogate the interpretation that renders Flaubert's irony a bit too systematic. Sensing his wife's boredom, he speaks more and more nervously, filling beforehand the silences he knows to be inevitable and, hence, accumulating stupidities. Thus, *bêtise* is shared. For us, it was important to take this work out of the moralism that leaves the viewer entirely out of the grasp of the work, yet caught in the paradox.[17]

Flaubertian *bêtise* is, here, not so much in the iteration of clichés but rather in the need to fill the radical void the clichés generate. This need gives the character more depth. The sonic image in which it results, and which sticks to Emma's face as its visual counterpart, is the product of the image produced by the narrative sentence. In this scene, Charles and Emma are more united than ever: by the boredom, the nervousness, the anxiety. When, at the end, Emma screams, Charles asks, astonished: 'But what's the matter?' (Ça va?), as if he thought that, if only he could transform boredom into an illness, he would be able to save his marriage. He is a doctor, after all. And not so much later, a Viennese doctor invented a way of considering such boredom an illness indeed – one in which especially women got caught. Which is why Germaine's superb acting that includes a slight rise of hysteria seemed well fitted. Flaubert is as prophetic, as proleptically interpreting, as Michael Holly attributes to the paintings she discusses.

This sonic image demonstrates another side of the performativity of the image that counters the flattening effect of repetition. The visual image, here, that of Emma's more and more exasperated face, is not the result of the look of the other. Instead, it is the product of the voice, of words, of the conversation with only one speaker, that Flaubert, also assigning it to a single speaker ('sa'), has characterized so effectively. Nevertheless, Charles is the generator, the character who brings about an invisible event: the one that transforms Emma, barely awoken to life, into a living cadaver, entering an agony that takes up the remainder of the story.

Her husband does not *cause* this agony; he only facilitates it, as its instrument, driven by the motor of Flaubertian *bêtise,* stupidity. The veritable cause is the expectation, the passivity, of she who is captured by a system that she fails to understand, but has been instilled into her from an early age. This system where capitalism and romantic love trade places, where commodities are invested with emotion and love is for sale, is what kills her, and, endlessly repeated, never ceased to kill or otherwise damage people. One look at the commercials in today's television or urban shop windows demonstrates it. Dismantling the mechanism of such unmarked repetitions is the work Flaubert does alongside the constant deployment of the stupidity, by means of the undecidability that refuses to let the reader off the hook as superior to the characters and their time. To grasp Flaubert's 'ghost', then, means not to judge his character Emma on the basis of the author's misogynistic reputation, and project on her the contempt that the undecidable passage discussed here refuses to attribute with any certainty, so that the bêtise can be contagious. Nor is there any cause to judge the author on the same basis. It means to grasp what his realism can be, beyond what the cliché interpretation makes of it. Like the eyes in Aptekar's painting, the comparison that characterizes Charles's conversation is so utterly telling, 'speaking', even if the question who speaks and what the eyes say must remain undecided. Leaving alone the man and his biography, it is in this meaningful refusal to decide that I locate Flaubert's ghost.

Cervantes's traumatic state

The ghost of Cervantes can only be glimpsed if we consider it more overtly present in his novel's chapters 39 to 41 of the first part (1605). However, had we not acquired the biographical knowledge so brilliantly offered by María Antonia Garcés's book (note 6), would we read these three chapters, the embedded novella in it, as external to the author's life? And does the difference matter? Yes, and yes. Although most critics now attribute the story told therein to the life experience of the author, little is said about what that means for the narrative and its meanings. The biographical fact in a nutshell: Miguel de Cervantes Saavedra (1547–1616) wrote one of the world's primary bestsellers after experiencing five and a half years of captivity as a slave in Algiers. The novel at first sight reads like a parody of medieval epics and romances, and that is how it has been mostly interpreted. It can also be seen as a precursor – one of those prophetic artworks so dear to Michael Ann Holly – of later novels that mock adventure stories, such as eighteenth-century *Jacques the Fatalist and his Master* (Denis Diderot, 1765–70) and *The Life and Opinions of Tristram Shandy, Gentleman* (Lawrence Sterne, 1759). But it also resonates with postmodern novels of the twentieth century. This is how films based on it have sometimes shaped it. The most recent example is Terry Gilliam's 2018 film Who Killed Don Quichotte?

Gilliam's beautifully made and witty film demonstrates postmodernist aesthetic at its best, although the ridiculing of Don Quichotte as a crazy old man repulses my anti-ageist sentiment. But more importantly, and for us, the motivation that drives the project, *El Ingenioso Hidalgo Don Quixote de la Mancha*, stands out in its intensity and creative expression of prolonged hopelessness. This resonates with what is termed *trauma*. This notion has recently been overused and, hence, is in danger of losing its specific meaning and, consequently, the social recognition and the possibility to help traumatized people. As is well known, trauma as such is unrepresentable. In our video project Don Quijote: Sad Countenances, we refrain, therefore, from representing trauma or the events that cause it. 'Trauma' is a state of stagnation and the impossibility of subjective remembrance that ensue from horrific, traumatogenic events, not the events themselves; it is the distortion of time and its resulting forms, rather than the violence that causes the trauma.[18]

In this project, I seek to be loyal to the ghost of the author whose spectral presence is visible only in what he/it cannot do. The incoherent, repetitive, wildly incongruous stories that follow each other in a hectic rhythm, in other words, the poetics of this narrative, make any attempt at a linear versioning of it hopeless. The novel carries not only the traces of the absurdity and madness that suggest the inevitably traumatic state in which its creator must have been locked, as transpires in the stories told but more clearly in the novel's poetics; it foregrounds this consequence of war and captivity in the madness of its literary form. One can barely read, let alone watch all those pointless attempts to help others, with oftentimes harrowing repercussions. In the exhibition, this is particularly foregrounded in the scenes 'Pointless Altruism' and 'The Failure of Listening'. Succinctly put: repetitiveness overrules narrative. Our loyalty to this mad poetic required that we abstain from making a feature film, which would inevitably impose linearity.

There are two ways of considering Cervantes's ghost in this jungle of narrativity. One belongs to the fiction, the other to the biography. In spite of some ghostly teasing, the tension between these two must remain undecidable.

One is implicit and must be teased out of our reading. The most illuminating path is the temporality, the repetitiveness and the endlessness of the range of adventures, none of which brings the story to an end. The narrative becomes its own captor. Captivity is not only a horrific experience, but the worst of it must be not knowing if it will ever end. Time loses its meaning. And it stretches endlessly. Into today. This harrowing temporality is at stake in the exhibition of the video project, in confrontation with the temporal liberty offered to the visitors. But amazingly, there is also an explicit reference, not only naming his (second, adopted) name, 'Saavedra', but also, in a short paragraph on a 'Spanish soldier, called something de Saavedra', presenting the untold tale of how this Cervantine ghost miraculously managed to evade the innate cruelty of the master. In these three chapters, but with that mysteriously biographical little note, the fictional narrator is told some things about the state of captivity by someone who has just escaped that horrendous-endless situation. Cervantes's novel is a meandering expression of trauma.

How can art, museums and theatre together help in the current situation of the world – mass migration, dictatorships, religious and nationalistic strife, destruction of the planet – to counteract violence's assault on human subjectivity, resulting in trauma? The question is broached through sixteen video installations and thirty-three photographs. They constitute a critical reflection on art's potential through experimental art-making. The project deploys art in museum practice in order to affect spectators, in this case with the otherness of a sociocultural state of violence-induced 'madness'. The tool is 'empathy'. This term indicates 'the capability to "think in the mind of another", to anticipate the reactions of another human being' (Assmann). This is not easy when that other is strange to us because they are 'mad'. If the public is willing, however, to bring empathy to madness, the figure of Don Quijote, the classical 'mad knight' will be transformed into a 'sad knight'.[19]

What I wish to foreground for undecidability is not so much the narrow escape from the slave-holder's cruelty that shimmers through the brief 'true-to-life' paragraph, of which the following is clear enough:

> The only one who held his own with him [the cruel master] was a Spanish soldier, called something de Saavedra; for his master never so much as struck him, nor bade anyone else strike him, nor even spoke a rough word to him, though he did things which those people will remember for many years, all in efforts to recover his liberty; and the rest of us were afraid that his least actions would be punished by impaling, as he himself feared they would be more than

once. And if it were not for lack of time I would tell you something of that soldier's deeds. (355–6)

Rather, I am interested in the play with pronouns, in which the escaped slave tells 'in the first person' an allegedly autobiographical tale of fairy-tale-like miraculous events, none too believable. He tells that tale right after evoking soberly, without telling any of it, the bold deeds of that other, 'third-person' character. Yet, this 'he' should be the 'I'. The name alone would make us prick up our ears if we were in search of that resonance of autobiography that points to the true, real, suffering author.[20]

In marked contrast to that slight evocation, without any narrative purposefulness, is the extensive tale that follows it immediately. This can only be characterized as a fairy tale – pure fiction. It begins with the coincidental viewing of something miraculous:

> It was by the merest chance that I looked up, and when I did I saw a cane with a handkerchief tied to the end of it appear through one of those little closed windows I spoke of. It was being waved and jerked up and down, as though it were summoning us to go and take it. We stared at it; and one of my companions went and placed himself just below it to see if it would be dropped, or what else would happen; but no sooner did he get there than the cane was raised and jerked from side to side, as if someone were shaking his head to say no. (356)

The apparition is mysterious, the objects magically personified, and the Captive with his comrades, awestruck. As focalizer, the speaking 'I' is rather clumsy – 'by merest chance', 'we stared at it', going 'to see if', and then what he sees is unclear, only barely liable to interpretation. The tale continues until the speaking 'I', who is talking to strangers met by chance, triumphantly finishes the story of his escape, along with the fairy, the most beautiful young woman on earth, equally held captive, by her overcautious father.

The ghost of the author hovers over the fictional character (here, the Captive) and inspires in this figure the implausible fairy-tale to imagine the possibility to escape. The 'real' Saavedra could have been a role model for him, but the dilemma is clearly too harsh: risking his life by such deeds as Saavedra performed, or waiting in abject passivity for the good fairy. Here, the undecidability sticks to the character himself and undermines his agency. This stark contrast is, in fact, the undecidability of that state that paralyses: trauma.

The alleged un-representability of trauma, serious as it is, might threaten to relegate it to incurability, which is intolerable, since it entails giving up on human beings. In this project, therefore, the attempt is to present, but not re-present trauma. For this purpose, we must distinguish, however difficult it may seem, between three aspects of trauma: its cause, the state that cause produces and the possibility to help people suffering from it to come out of it. This distinction can be formulated concisely as follows:

- *violence* – an event (that happens)
- *trauma* – a state (that results)
- *empathy* – an attitude (that enables)

The subjects of these three attitudes are different: the violence has a subject or agent (culprit, perpetrator); the traumatized subject is the victim of it; and the subject of empathy is the social interlocutor, who can potentially help to overcome it. In this project, this is the visitor, the primary target of the exhibition; this is its interlocutor, and the interlocutor of the fictional figures brought to life. The exhibition aims to activate visitors to become empathic subjects. The display is meant to have performativity towards that goal.[21]

There are some excellent publications on trauma that do not take it lightly as a catchphrase for anything sad or bad. But it remains difficult to grasp, especially in the face of narrative, since narrative is precisely what is disempowered by trauma. Earlier, I have collaborated with Michelle Williams Gamaker to make a video project – a feature film and installations – based on Françoise Davoine's groundbreaking book *Mère Folle,* which deploys her 'theoretical fiction' to argue with – not against – Freud about the possibility to analytically treat psychotic patients, something Freud considered impossible, because, he alleged, they cannot perform transference. Reversing the burden, Davoine claimed that the psychosis, the madness resulting from trauma, is mainly inflicted by social agents, and that, hence, society has the duty to help. For this purpose, she revised some tenets of the Freudian method, and with great success.[22]

How can we approach this challenge as social agents, not mental health professionals? In everyday life, images of violent events conducive to trauma are considered informative ('the news'). We take them in, even get bored by their repetitive nature, not even absorbing what that repetitiveness says about the world. According to the groundbreaking philosophy of language first developed by John Austin (mentioned in note 20), it is better to change gears and consider such images not informative but enhance their performativity. This can result in a shift from *activist* art, which focuses, informatively, on specific political issues, to *activating* art that seeks to strengthen the performativity of the images. The rationale of this shift is the insight that the trauma and the resulting powerlessness are not inherent in the violent events, objects of representation in the information formats. It is the impossibility to process, even experience extreme violence that generates the trauma and obstructs its representation. Violence is an *event* that is inflicted on people; trauma is a resulting *state*, in the victims. Between the two, no connection is possible.

Confusions and ethical problems threaten in attempts to show such horrid acts of violence. In our project we do not show these acts. A solicitation of feel-good identification ('trauma envy') always lurks and is utterly unhelpful, even ethically problematic. So does the risk of voyeurism. Davoine writes in her 2008 *Don Quichotte*: 'Cervantes doesn't try to arouse visions of horror for voyeuristic readers' (93). One moment where violence occurs in our videos is when a traumatized young man acts out, but that is already as a consequence of earlier violence. This is in the episode 'The Failure of Listening'. The young man Cardenio's attacks on his interlocutors are responses to the latter's failure to allow him to speak without being interrupted. But what happens to us, the beholders of the images that stage such situations? This is where trauma can be encountered by empathy. A counterpart to the episode is the one where Don Quijote is listening to witnesses who are deeply involved in contemporary situations of refugees. There, he is able to be sensitive and forget his own obsessions. This scene, 'Testimonial Discourses', updates the traumatic events hinted at in other scenes, to alert visitors to the actuality of the issues Cervantes was able to draw out from his own life experience, with the help of his imagination.[23]

Figure 6.4 A two-dimensional figuration of the traumatic state. Photo: Ebba Sund.

Instead of representing a traumatic state, which is both voyeuristic-exploitative and epistemically impossible, artists are able to 'image' it, or at least, clearly enough hint to it for audiences to be able to muster empathy. I want to include a photograph here, which was made in this vein. I was astounded when I saw it. Without any specific briefing, the young photographer has grasped what it means to be unable to speak and to implore onlookers with the eyes to help (Figure 6.4).

Notes

1 On the notion of *allo-portrait*, see my brochure *Allo-Portraits: On the Impossibility of Likeness in the Face of Movement,* for the exhibition 'Rendez-vous with Frans Hals', Haarlem: Frans Hals Museum 2018. Aptekar self-defines as a 're-painter', and the texts he mounts over his copies of old-master paintings are either poems or 'micro-narratives'. This is an understudied and underappreciated literary genre practised by, for example, Miguel Ángel Hernández, *Demasiado tarde para volver* (Barcelona: RiL Editores, 2019). In Japanese (-inspired) poetry, it would be a *haiku*, but less formally defined. For more on Aptekar's work, see Mieke Bal, *Quoting Caravaggio: Contemporary Art, Preposterous History* (Chicago, IL: University of Chicago Press, 1999) (esp. 11–127), and my essay from 1997, 'Larger than Life: Reading the Corcoran Collection', in *Ken Aptekar: Talking to Pictures* (Washington, DC: Corcoran Gallery of Art), 5–12, that includes this Shirlaw (self-?) portrait.

2 In Walter Benjamin, *Illuminations*, ed. and with an Introduction by Hannah Arendt and trans. Harry Zohn (New York: Schocken, 1968).

3 See the 1999 book mentioned in note 1. With the word '(re-)making' I refer to my videos in that they all have connections to the past made relevant for the present. See my website http://www.miekebal.org/artworks/films/ for further details.

4 For the original concept of the implied author, see Wayne C. Booth, *The Rhetoric of Fiction* (Chicago: University of Chicago Press, 1961). For a succinct statement of my position on the implied author, see my *Narratology: Introduction to the Theory of Narrative* (Toronto: The University of Toronto Press, 4th revised edition 2017).

5 *Discourse on Method and Meditations* [1637] Laurence J. Lafleur (trans.) (New York: The Liberal Arts Press, 1960); and *The Passions of the Soul*, [1649] trans. Stephen H. Voss (Indianapolis and Cambridge: Hackett Publishing Company, 1989). Descartes's most informative biographies are Desmond Clarke, *Descartes: A Biography* (Cambridge, UK: Cambridge University Press, 2006) and *Descartes: An Intellectual Biography* by Stephen Gaukroger (Oxford: Clarendon Press 1995). To make the film and video installation REASONABLE DOUBT, which was my

vindication of Descartes's precious tendency to doubt as his road to wisdom, I consulted many more sources, not relevant for my argument here.
On Flaubert, see Pierre-Marc de Biasi, *Gustave Flaubert. Une manière spéciale de vivre* (Paris: Le Livre de poche, 2009). See also for the film I made with Michelle Williams Gamaker as a *re-making* of *Madame Bovary*, http://www.miekebal.org/artworks/films/madame-b/ and the article about this project, 'Narrative Here-Now', in Marina Grishakova and Maria Poulaki (eds), *Narrative Complexity: Cognition, Embodiment, Evolution* (Nebraska: University of Nebraska Press, series Frontiers of Narrative, 2019), 247–69.

6   For the biography of Cervantes during his captivity, see the very well-documented study by María Antonia Garcés, *Cervantes in Algiers: A Captive's Tale* (Nashville, TN: Vanderbilt University Press, 2002). Although I am aware of the differences, I use 'ghost' as a synonym of 'spectre' (for the former's allusion to gothic literature) in the sense Esther Peeren has (re-)defined it so relevantly, *The Spectral Metaphor: Living Ghosts and the Agency of Invisibility* (London: Palgrave Macmillan, 2014).

7   For the term 'mise en abyme', see 52-27 in my *Narratology* (note 1). The spelling with a 'y' is a statement of the author-ghost kind: André Gide, who invented the term, spelled it that way. See Dällenbach, *The Mirror in the Text*, trans. Jeremy Whiteley with Emma Hughes (Chicago: University of Chicago Press, 1989 [1977]). The spelling historicizes the concept, not to search for Gide but for the meanings the concept has accrued during its, not his lifetime; Gide's ghost, not his intention.

8   Kyoo Lee's brilliant and bold book, *Reading Descartes Otherwise: Blind, Mad, Dreamy, and Bad* (New York: Fordham University Press, 2013), I encountered alas, after the fact; I thank philosopher and art historian Aron Vinegar of the University of Oslo for alerting me to Lee's book. I also revert and refer to my own article, 'Thinking in Film', in Jill Bennett and Mary Zournazi (eds), *Thinking in the World: A Reader* (London: Bloomsbury Academic, 2020), 173–201. For my audiovisual project, see http://www.miekebal.org/artworks/films/reasonable-doubt/ and further pages. For a reckoning with 'post-', see my article 'The Point of Narratology: Part 2', special issue of INDECS, 'Interdisciplinary Description of Complex Systems', 17, no. 2, part A (2019): 242–303 (242–58).

9   The connection between Descartes and 'madness', according to psychoanalysis, has been best demonstrated in Yaelle Sibony-Malpertu's *Une liaison philosophique. Du thérapeutique entre Descartes et la princesse Élisabeth de Bohême* (Paris: Stock, 2012). The fifth scene of my video installation is loosely based on this book.

10 See Michael Ann Holly, *Past Looking: Historical Imagination and the Rhetoric of the Image* (Ithaca and London: Cornell University Press, 1996). Yaelle Sibony-Malpertu's 2012 study (see footnote 9) makes the psychoanalytic skill of Descartes clear. But also, Michel Henry, *Généalogie de la psychanalyse* [1985] (Paris: P.U.F. 2015), begins with a chapter on Descartes. This has inspired the first scene of my video installation,

where Descartes's childhood learning is presented, with a special focus on the senses. Didi-Huberman's plea for anachronism is most clearly exposed in 'Before the Image, Before Time: The Sovereignty of Anachronism', in Claire Farago and Robert Zwijnenberg (eds), *Compelling Visuality: The Work of Art In and Out of History* (Minneapolis and London: University of Minnesota Press, 2003), 31–44.

11 I learned about the abandonment complex through the analysis by Han Verhoeff of Benjamin Constant's (semi-autobiographical) novel *'Adolphe' et Constant. Une étude psychocritique* (Paris: Klincksieck, 1976). Since I don't read Swedish – and Kristina's writings are sparse – I had to rely on secondary literature for the scene of their encounter. See especially the well-documented book by Veronica Buckley, *Christina Queen of Sweden: The Restless Life of a European Eccentric* (New York: Harper, 2005). I have also benefitted from an imaginative, 'first-person' novel by Françoise D'eaubonne, *Moi, Kristine reine de Suède* (Paris: Encre, 1979). This was as ghostly as it could get.

12 This heading alludes to Jonathan Culler's article from 2007 'The Realism of *Madame Bovary*', MLN 122: 683–96. Culler compels a radical rethinking both of realism and of Flaubert's deployment of it.

13 The only study of sound in Flaubert's novel I have found is by Michael Fried, *Flaubert's 'Gueuloir': On Madame Bovary and Salammbô* (Chicago, IL: The University of Chicago Press, 2012), which disappointingly consists mainly of long passages quoted.

14 In what remains in my view the best study of Flaubert, *Flaubert: The Uses of Uncertainty* [1974] (Ithaca: Cornell University Press, revised edition 2006), Jonathan Culler demonstrates how Flaubert deploys undecidability. Claudine Gothot-Mersch has argued convincingly that Flaubert loathed direct discourse, which he considered artificial. Gothot-Mersch, Claudine, 'De Madame Bovary à Bouvard et Pécuchet: Le discours des personnages dans les romans de Flaubert', *Revue d'Histoire Littéraire de la France*, 81 (4/5) (1981): 542–62.

15 Because there are so many editions and translations of this world-famous novel, and the chapters are short, I refer to quotes by part (in Roman numbers) and chapter (in Arabic numbers) instead of by page numbers. For more on this issue, see my article 'Intership: Anachronism between Loyalty and the Case', in Thomas Leitch (ed.), *The Oxford Handbook of Adaptation Studies* (New York and Oxford: Oxford University Press, 2017), 179–96, which I also cite to draw attention to the work of Leitch, the most prominent adaptation scholar I know of. See his 2003 article, 'Twelve Fallacies in Contemporary Adaptation Theory', *Criticism*, 45, no. 2: 149–71. We do not consider our film an adaptation, however, for reasons I explain in that article, and which agree with Leitch's diagnosis of the fallacies.

16 Loyalty, in this analysis, is distinct from fidelity, which we did not accept, with its literalizing and also its sexual connections. See Leitch's analysis of the fallacies (footnote 15), of which fidelity is the primary one.

17 The word 'contamination' alludes to the title of an exhibition of my video
    work held in Murcia, Spain, in 2019. See the (bilingual Spanish-English) book
    Contaminaciones: Leer, imaginar, visualizar, ed. Miguel Á. Hernández Navarro
    (Murcia: Cendeac, 2020). For a critical account that completely falls for the one-
    sided interpretation, see Marc Girard, *La passion de Charles Bovary* (Paris: Imago,
    1995). No wonder that this author dismisses Culler's brilliant work out-of-hand; he
    cannot bear undecidability. For the psychoanalyst that he is, this seems a handicap.

18 When I use the first-person plural personal pronoun, I am primarily referring to
    the initiator and main actor, Mathieu Montanier, and myself as the scriptwriter
    and director. We developed the project together until the moment of production,
    when Mathieu preferred to concentrate on his acting. On this project, see *Don
    Quijote: Sad Countenances*, ed. Niklas Salmose (Växjö, Sweden: Trolltrumma,
    2019) (available via Niklas@trolltrumma.se); Bilingual edition English-Spanish as
    Don Quijote: Tristes figuras; Don Quijote: Sad Countenances (Murcia, Cendeac (Ad
    Litteram), 2020).

19 The definition of empathy is from a collective volume that usefully opens up the
    concept and its uses for discussion: Aleida Assmann and Ines Detmers (eds),
    Empathy and Its Limits (London: Palgrave, 2016). 'From mad to sad' is my variation
    on Freud's view that psychoanalysis helps people to turn unbearable to bearable
    grief (*passim*). So, psychoanalysis contributes to making lives tolerable, manageable.

20 According to the thoroughly documented biography by Garcés (footnote 6), that
    allusive and elusive mention of the brave Spanish soldier is quite precisely and
    accurately autobiographical – of Cervantes, not of the staged 'Captive'.

21 On *performativity*, J.L. Austin, *How to Do Things with Words* [1962] (Cambridge:
    Harvard University Press, 1975). I consider the most lucid discussion the overview
    by Jonathan Culler, 'The Performative', in *The Literary in Theory* (Stanford, CA:
    Stanford University Press, 2007), 137–65. A brilliantly ground-shifting text focusing
    on trauma is Ernst van Alphen, 'The Performativity of Provocation: The Case of
    Artur Zmijewski', 81–96 in *The Journal of Visual Culture*, (2019): 18–1.

22 Van Alphen's article, 'Symptoms of Discursivity: Experience, Memory, Trauma',
    in Mieke Bal, Jonathan Crewe, and Leo Spitzer (eds), *Acts of Memory: Cultural
    Recall in the Present* (Hanover, NH: University of New England Press, 1999), 24–38,
    provides a lucid, systematic explanation of trauma in relation to narrative. Also,
    Françoise Davoine, *Mother Folly: A Tale,* by Judith W. Miller (Stanford: Stanford
    University Press, 2014 [1998]), a 'theoretical fiction' inspired by the author's
    psychoanalytic practice. We based our film and installation on this book, in which
    Davoine plays her own part. Widely known is Cathy Caruth, *Unclaimed Experience:
    Trauma, Narrative and History* (Baltimore, MD: Johns Hopkins University
    Press, 1996). Also an exchange between Ernst van Alphen, 'Second-Generation
    Testimony, Transmission of Trauma, and Postmemory', 473–88 in *Poetics Today* 27,
    no, 2 (2006), and Marianne Hirsch's reply, 'The Generation of Postmemory', 103–28

in *Poetics Today,* 29 (1): 2008. For more on the video project, renamed A LONG HISTORY OF MADNESS, see http://www.miekebal.org/artworks/films/a-long-history -of-madness/ and on the resulting exhibitions, page http://www.miekebal.org/ artworks/exhibitions/ from 'Saying It' to 'Landscapes of Madness'.

23 Françoise Davoine, *Don Quichotte, pour combattre la mélancolie* (Paris: Stock, L'autre pensée, 2008), and Françoise Davoine et Jean-Max Gaudillière, *A bon entendeur, salut! Face à la perversion, le retour de Don Quichotte* (Paris: Stock, L'autre pensée, 2013).

Works cited

Adorno, Theodor W., *Aesthetic Theory*, trans. Robert Hullot-Kentor. Minneapolis: University of Minnesota Press, 1997.

Adorno, Theodor W., *Can One Live After Auschwitz? A Philosophical Reader*, ed. Rolf Tiedemann and trans. Rodney Livingstone et al. Stanford: Stanford University Press, 2003.

Alphen, Ernst 'Symptoms of Discursivity: Experience, Memory, Trauma', in Mieke Bal, Jonathan Crewe, Leo Spitzer (eds), *Acts of Memory: Cultural Recall in the Present.* Hanover NH: University of New England Press, 1999, 24–38.

Assmann, Aleida and Ines Detmers (eds), *Empathy and Its Limits.* London: Palgrave, 2016.

Austin, J. L., *How to Do Things with Words.* Cambridge: Harvard University Press, 1975 [1962].

Bal, Mieke, 'Larger than Life: Reading the Corcoran Collection', in *Ken Aptekar: Talking to Pictures.* Washington, DC: Corcoran Gallery of Art, 1997, 5–12.

Bal, Mieke, *Quoting Caravaggio: Contemporary Art, Preposterous History.* Chicago, IL: University of Chicago Press, 1999.

Bal, Mieke, *Narratology: Introduction to the Theory of Narrative,* 4th revised edition. Toronto: The University of Toronto Press, 2017 [1985].

Bal, Mieke, 'Intership: Anachronism between Loyalty and the Case', in Thomas Leitch (ed.), *The Oxford Handbook of Adaptation Studies.* New York and Oxford: Oxford University Press, 2017, 179–96.

Bal, Mieke, 'Narrative Here-Now', in Marina Grishakova and Maria Poulaki (eds), *Narrative Complexity: Cognition, Embodiment, Evolution.* Nebraska: University of Nebraska Press, series Frontiers of Narrative, 2019, 247–69.

Bal, Mieke, 'The Point of Narratology: Part 2', special issue of INDECS, 'Interdisciplinary Description of Complex Systems', 17, no. 2, part A (2019): 242–303, 242–58.

Bal, Mieke, 'Thinking in Film', in Jill Bennett and Mary Zournazi (eds), *Thinking in the World: A Reader.* London: Bloomsbury Academic, 2020, 173–201.

Benjamin, Walter, *Illuminations*. Edited and with an Introduction by Hannah Arendt., trans. Harry Zohn. New York: Schocken, 1968.

Boletsi, Maria, 'From the Subject of the Crisis to the Subject in Crisis: Middle Voice on Greek Walls', *The Journal of Greek Media and Culture*, 2, no. 1 (2016): 3–28.

Booth, Wayne C., *The Rhetoric of Fiction*. Chicago: University of Chicago Press, 1961.

Buckley, Veronica, *Christina Queen of Sweden: The Restless Life of a European Eccentric*. New York: Harper, 2005.

Caruth, Cathy, *Unclaimed Experience: Trauma, Narrative and History*. Baltimore, MD: Johns Hopkins University Press, 1996.

Clarke, Desmond, *Descartes: A Biography*. Cambridge, UK: Cambridge University Press, 2006.

Crewe, Leo Spitzer, 'Second-Generation Testimony, Transmission of Trauma, and Postmemory', *Poetics Today*, 27, no. 2 (2006): 473–88.

Crewe, Leo Spitzer, 'The Performativity of Provocation: The Case of Artur Zmijewski', *The Journal of Visual Culture*, 18–1 (2019): 81–96.

Culler, Jonathan, *Flaubert: The Uses of Uncertainty*. Aurora, Colorado: Davies Group, 2006 [1974].

Culler, Jonathan, 'The Performative', in *The Literary in Theory*. Stanford, CA: Stanford University Press, 2007, 137–65.

Culler, Jonathan, 'The Realism of *Madame Bovary*', *MLN*, 122 (2007): 683–96.

Davoine, Françoise, *Mère folle: Récit*. Strasbourg: Arcanes, 1998. Translated as *Mother Folly: A Tale* by Judith W. Miller. Stanford: Stanford University Press, 2014.

Davoine, Françoise. *Don Quichotte, pour combattre la mélancolie*. Paris: Stock, L'autre pensée, 2008.

Davoine, Françoise and Jean-Max Gaudillière, *A bon entendeur, salut! Face à la perversion, le retour de Don Quichotte*. Paris: Stock, L'autre pensée, 2013.

D'eaubonne, Françoise, *Moi, Kristine reine de Suède*. Paris: Encre, 1979.

Descartes, René, *Discourse on Method and Meditations*, trans. Laurence J. Lafleur. New York: The Liberal Arts Press, 1960 [1637].

Descartes, René, *The Passions of the Soul*, trans. Stephen H. Voss. Indianapolis and Cambridge: Hackett Publishing Company, 1989 [1649].

Didi-Huberman, Georges, 'Before the Image, Before Time: The Sovereignty of Anachronism', in Claire Farago and Robert Zwijnenberg (eds), *Compelling Visuality: The Work of Art In and Out of History*. Minneapolis and London: University of Minnesota Press, 2003, 31–44.

Didi-Huberman, Georges, *Images in Spite of All: Four Photographs from Auschwitz*, trans. Shane B. Lillis. Chicago: University of Chicago Press, 2008.

Fried, Michael, *Flaubert's 'Gueuloir': On Madame Bovary and Salammbô*. Chicago, IL: The University of Chicago Press, 2012.

Garcés, María Antonia, *Cervantes in Algiers: A Captive's Tale*. Nashville, Tennessee: Vanderbilt University Press, 2002.

Gaukroger, Stephen, *Descartes: An Intellectual Biography*. Oxford: Clarendon Press, 1995.

Girard, Marc, *La passion de Charles Bovary*. Paris: Imago, 1995.

Gothot-Mersch, Claudine, 'De Madame Bovary à Bouvard et Pécuchet: Le discours des personnages dans les romans de Flaubert', *Revue d'Histoire Littéraire de la France*, 81, no. 4/5 (1981): 542–62.

Henry, Michel, *Généalogie de la psychanalyse*. Paris: P.U.F. 2015 [1985].

Hernández, Miguel Ángel, *Demasiado tarde para volver*. Barcelona: RiL Editores, 2019.

Hernández, Miguel Á. (ed.), *Contaminaciones: Leer, imaginar, visualizar*. Murcia: Cendeac, 2020.

Hirsch, Marianne, 'The Generation of Postmemory', *Poetics Today*, 29, no. 1 (2008): 103–28.

Holly, Michael Ann, *Past Looking: Historical Imagination and the Rhetoric of the Image*. Ithaca and London: Cornell University Press, 1996.

Lee, Kyoo, *Reading Descartes Otherwise: Blind, Mad, Dreamy, and Bad*. New York: Fordham University Press, 2013.

Leitch, Thomas, 'Twelve Fallacies in Contemporary Adaptation Theory', *Criticism* 45, no. 2 (2003): 149–71.

Peeren, Esther, *The Spectral Metaphor: Living Ghosts and the Agency of Invisibility*. London: Palgrave Mc Millan, 2014.

Sibony-Malpertu, *Une liaison philosophique. Du thérapeutique entre Descartes et la princesse Élisabeth de Bohême*. Paris: Stock, 2012.

Verhoeff, Han, *'Adolphe' et Constant. Une étude psychocritique*. Paris: Klincksieck, 1976.

Part III

Contemporary literary uncertainties

7

No-fault murder

Neoliberalism and Nordic noir

Bruce Robbins

In Jussi Adler-Olsen's *The Keeper of Lost Causes*, the original novel in the bestselling Danish Department Q series, the solution to the mystery is an automobile accident. At the end of the novel, we find out that many years earlier two cars had collided, with fatal consequences, and that a child in one car had decided to kill a child in the other car, whom he had glimpsed through the window, as they passed, misbehaving, and whom he therefore held responsible. For obvious reasons his revenge is delayed; when the crime happens, both criminal and victim are in their thirties. This long delay helps obscure the criminal's motive, which of course for narrative reasons needs to be obscured. The victim has become a political figure, and here, as so often in crime fiction, a political motive is at first suspected, only to be replaced in the ending by a merely private motive. This is a disappointment for those of us who would like crime fiction, a phenomenon of mass entertainment, to turn out to be doing significant political work at the level of mass consciousness, but it is not surprising; the displacement from public motive to private motive happens more often than not. Yet there is a kind of politics in the very fact that the motive, though private, is indeed so obscure. Department Q specializes in cold cases – 'cases that have been shelved, but are of particular interest to the public welfare'.[1] Here, with so much time having passed, we have a case that is cold *for the criminal* as well as for the police. It's not just that the motive has been buried; there is also a certain coldness in its very nature. To say that the motive was an accident and that the responsibility for it fell on a child playing in the back seat is to suggest in two different ways that there was no true responsibility for it at all. When we call something an accident, as when we point the finger at a small child, what we mostly mean is that, however great the misfortune, it is not a misfortune for which the concept of criminal responsibility is relevant.

This use of an accident to explain a Danish murder story seems intriguing, first, because of the salience of 'the public welfare', and the state that claims to institutionalize it, in discussions of Scandinavian crime fiction, and also because treating misfortune as an accidental condition rather than as someone's personal responsibility – that is, treating responsibility as undecidable – is arguably the dominant moral principle on which the welfare state was founded. Before the welfare state, a man's inability to support his family (at the outset the burden of support was held to fall on men alone) was largely considered as his personal failing, as a lack of moral virtue. Great efforts were made to discourage the supposed vices that were thought to lead to misery and demands for assistance. It is only with the emergence of the welfare state that unemployment, say, is no longer seen as proof of moral turpitude in the unemployed. Or perhaps I should say *was* no longer seen – criticism of the welfare state in recent years has of course involved direct and successful attacks on this moral principle. For the neoliberal critics of the welfare state, responsibility is the decisive word. Unemployment and related misfortunes should never have been removed from the domain of individual responsibility. We need more responsibility, not less. For them, poverty and unemployment are *not* accidental conditions that could happen to anyone and that should therefore invite social solidarity. They are the result of personal decisions.

It is possible to imagine that in this novel, Jussi Adler-Olsen was deliberately presenting an allegorical defence of the welfare state, or to be more precise a critique of neoliberalism's critique of the welfare state. From this perspective, the would-be murderer is making exactly the political mistake that the neoliberal critics of the welfare state make: he is treating an accident as if it were a proper matter of personal responsibility. If so, it is possible to generalize the speculation. The allegory might be extended, in other words, to suggest that motives for murder are *always* mistakes. By supplying everyone's basic needs, so the argument might run, the welfare state has in effect eliminated proper or reasonable motives for murder. For the welfare state, society would thus have become a kind of universalized childhood, a world of children at play in which criminal responsibility is not entirely unknown but is a very rare exception. The result would be what I was reaching for in my title: a no-fault view of murder.

In at least one respect, this formula is obviously unsatisfactory. In the Adler-Olsen novel, as in every example of the genre I can think of, the murderer or would-be murderer *is* eventually discovered, stopped and in one way or another held responsible for his actions. Without that plot dynamic – without the individual perpetrator who is eventually held responsible – it is arguable that the crime fiction genre could not exist. In that sense, you'd have to say that *The Keeper of Lost Causes* is on both sides of the issue of responsibility. It evokes the image of an 'everything-is-childhood' principle in which responsibility would be social rather than individual, but it does not fully accept that principle. And to the extent that it doesn't, it is expressing hostility at the premises of the welfare state, or butting up against its limits. Or perhaps you could say that, as a novel that's composed both in and for the welfare state, it's at war with itself. Not a very satisfying conclusion, though it does mark an advance over the received wisdom on the genre, which assumes that the hostility is one-sided – that Scandinavian crime fiction is deliberately and overwhelmingly critical of the Scandinavian welfare state.

But let me take the argument further. When the perpetrator in *The Keeper of Lost Causes* is held responsible, *how* is he held responsible? How is he penalized? (Spoiler alert, for those who care.) He is not apprehended, tried, convicted and imprisoned, according to the law. Neither is he executed by the state according to an eye-for-an-eye logic of vengeance or ethical equivalence (more American than Scandinavian) that dictates endings which have little to do with the probable result of eventual legal judgement. He is killed, yes, but the means of the killing are the same means by which he had planned to commit violence against others. In other words, he kills himself and he does so unintentionally. His death, too, is an accident. If there is accident on the side of *motive* for the crime, there is also accident on the side of its *punishment*.

All this accident cannot itself be accidental. Again, it seems to fit quite snugly into the ideology of the Scandinavian welfare state. What is achieved by this coincidence is a lifting of the state's burden to punish. We say, customarily, that the state cannot exist without inheriting and monopolizing the desire for revenge that will naturally or presumably be felt by the individual victim of injustice or the victim's kin. The story goes back to Greek tragedy: the polis can only come into being if the individual is willing to surrender the prerogative of personal vengeance and instead allow the role of administering justice to be transferred to the impersonality of the law. That's the only escape from a cycle of individual violence or family vendetta, as in the *Oresteia*, that (so the law argues) would otherwise be endless and that would render impossible the civility of civil society. What I'm suggesting is another twist to this foundational story. What if the state in its most advanced, social-welfare embodiment no longer *wants* to punish? What if the welfare state, believing that the motives for crime are social and having extended its own range of responsibility to cover as much as possible of society as a whole, posits that the motives for crime too are its own responsibility, not the responsibility of the individual? What if the state no longer *believes* in its authority to decide on the individual's punishment? What if it has come to believe in a sort of no-fault view of crime? If so, this belief would go beyond the desire to soften and civilize punishment, substituting some sort of corrective rehabilitation. It would be the logical outcome of the idea that what had been termed 'crime' – and remember that once upon a time, before the welfare state, poverty itself was closely associated with criminality – is now seen as something more like an accident.

This line of argument finds strong support in Jakob Stougaard-Nielsen's recent book, *Scandinavian Crime Fiction*.[2] For Stougaard-Nielsen, what is unique to the genre in Scandinavia is the breakdown of the victim/perpetrator binary. Reflecting on the 1973 bank robbery that led to the coining of the expression 'Stockholm syndrome', he suggests that the psychological identification of the hostages with the robber and hostage-taker, the identification of the victim with the perpetrator (the syndrome's barebones definition), must be reconceived in social rather than psychological terms. Identification with the perpetrator is a distinctive fact about the genre. It happens in the novel's reader as well, and it happens not because of some vague psychological perversity having to do with power and submission, but because in Scandinavia it is recognized, and even recognized by the victim, that the perpetrator should be seen as *himself a fellow victim*. It is not accidental, then, that the syndrome should be named for Stockholm: such a recognition depends on the unusually strong belief in social democracy, and such a belief is not equally available everywhere in the world.

Stougaard-Nielsen also makes it possible to see something else about the genre. The perpetrator is a victim, but he is a victim of circumstances, not a victim of any individual's intentionally malevolent acts. This is as close as one can get to victimhood without criminality, that is to a version of citizenship – perhaps no longer recognizing the concept of victimhood any more than the concept of criminality – that also stands outside the binary of criminal/agent of punishment. From this angle, it's no wonder that the genre hesitates in the face of its apparent responsibility to decide on responsibility and to punish accordingly.

I have not done a systematic examination of Scandinavian crime fiction, a genre so rich and rapidly expanding as to make generalization impractical, if not impossible. I cannot say with confidence how characteristic this hesitation is. But given the genre's remarkable international success and its ongoing association with the critique of the welfare state both inside and outside Scandinavia, especially since *The Girl with the Dragon Tattoo*, the hypothesis seems worth pushing in this direction. I notice, for example, in two excellent Liza Marklund stories, *Nobel's Last Will* and *Borderline*, that while something resembling violent revenge against the murderer happens in both endings, in both cases the violence is not decided on by any of the parties whose involvement we have been following. In *Nobel's Last Will*, it happens, again, by accident. In *Borderline*, the violence is performed by a third party that up to now has not been part of the story. This looks like punishment as, again, a sort of fate or accident, delivered to the reader without the relevant human agents, individual or collective, having to dirty their hands, or perhaps so that they *don't have* to dirty their hands. If so, it would suggest again a taking of distance from the state's role as punisher and decider. On the one hand, it indicates a failing of belief on the part of the state that punishment, particularly violent punishment, belongs in its hands – that only by taking over the function of punishment can it stop private individuals from doing the punishing themselves. On the other hand, it also indicates a residual belief that the reader, or society, still demands some sort of punishment, even sometimes a violent one, that will hold some individual responsible.

As it happens, interpreters of neoliberalism run up against a closely related set of issues. In the United States, the period of neoliberalism's astonishing political rise, since the 1970s, has seen an equally astonishing expansion of the prison system and the population of the incarcerated, who are largely people of colour. This exacerbated punitiveness seems consistent with neoliberalism's frontal assault on the ameliorative principles of the welfare state. But it is not anti-statist, of course – on the contrary – and neoliberalism has often seemed anti-statist at its very heart. What then is the neoliberal position on the state's responsibility to deal with crime? Gary Becker's classic 1968 paper 'Crime and Punishment: An Economic Approach', an extremely influential statement of neoliberal ideology, argued explicitly against thinking of crime and punishment in moral terms.[3] His approach, Becker says, 'assumes that a person commits an offense if the expected utility to him exceeds the utility he could get by using his time and other resources at other activities. Some persons become "criminals", therefore, not because their basic motivation differs from that of other persons, but because their benefits and costs differ'.[4] Becker is anti-imprisonment, arguing that 'social welfare is increased if fines are used whenever feasible' because 'probation and institutionalization use up social resources', while 'fines do not', and fines have the added advantage of providing compensation to victims, which the offender's imprisonment does not.[5] In making this argument, he brushes off the moral objection that fines 'are immoral because, in effect, they permit offences to be bought for a price in the same way that bread or other goods are bought for a price'.[6] Becker's amorality has won grudging admiration, even from unexpected quarters. 'For Foucault', François Ewald tells Becker in 2013, 'your critique of governmentality produces the capacity to be true without or outside of moral considerations'.[7] Becker makes an exception for rape and murder, which he concedes might not be adequately dealt with by fines. But you could hardly say he is moralistic even about murder: 'the cost of murder is measured by the loss in earnings of victims and excludes, among other things, the value placed by society on life itself'.[8] The point is clear. Like the welfare state that appears to be its insistent target, and like the Scandinavian murder mysteries that, I have suggested, embody much of the welfare state's characteristic morality, neoliberalism is drawn to a no-fault view of criminality.

Foucault's qualified but real admiration for Gary Becker, expressed in the lectures at the Collège de France in 1978–9 and posthumously published in 2008 as *The Birth of Biopolitics*, demonstrates to the satisfaction of many that there is a real complicity between neoliberalism and anti-normative identity politics.[9] Becker's bold anti-moralism and his anti-statism, which induces him to find even prisons too much of an imposition on the taxpayer, certainly resonate with Foucault's signature concern for excluded minorities and 'revolts of conduct' as well as his own powerful anti-statism, which has unfortunately discouraged his admirers from seeing the point of conventional parliamentary politics. It's because of the anti-statism, of course, that the very idea of common ground between neoliberalism and the welfare state seems even more outlandish. But perhaps it is not as outlandish as it might seem. Consider Nancy Fraser's view of what American voters were voting on in the presidential election of 2016. According to Fraser (a staunch defender of the welfare state), the vote that put Donald Trump in the White House was a vote for 'The End of Progressive Neoliberalism'. 'Progressive neoliberalism', as Fraser defines it, is:

> An alliance of mainstream currents of new social movements (feminism, anti-racism, multiculturalism, and LGBTQ rights), on the one side, and high-end 'symbolic' and service-based business sectors (Wall Street, Silicon Valley, and Hollywood), on the other. In this alliance, progressive forces are effectively joined with the forces of cognitive capitalism, especially financialization. However unwittingly, the former lend their charisma to the latter. Ideals like diversity and empowerment, which could in principle serve different ends, now gloss policies that have devastated manufacturing and what were once middle-class lives.[10]

This may sound like a familiar complaint against identity politics – the complaint that the liberationist movements of 1960s counterculture proved open to co-optation by consumerism, financialization, neoliberalism or whatever inflection of contemporary capitalism you prefer. But that is not all it says. It is the 'ideals', the cultural values, the moral norms that for Fraser explain why progressive neoliberalism can be or has to be called progressive. She is glad to see the end of progressive neoliberalism, with its tilt towards recognition at the expense of redistribution, and of the Clinton coalition that embodied it, but she does not assert that these ideals are not or never were genuinely progressive. The fact that they are compatible with neoliberalism does not erase the fact that, as she says, they 'could in principle serve different ends'. To this I would add, first, that they help explain the attraction and success of neoliberalism, and second, that historically they *have* served different ends, including the ends of the welfare state – which are also redistributionist. As I've noted, the welfare state requires and encourages the de-moralizing of poverty and, more generally, the de-activating of a great deal of conventional morality. It too has been 'co-opted' – if that is the right word – into institutions that are or were parts of the political status quo, which is to say have made a measurable difference in actual lives. Other real-world consequences of the movements of the 1960s include no-fault divorce, which allowed women to escape from otherwise hopeless conjugal entrapments and, especially when government assistance was also available, to pursue more independent paths. That is, it encouraged what Fraser calls, ventriloquizing neoliberalism, 'diversity and empowerment'.

The paradigmatic example of moral overlap between the welfare state and neoliberalism is also the one that is most relevant, at least at the level of surface detail, to *The Keeper of Lost Causes*: no-fault insurance for automobile accidents. No-fault automobile insurance was first proposed by then Massachusetts state representative Michael Dukakis in 1967. When it was adopted in 1970, it was greeted as a progressive measure. There was and is opposition to it, especially on the right. But there is no doubt that it would not have had the success it has had in a number of states if the big insurance companies had been 100 per cent against it. Wall Street clearly did the math and saw in it benefits for its bottom line. They may even have been behind it all along. If so, it would not be shocking: the birth of modern corporate capitalism can arguably be matched up quite closely with the nineteenth-century invention of limited liability and the phasing out of imprisonment for debt, in both cases a pulling back from the traditional understanding of moral accountability.

The moral of my argument is not: come home, neoliberalism, all is forgiven. What I am saying is that those of us who are quick on the draw where accusations of closet neoliberalism are concerned (e.g. about Foucault) should perhaps keep our guns in our holsters a bit longer. You don't have to be an eager exploiter of your fellow man to feel a twinge of sympathy, say, at the word 'austerity' as you pause to remember that it also has environmental and anti-consumerist connotations. There are reasons why this ideology works, and not all of them are bad reasons. No account of neoliberalism that does not explain why it has won as much consent as it has will be very useful for those of us who are looking for its points of vulnerability.

Neoliberalism's success and the success of Nordic noir as a genre again seem to have more points of contact than one might have predicted. In spite of their bold amoralism, both also make a surreptitious but forceful appeal to nostalgic and reactionary values. This is the argument made about neoliberalism by Melinda Cooper in her *Family Values: Between Neoliberalism and the New Social Conservatism.*[11] Neoliberalism seems to take a very different position from the so-called neoconservative or traditional right, Cooper says. They differ on the state, to which the neoconservative right, being moralistic and paternalistic, is not totally opposed. And they differ on the family, a traditional normative institution to which the neoliberals seem indifferent, as they are indifferent to other moral norms, but that the traditional right of course supports. In spite of these apparent differences, however, neoliberalism has in fact made common cause with the traditional right again and again both about the family and about the state. Why? Because while the supposedly free market can and must dissolve all other forms of trust and solidarity, it simply won't work without preserving one basic non-market, noncontractual sphere: the sphere of the family. The family's true agents are not after all self-interested entrepreneurial individuals but fellow family members who do not act like self-interested individuals in relation to each other. Neoliberalism *says* that it needs the economic *individual*, prepared to enter into contractual relations with other individuals, but in fact it needs the intimate, trusting, *non*contractual sphere of the family, and thus it must oppose any attempts by women to liberate themselves from their traditional role within the family. To avow it, then, would be to admit self-contradiction. It can get away with this self-contradiction because, or to the extent that, the family is taken for granted, as the individual is. Aiming her polemic at Nancy Fraser and others who accuse identity politics of complicity with neoliberalism, Cooper argues that feminists, by encouraging women to liberate themselves from the family, expose the contradiction, subvert the basis of capitalism and are thus anti-capitalist revolutionaries by definition.

Cooper's point about neoliberalism's unavowed dependence on 'family values' echoes a confusion point that has been noticed by Scandinavian critics like Jakob Stougaard-Nielsen in Nordic noir's critique of the welfare state. Is that critique indeed a left-wing critique as it appears to be? Or is it, sometimes, a critique from the right? And if it is from the right, which version of the right does it represent, the neoconservative right or the neoliberal right? According to Stougaard-Nielsen, beginning with the strong critique of the Swedish welfare state in Sjöwall and Wahlöö's Martin Beck novels, there is an ambiguity between critique from the left and critique from the right, the critique from the right being a nostalgic, past-oriented 'anti-modern cultural critique'[12] – as if the good old days involved social justice for all genders and races – that stands out against the authors' socialism. 'The political rhetoric here', Stougaard-Nielsen writes, 'resembles that of populist right-wing agitation in later decades (outside forces threatening national harmony with the elderly as primary victims)'.[13] He goes on to suggest that the appeal of the genre comes in part from its political ambiguity, which includes 'national and cultural conservatism'.[14] To this can be added one more ambiguity. It seems possible and even inevitable that some of the critique from the right is not after all based on 'cultural conservatism' but on neoliberalism, which is much less traditional about culture but, in its insistence on the 'modern' autonomous and entrepreneurial individual, no less an ideology of the right.

When the Scandinavian crime story is read as critique of the welfare state, is it a critique from the left (as has usually been assumed, based on the known left-wing views of the classic authors) or is it perhaps a critique from the right – even a neoliberal critique? In the Adler-Olsen novel, the attempted murder is in effect the work of an entire family, which is in angry revolt against the state and the law. In that sense, the novel can appear to be taking the side of state and law against family loyalty, considered as a vestigially personalistic ethic. Yet two members of that family have spent time in state institutions, and we are not encouraged to think it was time well spent. Thus, the responsibility for their criminality could also be attributed in part to the state. Anti-statism is an everyday affair. A neighbour tells Carl Mørck, the detective in charge of Department Q,

> Down at social services we spend more time filling out stupid forms than helping citizens. Did you know that, Carl? Let those smug government ministers give it a try. If they had to fill out forms to get their free dinners and free chauffeurs and free rent and their enormous salaries and all that other shit, they wouldn't

have any time left for eating or sleeping or driving or anything else. Can't you just picture it?[15]

It's as if one of the novel's readers were speaking up within its pages, channelling tabloid complaints about 'excess regulation' and 'big government'. Mørck himself finds police bureaucracy absurd or worse, and says so on many occasions. On the other hand, he is extremely attracted to the official 'crisis counselor' assigned to him after a traumatic incident by that same welfare-state bureaucracy, and he is not wrong to find her very insightful. He ends up solving the case with her help, as well as the help of a Syrian refugee whom the Danish state has generously taken in, suffering through his comical Danish but benefiting from his special skills, and by virtue of Mørck's own ability to get through to a brain-damaged character who has been long unable to communicate with anyone else. In this sense, Mørck acts out the state's proper responsibility to deal with disability, a theme that is touched on again by the role of that brain-damaged character in the ending, and for that matter also by the fact that the case itself serves as therapy for another policeman who has been paralysed in an earlier shooting. To anyone looking from outside Scandinavia, these items seem evidence offered in defence of the welfare state.

The cold case can be described as a case in which no decision is called for. I began by aligning the cold case with the coldness of the welfare state, conceived of as a state which hesitates to judge the individual and thus creates a maximum of social space in which no decision is expected or called for. In other words, the welfare state maximizes the zone of social undecidability – if you prefer, a zone in which we assume in advance that, like a mother trying to protect her children from bombers overhead, we have to see that there are no good choices and no good decisions. In making this connection, my point was to contrast the welfare state with neoliberalism, which preaches the doctrine of accountability at all levels and thus *minimizes* the social space of undecidability. That seems to me a useful contrast, a way of reminding ourselves that neoliberalism does not fill every square inch of social space, as some of its theorists seem to suggest, and that popular genres like Nordic noir don't merely reflect neoliberalism's assumptions but serve as sites of valuable argument about those assumptions.

Without idealizing the Scandinavian status quo or the history that led to it, I think it is fair to say (especially for an American like me) that expanding the zone of individual undecidability, as I think has happened in Scandinavia, has required expanding the scope and power of *collective decision-making*: call it socialism or even social democracy. In other words, it's not the result of a universal or philosophical position on decidability as such, but a historical and political preference for certain decisions and deciders over others. If we don't want the responsibility to decide to fall either on individuals or on the market, neoliberalism's secular divinity, then it's better not to trust undecidability as a principle, but to take the money out of decision-making and thus arrange for decisions to be made in a genuinely democratic manner.

Note: A somewhat different version of this chapter was published in boundary 2 46:1 (2019) DOI 10.1215/01903659-7271387, 2019, by Duke University Press.

Notes

1 Jussi Adler-Olsen, *The Keeper of Lost Causes: A Department Q Novel*, trans. Lisa Hartford (New York: Penguin Plume, 2007 [2011]), 21.
2 Jakob Stougaard-Nielsen, *Scandinavian Crime Fiction* (London: Bloomsbury, 2017).
3 Gary S. Becker, 'Crime and Punishment: An Economic Approach', in Gary S. Becker and William M. Landes (eds), *Essays in the Economics of Crime and Punishment* (New York: National Bureau of Economic Research. Distributed by Columbia University Press, 1974).
4 *Crime and Punishment*, 9.
5 Ibid., 28.
6 Ibid., 29.
7 Gary S. Becker, François Ewald and Bernard E. Harcourt, 'Becker and Foucault on Crime and Punishment', 6 September 2013, University of Chicago Coase-Sandor Institute for Law and Economics Research Paper No. 654; University of Chicago, 2013, Public Law Working Paper No. 440; Columbia Law and Economics Working Paper No. 456. Available at SSRN: https://ssrn .com/abstract=2321912 or http://dx .doi.org/10.2139/ssrn.2321912: 3.
8 Ibid., 6.
9 Michel Foucault, *The Birth of Biopolitics: Lectures at the Collège de France 1978–79*, ed. Michel Senellart, trans. Graham Burchell (New York: Picador, 2008).
10 Nancy Fraser, 'The End of Progressive Neoliberalism', *Dissent*, 2 January 2017. https://www.dissentmagazine.org/online_articles/progressive-neoliberalism -reactionary-populism-nancy-fraser
11 Melinda Cooper, *Family Values: Between Neoliberalism and the New Social Conservatism* (New York: Zone Books, 2017).
12 *Scandinavian Crime Fiction*, 43.
13 Ibid.
14 Ibid.
15 *The Keeper of Lost Causes*, 211.

Works cited

Adler-Olsen, Jussi, *The Keeper of Lost Causes: A Department Q Novel*, trans. Lisa Hartford. New York: Penguin Plume, 2011 (2007).

Becker, Gary S., 'Crime and Punishment: An Economic Approach', in Gary S. Becker and William M. Landes (eds), *Essays in the Economics of Crime and Punishment*. New York: National Bureau of Economic Research. Distributed by Columbia University Press, 1974.

Becker, Gary S., François Ewald and Bernard E. Harcourt, 'Becker and Foucault on Crime and Punishment', 6 September 2013. University of Chicago Coase-Sandor Institute for Law and Economics Research Paper No. 654; University of Chicago, Public Law Working Paper No. 440; Columbia Law and Economics Working Paper No. 456. Available at SSRN: https://ssrn .com/abstract=2321912 or http://dx.doi.org/ 10.2139/ssrn.2321912.

Cooper, Melinda, *Family Values: Between Neoliberalism and the New Social Conservatism*. New York: Zone Books, 2017.

Foucault, Michel, *The Birth of Biopolitics: Lectures at the Collège de France 1978–79*, ed. Michel Senellart, and trans. Graham Burchell. New York: Picador, 2008.

Fraser, Nancy, 'The End of Progressive Neoliberalism', in *Dissent*, 2 January 2017. https://www.dissentmagazine.org/online_articles/progressive-neoliberalism-reactionary-populism-nancy-fraser

Harcourt, Bernard E., Gary S. Becker and François Ewald, '"Becker and Foucault on Crime and Punishment": A Conversation with Gary Becker, François Ewald, and Bernard Harcourt: The Second Session', University of Chicago Public Law and Legal Theory Working Paper, 15 May 2013. https://chicagounbound.uchicago.edu/cgi/ viewcontent.cgi?referer=https://www.google.com/&httpsredir=1&article=1409 &context=public_law:and_legal_theory.

Stougaard-Nielsen, Jakob, *Scandinavian Crime Fiction*. London: Bloomsbury, 2017.

8

Collage forms and undecidability in Emine Sevgi Özdamar's *Seltsame Sterne starren zur Erde*

Hannah Vinter

Durch die hohen Häuser auf der Karl-Marx-Allee wirkten die Menschen ganz klein. Die Allee sah wie eine Collage aus, so als hätte man aus einem Bild kleine Menschen herausgeschnitten und mit Uhu auf ein Bild mit großen Häusern geklebt.[1]

(Through the high buildings on Karl-Marx-Allee, the people appeared very small. The avenue looked like a collage, as if someone had cut little people out of a picture and stuck them onto a picture of big houses with Uhu glue.)

The narrator of Emine Sevgi Özdamar's autofictional novel *Seltsame Sterne starren zur Erde* (Strange Stars Stare to Earth) – published in 2003 and set in the divided Berlin of the 1970s – makes this observation as she walks down East Berlin's iconic central avenue. Her description, which appears amid a series of fragmentary musings about the things she sees, the scents she smells and the memories they provoke, is easily passed over. Nevertheless, it merits a closer look. The narrator's reference to collage denaturalizes the perspective of what she observes; it is self-evident that, compared to the tall tower blocks of Karl-Marx-Allee, people appear small, but by suggesting the scene looks like tiny people stuck to big houses, it seems as if their relative sizes have been intentionally selected and juxtaposed. The narrator's words also create tension between the materiality of the scene and that of its representation; her reference to looking 'through' the looming buildings makes the physical landscape appear vaguely insubstantial, whereas her collage simile is developed in such concrete terms – including the brand of glue used to stick it down – that it is endowed with the material qualities of something directly experienced. The description of the collage also puts the narrator both inside and outside the image; she is simultaneously externally observing the scene and imagining creating it. This passage thus creates a sense of undecidability between the categories of large and small, real and imaginary, productive and receptive, revealing these labels as contingent and in flux.

Such perspectival ambiguity is common in *Seltsame Sterne*, a text that employs a dizzying range of forms – episodic prose, poetic quotation, newspaper headlines, text from found objects, diary entries, rehearsal sketches and theatre notes – to evoke its narrator's life Berlin. *Seltsame Sterne* also takes in a broad array of historical, personal and artistic themes, including the narrator's experience of violence in Turkey, where she was born and grew up, her observations of the politically fraught landscape of divided Berlin, her friendships and romantic relationships and her work at the East German theatre, the Volksbühne. In this chapter, I explore how the heterogeneity of *Seltsame Sterne* relates to Özdamar's little-studied practice of creating theatre collages. As Özdamar described in a conversation in 2019, collages formed part of her dramaturgical process; when working on a play as a director's assistant, she would first read the script, and then make collage works using images from magazines and books, photographs of actors and other materials, and these would help shape her ideas as she went into rehearsals.[2] The first time she used collage in this way was for the production of *Hamlet* that features extensively in part two of *Seltsame Sterne*, and the narrator refers directly to making these collages in the text.[3] In this chapter, I analyse Özdamar's *Hamlet* collages – two of which are published here for the first time – and show how their disruptive aesthetics and anti-authoritarian politics illuminate *Seltsame Sterne*. In her text just as in her collages, Özdamar experiments with material fragments in order to destabilize conceptual boundaries, for example between past and present, or between art and life. In deconstructing these binaries, Özdamar insists on the presence of paradox in our understanding of the past, creating an engagement with Cold War history that simultaneously acknowledges losses and suggests possibilities for new beginnings. *Seltsame Sterne* also uses the material ambiguity of collage to challenge ideologies that impose fixed images of the world. The text's undecidable forms provoke idiosyncratic associations that suggest the power of personal connections to undermine authoritarian categories.

Seltsame Sterne and its reception

Özdamar's multi-award-winning oeuvre has established her reputation among scholars as 'one of the leading lights of Turkish–German literature', as Lizzie

Stewart and Frauke Matthes write.[4] Born in Eastern Anatolia in 1946, Özdamar rose to prominence as a German-language writer after winning the prestigious Ingeborg Bachmann prize in 1991 for extracts from what would become her first autobiographical novel, *Das Leben ist eine Karawanserei – hat zwei Türen – aus einer kam ich rein – aus der anderen ging ich raus* (Life is a Caravanserai – Has Two Doors – I Came in One – I Went Out the Other).[5] Published in full in 1992, this text was a fictionalization of her childhood in Turkey. It was followed in 1998 by a second autofictional novel, *Die Brücke vom goldenen Horn* (The Bridge of the Golden Horn), which was based on her first experience of coming to Germany in the 1960s as a teenage industrial worker, before returning to Turkey and training as an actress.[6] *Seltsame Sterne*, published in 2003 and inspired by the period in the mid-1970s when Özdamar came back to Berlin and worked at the Volksbühne, follows on from these precursors, and the three texts have subsequently been published together as a trilogy.[7]

Seltsame Sterne consists of two parts, both structured around episodic encounters rather than a conventional narrative arc. Part One is divided into three sections of first-person prose, scattered with intertextual elements, ranging from snippets of poetry to text from bottle labels. It begins in 1976 after the narrator, a Turkish actress and theatre-maker, has arrived in Berlin. She stays in a left-wing commune in West Berlin, but commutes to the East, where she interns at the Volksbühne, working under Brechtian director Benno Besson. Part One soon jumps back in time to show the narrator before she left Turkey, as she grapples with emotional and political turmoil. The reader learns that the authoritarian crackdown unleashed after Turkey's 1971 military coup led to the closure of the theatre where the narrator worked and served as the background to the break-up of her marriage. Wanting to escape, she moves to Berlin, where she meets Besson and begins work in the theatre. The remainder of Part One focuses on the narrator's experiences in the West-Berlin commune where she lives, her relationships and her encounters in the city. The focus on theatre work also begins to intensify, as the narrator participates in a production of Heiner Müller's *Die Bauern*, and gets a visa allowing her to live in East Berlin.

Part Two of *Seltsame Sterne* switches to diary format, interspersed with rehearsal sketches and notes, and it focuses more consistently on the Volksbühne, even as the narrator continues to move between East and West. The narrator's relationships with friends and lovers feature particularly prominently, as does her work on Volksbühne productions of Shakespeare's *Hamlet* and Goethe's *Der Bürgergeneral*. Political turbulence also forms a backdrop to the narrative, from police crackdowns on members of the militant left-wing group, the RAF, in the West, to the expulsion of the dissident singer Wolf Biermann from the East. Partly influenced by these tensions (though the connection is never made explicit[8]) the creative team at the Volksbühne starts to scatter by the end of the text, just as the West German commune is also disintegrating. Besson moves to France to work on a production of Bertolt Brecht's *The Caucasian Chalk Circle*, and the novel ends as the narrator goes to join him.

As this summary suggests, *Seltsame Sterne* resists easy categorization, and as such it offers an intriguing example of literary undecidability. Most obviously, like much of Özdamar's oeuvre, the work destabilizes genre boundaries. Lacking any overarching plot, it does not resemble a conventional novel, and the subject matter is clearly autobiographical as the narrator shares names, traits and a personal history with the author.[9] Real individuals with whom Özdamar worked appear as characters, and the text incorporates rehearsal sketches, notes and other realia from Özdamar's time in 1970s Berlin. On the other hand, *Seltsame Sterne* offers no guarantees of its own factuality; Laura Bradley points out that the text is clearly not packaged as memoir, and Gizem Arslan adds that 'the whimsy of fiction permeates the novel'.[10] *Seltsame Sterne* also creates uncertainty about how far it should be seen as a fragmentary component of Özdamar's writings and how far as a composition in its own right. The book's profound interconnectedness with Özdamar's other work is clear; the text has been incorporated into her autofictional 'Istanbul-Berlin-Trilogy', and it also expands material that appears in the short narrative 'Mein Berlin' (My Berlin), which is included in her 2001 story collection *Der Hof in Spiegel* (The Courtyard in the Mirror).[11] Such connections are characteristic of Özdamar's oeuvre, in which, as Liesbeth Minnaard describes, 'the novels and the shorter pieces of prose refer to, and even pre- and re-tell, each other'.[12] At the same time, *Seltsame Sterne* distinguishes itself from many of Özdamar's other autofictions in the radical extent to which it combines different textual and visual forms. The text's formal diversity also recalls the performance traditions it thematizes – as Ela Gezen discusses with reference to Brechtian staging, and Claudia Breger highlights in relation to the development of postmodernist performance – and it thus disrupts the division between textual narrative and theatre.[13]

Many critics have sought to explain the significance of *Seltsame Sterne*'s formal ambiguities, and in doing so several have characterized the text as a 'montage'. Gezen, for example, argues that Özdamar creates a Brechtian montage that shows the need for critical input in the past she evokes: 'By employing literary montage as a structural principle in *Seltsame Sterne*, Özdamar, like Brecht, draws attention to the unraveling of social, historical, and political processes', Gezen writes, arguing that, 'Özdamar's text stages the incompleteness and ongoing construction of the narrator's past and present'.[14] Breger – drawing connections between *Seltsame Sterne*, late-twentieth-century experimental theatre and pop art objects – argues that Özdamar creates a montage of elements which transmit a sense of unmediated presence and which at the same time are held at a critical remove.[15] Breger argues that the effect of this process, which she terms 'presentification-at-a-distance', is to preclude conclusive judgements about *Seltsame Sterne*'s subject matter, for example about the 1970s left-wing movements portrayed in the text, which are shown simultaneously in an affectionate and a critical light. The reader is thus constantly 'reevaluat[ing] the complex, overdetermined constellations', unable to arrive at a definitive image of the past, while nevertheless continuing to grapple with it.[16]

These readings are important in emphasizing the connection between Özdamar's undecidable forms and her refusal to offer one-sided images of Cold War Berlin. As such, they resonate with established studies of Özdamar as a writer who undermines fixed boundaries.[17] While in broad agreement with these analyses, I believe further light can be shed on *Seltsame Sterne* by moving from a discussion of 'montage' to a focus on 'collage', a term that other critics have used in a general sense to describe *Seltsame Sterne*'s formal heterogeneity, but which none has probed in depth.[18] Calling for a shift from montage to collage immediately raises the question, what is the difference between the two? The *OED* suggests that montage is a broader label, used to describe spliced shots in film as well as assembled flat images (as in photomontage), and which is extended to refer to other types of medleys; obvious examples are discontinuous scenes on stage, or fragmented elements in a written text. Collage, by contrast, is more narrowly associated with visual art forms in which assembled elements are stuck down on a flat ground, or with figurative references to such art.[19] These descriptions make clear why critics have favoured 'montage' to describe *Seltsame Sterne*, which, as a prose work that draws on dramatic techniques, resonates with the wider associations of that term. However, it is notable that common aspects of collage – the insertion and juxtaposition of realia, the use of paper fragments – are found in *Seltsame Sterne*, and this merits further attention.

Beyond any attempts to pin down differences between 'montage' and 'collage' – terms which inevitably overlap – collage offers a relevant lens of analysis because Özdamar herself produced collages, and she began doing so during her work on the 1977 production of *Hamlet* that features in *Seltsame Sterne*. Özdamar's collages have only lately begun to attract scholarly attention, with Bernard Banoun having recently published and analysed some of her later graphic works, and Bettina Brandt also discussing her collage production, and stressing the importance of avant-garde forms to her work.[20] Thanks to contact with Özdamar, I make two of her *Hamlet* collages available here for the first time. These works offer insight into *Seltsame Sterne* not only because they relate to a production thematized in the text but also because they illustrate how Özdamar uses physical fragments to destabilize wider conceptual categories – a process that sheds light on the function of paper elements and other realia in her novel, and that reveals connections between these interpolations and ideas circulating in her theatre milieu. Analysing Özdamar's experiments with paper fragments thus reformulates previous critics' observations about montage in *Seltsame Sterne* from a new angle, while also suggesting novel resonances between her textual and theatrical work.

Özdamar's collages

Özdamar made around nine collages for *Hamlet* and – as with all her collage works – she did so in order to develop dramaturgical ideas, not with the intention that they should be viewed as independent pieces of art. Describing her work in an oral interview, she stated:

> Um sich an ein neues Stück anzunähern, das ist ein sehr guter Weg gewesen für mich – mit Collagen. Ich musste erst selber kapieren, welches Gefühl vermittelt mir das Stück – also Hamlet – und natürlich das bildlich machen und durch einen Klebeprozess, wählen, wählen, wählen und kleben. Machst du jetzt stundenlang. Nimmst du das und dann tust du weg, tust du weg. Du klebst nicht erst, sondern stellst du her auf dem Papier, also lose. Und dann wenn du sicher bist – oh das Bild vermittelt dir was – dann klebst du es, und dann ist die Collage da.[21]
>
> (Collages were a very good way for me to get closer to a new play. First I had to understand what feeling the play – say, *Hamlet* – communicates to me and to make that visual, of course, through a process of gluing, choosing, choosing, choosing and gluing. You do it for hours. You take this, and then you put it aside, put it aside. You don't glue at first, but you put things here on the paper, unfixed. And then when you're sure – oh! that picture says something to you – then you glue it, and then the collage is there.)

Özdamar thus characterizes collage as an immersive procedure of experimenting with fragments in order to feel out their connections – with one another, with herself and with the play. Her description highlights the practical nature and material focus of her work, in which these associations are not theorized but sensed. But while Özdamar's collages are primarily a tool for dramaturgical exploration, they also hint at an interest in the form's history as part of an artistic tradition; for example, some of her later works incorporate collages by Max Ernst, and use imagery that recalls other surrealist and dadaist collage.[22] Bettina Brandt, who describes Özdamar's own first play, *Karagöz in Alamania*, as a 'Theatercollage' incorporating folkloric and avant-garde elements, notes that both Modernist traditions, such as surrealism, and popular theatre forms were influential in Özdamar's artistic milieu, and played a central role in shaping her work.[23] Özdamar's *Hamlet* compositions resonate with these intersecting currents, as they use folk motifs to challenge aesthetic categories – an exercise resulting in multilayered deconstructions that also recall the avant-garde movements that fostered collage's twentieth-century development.

A striking example of these concerns is found in the collage that shows a moment from Act 3, Scene II of *Hamlet*, in which Horatio is imagined entering on a flying carpet (Figure 8.1). A crude interpretation might be that Özdamar challenges the division between 'East' and 'West' by inserting an iconic element of Middle Eastern folklore (the flying carpet) into a canonical work of European literature (*Hamlet*). Such a reading, however, would reinforce the division it pretends to deconstruct, in that it reiterates the problematic binary that Claudia

Figure 8.1 *Hamlet* collage, by Emine Sevgi Özdamar, © Emine Sevgi Özdamar, 1977. Reproduced with permission of the author.

Breger observes in Özdamar scholarship, where she laments the 'repeated characterization of Özdamar's transnational poetics as a connection of (Turkish) oral tradition with (European) modernity and literariness'.[24] Özdamar's collage, by contrast, creates a more complex disruption as it challenges the equation of the East with folk traditions and the West with 'high' culture by bringing out the folk elements embedded in *Hamlet* itself. The image of Hamlet calling for his friend, 'Heda Horatio', who suddenly materializes from the air, assumes a fairy-tale quality of wishes being granted on command – a folk motif by no means confined to an Eastern context, and which serves as a reminder that *Hamlet* has roots in the oral tradition.[25] Thus, the collage shows the labels of 'popular' and 'fine' art to be fluid in a way that simultaneously challenges Orientalist notions of 'East' and 'West'.

This dismantling of categories resonates with ideas explored in Besson's production. Besson's thinking as a director was partly informed by the Shakespeare scholar Robert Weimann, who acted as a consultant on the 1977 staging of *Hamlet*,[26] and who argued that Shakespeare drew on a legacy of folk performance in which there was no fixed barrier between actors and audience.[27] Weimann posits that Shakespeare borrows structures from popular theatre that create mutually interactive relationships between viewers, performers and social structures, producing plays that do not reflect society, but that simultaneously shape and are shaped by society. In this interplay, he argues, the plays also create an evolving reaction between past and present. 'For Shakespeare, the art and experience of playing handed down via the popular stage was part of a meaningful cultural past in the process of its present reawakening, assimilation and change', Weimann writes in a revised English version of his influential text, *Shakespeare und die Tradition des Volkstheaters* (Shakespeare and the Popular Tradition in the Theater), in which he names Besson in the dedication.[28] The folkloric influences in Özdamar's collage recall the dynamic relationships Weimann describes between audience and performer, and between past and present.

At the same time, the use of popular motifs to destabilize boundaries also recalls theories underlying collage's development as a Modernist form. The insertion of everyday objects into the realm of 'high' art to challenge the boundary between 'inside' and 'outside' the artwork was a key feature of the first avant-garde collages, as art historian Christine Poggi describes in her analysis of Pablo Picasso's foundational collage work, *Still Life with Chair Caning* (1912).[29] Picasso's oval-shaped composition evokes a still life with a newspaper and other objects on a table. It is framed by a piece of rope, and includes a scrap of oilcloth – a material used for tablecloths – with a pattern resembling furniture caning. Poggi describes how Picasso's combination of these elements confuses the traditional binary between object and representation. She writes: 'Picasso made it impossible for the viewer to determine which representational paradigm governs the appearance of the oilcloth. Is the oilcloth to be taken as a literal or real object, that is, does the oilcloth refer to the surface of the table? or to a tablecloth resting upon it?'[30] Without wanting to claim that Özdamar is a Cubist, I argue that her Horatio collage also plays with this material undecidability. Its most striking feature is the carpet Horatio is pictured riding, which is not an image, but a real piece of woven fabric. Like Picasso's oilcloth, the fabric troubles the boundary between object and representation, seeming to occupy both positions at once, and the question of how to interpret its role in the wider composition remains open in the mind of the viewer.

Thus, Özdamar's collage suggests a sense of undecidability between inside and outside the artwork, and in doing so it also resonates with previous scholarly analyses that have linked Özdamar's writing with the anti-representational philosophy of Gilles Deleuze. See, for example, Margaret Littler's Deleuzian analysis of *Die Brücke vom goldenen Horn*, which, Littler argues, emphasizes 'art's relationship to life, not as representation, imitation or mimesis, but as directly continuous with the material world'.[31] Links between Deleuze and Özdamar's collages are especially intriguing because there are some structural resonances between the two. In *A Thousand Plateaus*, which Deleuze jointly authored with Félix Guattari, the philosophers suggest that the dynamic relationship between art and life can best be seen when elements are not built up into inevitably hierarchical structures, but spread out on a continuous surface.[32] 'The ideal for a book would be to lay everything out on a plane of exteriority . . . on a single page, the same sheet: lived events, historical determinations, concepts, individuals, groups, social formations', they write.[33] Their description recalls the form of collage, which art historian Diane Waldman sums up as having transformed painting 'from a window into a flat plane',[34] and it also evokes the space of the stage, on which different places, times, characters and objects are constantly refigured. Thus, the Deleuzian thought that has previously been traced in Özdamar's work offers another lens through which to view the ongoing interactions that her collages create between the artist, the material fragments she handles, and the theatre setting within which she works. Moreover, these Deleuzian resonances suggest the politically subversive potential of Özdamar's collages, for, as Littler points out, in refusing to operate according to the logic of preformed political frameworks, Deleuze's anti-representationalism suggests new possibilities for conceptualizing social relationships.[35]

In Özdamar's *Hamlet* collages, the destabilization of categories certainly has a rebellious political effect. As Robert Weimann describes in a 1998 retrospective of the East German stage, the *Hamlet* production arose in a context in which there was pressure on theatre makers to present Shakespeare's works as prefiguring the socialist present.[36] However, by continually emphasizing disjuncture, Besson's *Hamlet* rejected this authoritarian insistence on using Shakespeare to portray the German Democratic Republic (GDR) as a utopian culmination of history.[37] Özdamar's other *Hamlet* collages also suggest that this aesthetics of juxtaposition had an anti-fascist thrust. This is evident in one of several collages that show the ghost of Old Hamlet as a composite of a suited man and a Roman centurion (Figure 8.2). Özdamar's unusual combination prompts the viewer to search for the connection between the elements, which is found in their mutual evocation of patriarchal authority, with the military and imperial dominance of Rome figured on the one hand and the financial dominance of the twentieth-century man in a suit on the other. However, while suggesting a connection between the suit and the Roman uniform, the collage also emphasizes their visual incongruity, showing how ridiculous they look together. The result is an image that parodies an ideology that sought to conflate classical aesthetics and twentieth-century masculinity: fascism. Thus, in the collages of Old Hamlet, Özdamar's confounding of

Figure 8.2 *Hamlet* collage, by Emine Sevgi Özdamar, © Emine Sevgi Özdamar, 1977. Reproduced with permission of the author.

boundaries between past and present plays a wider political role, both pointing to the pervasiveness of patriarchal dominance across space and time, and lambasting fascist ideology that sought to portray this dominance as natural and desirable.

However, while suggesting both a break from East German orthodoxy and a satire of fascism, Özdamar's collages do not impose their own strict political vision. Rather, as in Deleuze and Guattari's description of the ever-dynamic flat plane, they create an awareness of openness. Lawrence Guntner writes that part of the innovation of Weimann's thought in East Germany was that while Shakespeare reception had previously insisted on the 'authority of the written word and excluded the player and the spectator in the constitution of meaning', Weimann demonstrated that 'the player and the spectator were, in fact, the essential elements and equal partners in this process. Thus, the meaning negotiated during performance is not constituted for all time but, like translation, varies according to the historical situation.'[38] This is to say that the idiosyncratic meetings of people and things in the space of the theatre could unsettle notions of continuity through being open to interaction with their context. Guntner's description recalls Özdamar's account of using her collages to sense unpredictable physical connections between different elements, and it further implies the anti-authoritarian political undercurrent of this process.

An analysis of Özdamar's *Hamlet* collages thus suggests several, interconnected ideas. First, Özdamar uses collage to explore evolving connections between herself, a theatrical work and material fragments, and – in the wider tradition of collage – she creates multiple undecidabilities in the process: between 'high' and 'low' art, between object and representation and between different times and places. Second, her process of doing so resonates both with the aesthetic concerns of her theatre milieu and with the wider traditions of collage art. And thirdly, such experimentation had anti-authoritarian political aims. All three of these ideas come through in Özdamar's play with paper elements in *Seltsame Sterne*, to which I now turn.

Collage forms in *Seltsame Sterne*

A striking resonance between Özdamar's collages and *Seltsame Sterne* is found in the text's many allusions to paper fragments. And just as Özdamar's visual collages use such fragments to trace dynamic interactions between artist, material objects and theatre, her textual references to paper create an ongoing interplay between world, page and stage. The fluidity between textual and material spheres – which Gizem Arslan likewise notes in her analysis of 'translation' in *Seltsame Sterne*[39] – is reinforced by the narrator's frequent descriptions of her surroundings being made out of paper or card. See, for example, her reference to the November sky hanging 'wie eine schmutzige Fotokopie eines Himmels über Berlin' (like a dirty photocopy of a sky over Berlin), her characterization of the politically fraught landscape of West Berlin as a fairground shooting game full of 'Menschen aus Pappe, und andere Menschen aus Pappe schießen Löcher hinein' (cardboard people, and other cardboard people shoot holes into them) and her allusion to the doors of the West-Berlin commune being made out of cardboard (*Seltsame Sterne*, 32, 65, 68). While these descriptions resonate generally with other works by Özdamar that compare landscapes to photos,[40] in the context of this text about the Volksbühne they are, more than ever, suggestive of theatrical scenery. Such imagery affirms the arguments of previous critics who posit that *Seltsame Sterne* presents Berlin as a stage set.[41] At the same time, Özdamar's references to the paper landscape also suggest a continuum between the narrator's environment and the pages of the book. This impression is reinforced by descriptions of graffiti scrawled on walls in the West, which figure the city as a page to be read (*Seltsame Sterne* 64–5).[42] It is also suggested by the rehearsal sketches that Özdamar inserts into the text, which simultaneously evoke the space of the theatre and show up their own status as material objects, bringing both together on the page of the novel.

As with Özdamar's collages, the undecidability that these paper fragments create between different material spheres also challenges the bounds between conceptual categories – for example, between past and present. Her insertion of rehearsal sketches into the text offers a clear example. On one level, these drawings show the dynamic motion of actors (see *Seltsame Sterne* 122, 172, 198), and they thus suggest the immediate experience of unfolding action. At the same time, they are printed in a way that highlights their faded historicity. In almost every case, Özdamar's drawings are reproduced to show not just the sketch, but to emphasize the paper it has been made on. Sometimes this means that the drawing itself is rather small, in the centre of a sheet that has nevertheless been reproduced in its entirety, showing up its darkened edges, or torn, hole-punched holes (*Seltsame Sterne* 205, 214). Notably, when the narrator refers to buying the notebooks on which these sketches are made, their pages are already 'gelblich' (yellowish), and thus appear new and old at the same time (*Seltsame Sterne*, 81).

These ambiguous fragments create the impression of objects seen from several temporal perspectives simultaneously, and this, in turn, shapes the way that *Seltsame Sterne* figures the now-vanished landscape of the socialist GDR. In the following description of goods displayed in shop windows, for example, the objects that the narrator references appear both in and out of their East Berlin setting:

> Die wenigen Waren in den Ostberliner Schaufenstern beruhigten mich, eine kleine Waschwanne, ein Fahrradspiegel oder ein Fahrradschloß sahen aus wie archaische Gegenstände, und ich kam mir so vor, als sähe ich mir gerade in einem kleinen Museum Gegenstände aus einer anderen Zeit an. Manche Verpackungen für Kaffee, Bohnen oder Salz sahen aus, als hätten Kinder auf der Straße vergilbte Papierstücke oder Pappe gesammelt und daraus Pakete gebastelt. Darauf haben sie dann IMI oder *Eisbecherset-Stieleisbereiter* oder *Weizenin* oder *Jensisal Speisevollsalz* oder *Solzenkuchen* oder *Putzi* oder *Mondos aus reinem Naturgummi* geschrieben. (*Seltsame Sterne* 19)
>
> (The sparse goods in the East Berlin shop windows soothed me; a small washtub, a bike mirror or a bike lock looked like archaic objects, and I seemed to myself as if I were, in this moment, looking at objects in a little museum from another time. Some packaging for coffee, beans or salt looked as if children had collected yellowed pieces of paper or cardboard in the street and fashioned packets out of it. Then they had written IMI or *Sundae Dish Set – Ice-Lolly Kit* or *Wheat Powder* or *Jensisal Whole Table Salt* or *Solzen-cakes* or *Putzi* or *Mondos, made from pure natural rubber.*)

On one level, the passage evokes a first-hand experience of the GDR, as the narrator is confronted with the distinctive items on sale in East Berlin. The packaging and brand names given are all real objects that are now unfamiliar ('IMI' heavy duty washing detergent, 'Weizenin' wheat powder) and that have a simplicity that contrasts with more sophisticated capitalist branding (Mondos condoms 'made from pure natural rubber'). The narrator's description thus conjures up an immediate encounter with this now-lost world. At the same time as being introduced as present, however, these objects appear already past, with the packaging yellowed, and the goods compared to archaic museum pieces. The layered temporality of the sentence in which the narrator imagines herself looking 'in this moment' (placing herself in the present) at items 'from another time' (presumably placing herself in the future and them in the past) creates multiple simultaneous perspectives on the same objects. This ambiguity chimes with the collage structure of the items themselves, which are imagined as fashioned together from paper scraps, suggesting a Cubist-style uncertainty over whether the packaging should be read as object or as representation – is it the original, or a reconstruction? These proliferating undecidabilities destabilize the perspective of the modern-day reader who, paradoxically, is reminded through direct contact with objects from the past how mediated their experience of that past is.

The uncertain space and time created by these objects calls into question the reader's ability to make definitive judgements about what life in East Germany was like, supporting Claudia Breger's assertion that *Seltsame Sterne* balances 'presentification with historicization' in order to 'disrup[t] nostalgia but also counteract[t] wholesale attacks' on leftist politics during the Cold War.[43] This idea is illustrated by striking resonances between Özdamar's passage and notable museum displays featuring GDR products. Her description partly recalls an art installation titled *Wirtschaftswerte (Economic Values)* by the avant-garde West German artist Joseph Beuys, whom Özdamar has occasionally referenced elsewhere.[44] First displayed in 1980, *Economic Values* was assembled from GDR goods notable for their crude, faded paper packaging. The title of Beuys's work plays with the notion of 'value' between capitalist and non-capitalist systems, and according to London's Tate Modern, which hosted the installation in 2005, Beuys saw these sparse objects as an attractive alternative to the commodification that dominated the West; for him, they 'represented a simplicity and authenticity that reminded him of his childhood'.[45] Beuys's approach initially resonates with the narrator's description of finding the East German products soothing and reminiscent of children's handiwork. This seemingly positive association is ambiguous, however. Charity Scribner writes in a commentary on *Economic Values* that Beuys, a West German, spent little time in the GDR and relied on others to bring him the items that made up his installation, from which he selected those that, in their plainness, conformed with his idea of the East.[46] His installation was thus an idealization of the GDR shaped by a Western gaze, and, as Scribner comments, it 'anticipated the current race to curate the socialist past,' which has gathered pace since the state's demise.[47] This wider curation of East Germany's image is evoked in Özdamar's description, which directly recalls another exhibition of GDR design, created by Matthias Dietz and Christian Habernoll in 1989 near Frankfurt on Main, and bearing the sarcastic title 'SED: Schönes Einheits Design' (SED: Stunning Eastern Design).[48] As Scribner writes, this display 'lampooned the "pallid universe" of démodé East German consumer goods,'[49] and it is striking that all of the items listed in the *Seltsame Sterne* passage feature in the exhibition catalogue.[50] Moreover, the goods Özdamar names are, in two instances, shown on the same double-page spread of catalogue, and, in the case of the '*Sundae Dish Set–Ice-Lolly Kit*', she hyphenates two separate products shown on facing pages, strongly suggesting that this was the source for her text.[51] Thus, in recalling this scornful presentation of GDR goods at the same time as evoking more idealized associations with Beuys, the objects in Özdamar's description waver uncertainly between different gazes, appearing reassuringly simple, but also comic and bizarre. By overlaying mockery and fetishization of East German goods, the text undoes both positions, making it hard to identify with either a triumphalist capitalist or a nostalgic pro-GDR view.[52]

Beyond undermining simplistic narratives about East Germany, Özdamar's paper fragments also insist more broadly on the contradictory quality of the past, which simultaneously is shown to contain irretrievable losses and new, unfolding realities. The co-presence of loss and gain is central to the fluidity that Özdamar's paper fragments create between world, page and stage – something evident, once again, in the narrator's references to the Berlin landscape being made out of paper. In suggesting a connection between the urban surroundings and a stage set, these references can be seen, on one level, to paint the city as a space of renewed life, since the theatre is associated in *Seltsame Sterne* with resurrection. For example, the narrator channels a famous statement by Heiner Müller when she states, 'Im Theater stehen die Toten auf' (the dead rise in the theatre),[53] and she goes on to describe the stage as a place where the dead reassert themselves, coming into dynamic contact with the present and future: 'Die Toten wollen weiterleben, um sich in die kommenden Geschichten der Welt einzumischen' (The dead want to carry on living so that they can intervene in the coming stories of the world) (*Seltsame Sterne*, 170). This description of the inanimate coming to life on stage is also evoked in a reference to the paper rehearsal sketches: 'Ich sah die Kollegen, die als Zeichnungen in meiner Tasche steckten, ins Theater gehen' (I saw the colleagues, who were tucked into my pocket as drawings, go into the theatre) (*Seltsame Sterne*, 169). This reference again strengthens the reader's impression of the porous relationship between stage and page, and suggests that the continuum between them is an animated space, a Deleuzian 'plane of exteriority', in which lively transformations take place.[54] At the same time, however, the identification of the city with stage scenery emphasizes its frailty as much as its vitality; the paper sky is dirty, the cardboard doors of the shared flat offer no protection from intruders and the paper figures of West Berlin's inhabitants are riddled with holes (*Seltsame Sterne*, 32, 68, 65). Thus, the narrator's paper surroundings point simultaneously to dynamic reanimation, and to an acknowledgement of material fragility that cannot be overcome.

This tension allows Özdamar to create an approach to history that folds together an awareness of real loss with an understanding that, even though events in the past cannot be brought back, they are also never finished. This undecidability is central to *Seltsame Sterne*'s approach to traumatic histories and is clearest of all in the narrator's references to victims of the authoritarian crackdown that followed Turkey's 1971 coup. Here, once again, contradiction is embodied in references to paper fragments. Thus, when the narrator describes how, after the military takeover, 'Menschen verschwanden ganz plötzlich und wurden zu Fotos. Die Eltern liefen mit Fotos in den Händen herum und fragten: "Wo sind unsere Kinder?"' (People disappeared quite suddenly and became photos. The parents ran around with photos in their hands and asked: 'Where are our children?'), the transformation of living humans into paper images stands as a distillation of the parents' loss (*Seltsame Sterne*, 26). Özdamar develops the sense of mourning that is bound up with paper pictures when she describes a boy, imprisoned and tortured by the Turkish regime, trying to connect with the picture of a village girl in his cell:

> [M]it wem sprach der Junge, der zwanzig Jahre alt war, aber auf seinem Foto aus der Zeitung wie fünfzehn aussah? Er schnitt im Gefängnis aus einer Zeitung ein Bild aus. Ein Mädchen. Ein Dorfmädchen. Wenn man diesen Jungen nach der Folter zu seiner Zelle zurücktrug, legte er sich nicht ins Bett, sondern unter das Bett und sprach mit dem Bild des Mädchens. 'Heute haben sie mit mir das gemacht . . . das gemacht.' (*Seltsame Sterne*, 25–6)
>
> (Who did the boy, who was twenty years old but who looked fifteen in his photo in the paper, speak to? In jail he cut a picture out of the newspaper. A girl. A village girl. If this boy was brought back to his cell after the torture, he didn't lie in the bed but under the bed and spoke to the picture of the girl. 'Today they did that to me . . . did that.')

The picture of the girl is both the site of the boy's fantasy and a sign of the absence of any real sympathetic figure to comfort him; the caesura in the description of his torture corresponds with a gap created by her image, which highlights that there was no one there to break his isolation. Likewise, the boy's own photograph in the newspaper, which looks much younger than the age attributed to him, creates an impression of lost innocence and points to unreliable information distributed under the regime, suggesting that the real facts of his life have been submerged. Thus, on multiple levels, the paper fragments emphasize traumatic losses wrought by right-wing brutality.

At the same time, however, these images are explicitly generative. At a later point in the text, after the death of her grandmother, the narrator mourns: 'Ihre blauen Augen sind geschlossen. Mit diesen Augen hatte sie geweint, als junge Leute von den Faschisten getötet wurden. Sie sah ihre Fotos in den Zeitungen, sie konnte nicht lesen und nicht schreiben' (Her blue eyes are closed. It was with these eyes that she had cried when young people were killed by the fascists. She saw their photos in the newspapers, she couldn't read and couldn't write) (*Seltsame Sterne*, 227). Here, the newspaper pictures do not just stand for lives lost, but also create living encounters with the past, becoming a focal point for the grandmother, who cannot read, to form an affective connection with those who died. The grandmother's mourning for these young people becomes entangled, in turn, with the narrator's mourning for the grandmother; paper images are at the centre of this network of connections, which unfold in the living even as they look back at the dead. The result creates a complex dynamic which unsettles previous analyses that either have approached *Seltsame Sterne* as a text that primarily grapples with traumatic histories (see Kader Konuk or Withold Bonner) or, as is the case with Gizem Arslan, have stressed that it 'points to animation and gain' and is 'irreducible to themes of trauma, grief, and loss'.[55] Showing both sides as intertwined, *Seltsame Sterne* challenges despair's passivity, as well as optimism's potential to brush over losses, and it insists on paradox in our experience of the past.

In Özdamar's visual collages, the presence of such contradictory forms is used to challenge totalitarian thought, and in *Seltsame Sterne* too the insertion of material fragments disrupts reductive master narratives. See, for example, the following passage from the beginning of the text, in which the narrator, having just arrived in East Berlin, goes to a bar where she meets a young man, who lights her cigarette:

> Er blieb an meinem Tische sitzen, warf mit halbgeschlossenen blauen Augen seinen Kopf nach hinten und strich mit seinen Händen durch seine Haare, mit Fingern, die so lang wie Stifte waren. Albrecht Dürer, Selbstportrait als junger Mann. Ich stehe vor diesem Bild, und Dürers Hände haben mir Feuer gegeben. Was dachte Albrecht damals? Wie war seine Mutter? Was haben sie damals gegessen? Wie war die Liebe damals? Wie sprach man damals mit Kindern? Und die Großmutter von Dürer – wenn sie aus dem Fenster schaute, was sah sie damals? An was blieben ihre Augen kleben? 'Müssen Sie nach Westberlin?' fragte Albrecht Dürer. (35–6)

> (He stayed sitting at my table, threw his head back with half-closed blue eyes and combed through his hair with his hands, with fingers as long as pens. Albrecht Dürer, Self-Portrait as a Young Man. I stand in front of this picture, and Dürer's hands give me a light. What did Albrecht think back then? What was his mother like? What did they used to eat then? What was love like then? Back then, how did you speak to children? And Dürer's grandmother – when she looked out of the window, what did she see at that time? What did her eyes stick to? 'Do you have to go back to West Berlin?' asked Albrecht Dürer.)

In this passage, the insistence on the young man as the German renaissance painter Albrecht Dürer disrupts the temporal and spatial coherence of the scene, creating a collage-like effect of a found image being inserted into an incongruous context. The young man is not compared to Dürer; rather, he becomes his portrait, and the narrator thus appears to be in two places at once, both immersed in questions about the painter's life and still in her contemporary setting.

The temporally and spatially disruptive effect evokes the anti-totalitarian Volksbühne dramaturgy recalled in Özdamar's collages. Like Shakespeare, Dürer had been co-opted into coercive narratives of order and progress. Under the Nazis, he was presented in fascist publications as a master who embodied a tradition of German cultural superiority.[56] In the GDR, he was hailed as someone who prefigured the inevitable rise of socialism; official GDR celebrations to mark the painter's fifth centenary proclaimed, 'Die Werke Albrecht Dürers sind hervorragende künstlerische Zeugnisse für die geschichtsverändernde Kraft des Menschen in der Epoche der frühbürgerlichen Revolution, sie sind ein kostbarer Besitz und damit ein mitgestaltender Faktor unserer revolutionären sozialistischen Gegenwart' (The works of Albrecht Dürer are superb artistic testaments to the history-altering power of people in the epoch of the Early Bourgeois Revolution. They are a precious possession and, as such, a factor shaping our revolutionary socialist present).[57] Özdamar, by contrast, uses Dürer's image to create a disruption that undermines the narratives of continuity underlying both Nazi and GDR appropriations of the artist, and that resonates with Besson's temporally disjunctive staging of *Hamlet*. Instead of being a figure who attests to a particular teleological view of history, Dürer appears in Özdamar's text in the midst of an unpredictable historical assemblage between past and present, here and there.

In addition to temporal and spatial disruption, Özdamar's description of an encounter with Dürer is distinguished by its focus on idiosyncratic detail. When the narrator imagines Dürer, she focuses on his intimate experience – 'What did Albrecht think then? What was his mother like? What did they eat then?' – and the effect is to undermine the ideological view of the artist as a one-dimensional representative of tradition and to introduce the multifaceted particularities of his life. This focus on the personal magnifies the passage's anti-totalitarian impetus, as the Dürer character turns out to be pining for his boyfriend in West Berlin, a characterization that resonates with homoerotic overtones in Dürer's letters and work,[58] and which brings out a queer side of the artist that runs counter to the ideologies that co-opted his image. It is notable, however, that even as Özdamar disrupts totalitarian narratives through a focus on the personal, she does so in a way that also challenges the notion of personality existing as a discrete entity. The narrator does not imagine Dürer as an isolated figure, but as part of a network constituted by an array of different elements – his mother, his grandmother, his food, his environment – and she thus shows the specificity of his experience as part of these unpredictable constellations. Her description recalls Margaret Littler's Deleuzian reading of *Die Brücke vom goldenen Horn* as a text that shows 'the self as an enfolding of the outside, rather than the interiority of a psyche'.[59] As such, *Seltsame Sterne* creates a further political intervention, for it not only disrupts false narratives of coherence imposed by the GDR, it also undermines the individualism glorified in American discourse attacking the Soviet Bloc. The unpredictable connections created by Özdamar's networks of images thus serve to dismantle narratives imposed by warring Cold War ideologies and to suggest new possibilities outside such structures.

A final example shows how Özdamar's interest in the subversive power of unfolding personal connections is manifest in her experimentation with paper fragments. Towards the end of *Seltsame Sterne*, the narrator is applying for a doctoral degree in Paris on the topic of the 'people's theatre movement', and her friend, Frank Castorf, writes a series of notes for her application. Castorf, who later became artistic director of the Volksbühne, is one of the many recognizable historical figures who appear as characters in the narrative, and a page of typed notes he wrote for Özdamar is scanned into the text (*Seltsame Sterne*, 241). Castorf's observations begin with a reference to the fluidity between art and reality: the words 'Wirklichkeit als Gegenstand' (reality as object), 'Künstler' (artist), 'Kunstwerk' (artwork) and 'Publikum' (audience) are all printed and embellished with a series of double-sided arrows, drawn on in pen, showing feedback processes between these categories. The fact that an image of this document appears in the text enacts the interaction it describes, as it suggests a continuum between the page of the book, the space of the stage that is being referenced and the material world of this real historical fragment. Moreover, the paper object emphasizes the personal nature of these connections. When the narrator goes to take these notes back to West Berlin, she is worried that they will be confiscated by GDR border guards, and so she hides them under her clothes:

> Weil ich Angst hatte, der Grenzpolizist könnte mir Franks Notizen wegnehmen, steckte ich sie unter mein Hemd, es knisterte, wenn ich atmete, deswegen hustete ich dauernd künstlich ...
>
> Wieder in West Berlin. Die Notizen unter meinem Hemd schützten mich gegen den Wind. Meine Großmutter hatte uns früher im Winter immer eine Zeitung unter die Pullover gesteckt. (*Seltsame Sterne*, 240)

(Because I was worried that a border officer might take Frank's notes away from me, I stuck them under my shirt. It rustled when I breathed and so I faked constant coughs.

In West Berlin again. The notes under my shirt protected me against the wind. My grandmother always used to tuck a newspaper under our sweaters in winter.)

As an object, the notes take on an intimate quality; they become integrated with the narrator's body, responding to her breath. They fortify her against the cold, and they forge an unexpected temporal and spatial link with her childhood in Turkey, when her grandmother used newspaper to keep her warm. These personal connections play out against the background of state apparatus on each side of the Berlin Wall, referenced both through the overbearing GDR guards and, a few lines later, through the narrator's description of a West Berlin official who asks to check her passport, making her panic that she will be caught without a proper residency permit (*Seltsame Sterne*, 242). Among these rigid demands for valid papers, the narrator's unruly papers create evolving links between her body, her friends, her family and her experience, cutting across the authoritarian structures of Cold War Berlin and testifying to the subversiveness of the idiosyncratic fragments that she assembles.

Thus, these paper notes are an exemplary illustration both of the unde-cidabilities created by Özdamar's collage forms and of their political effects. Much as Özdamar's visual collages trace evolving connections between material objects, the theatre and the author herself, so too her use of paper fragments in *Seltsame Sterne* creates these dynamic links. As these fragments refuse to rest in particular material categories, they also unsettle conceptual categories, disrupting labels – past and present, here and there – that normally structure our understanding of the world. In so doing, they create space for paradox, allowing for nuanced emotional responses in the face of complex or traumatic histories. Moreover, they become nodes in a network of idiosyncratic personal connections, undermining rigid narratives of the past that attempt to impose control, and showing the rebellious force of undecidability.

Notes

1 Emine Sevgi Özdamar, *Seltsame Sterne starren zur Erde: Wedding – Pankow 1976/77*, 2nd edn (Cologne: Kiepenheuer & Witsch, [2003] 2008), 81. All further references from this edition are given within the text. All translations are my own unless otherwise stated.

2   Emine Sevgi Özdamar, oral interview by Hannah Vinter, 10 November 2019.

3   Ibid.; Özdamar, *Seltsame Sterne*, 190–1.

4   Lizzie Stewart and Frauke Matthes, 'Introduction: Emine Sevgi Özdamar at 70', *Oxford German Studies*, 45, no. 3 (2016): 238.

5   Emine Sevgi Özdamar, *Das Leben ist eine Karawanserei – hat zwei Türen – aus einer kam ich rein – aus der anderen ging ich raus* (Cologne: Kiepenheuer & Witsch, 1992). Translated as Emine Sevgi Özdamar, *Life Is a Caravanserei – Has Two Doors – I Came in One – I Went Out the Other*, trans. Luise von Flotow (London: Middlesex University Press, 2000).

6   Emine Sevgi Özdamar, *Die Brücke vom goldenen Horn* (Cologne: Kiepenheuer & Witsch, 1998). Translated as Emine Sevgi Özdamar, *The Bridge of the Golden Horn*, trans. Martin Chalmers (London: Serpent's Tail, 2007).

7   Emine Sevgi Özdamar, *Sonne auf halbem Weg: Die Istanbul-Berlin-Trilogie* (Cologne: Kiepenheuer & Witsch, 2006).

8   See Ela E. Gezen, *Brecht, Turkish Theater, and Turkish-German Literature: Reception, Adaptation, and Innovation after 1960* (Rochester, NY: Camden House, 2018), 100–1.

9   The narrator is addressed as both 'Svegliati' and 'Emine'. Özdamar, *Seltsame Sterne*, 136, 240.

10 Laura Bradley, 'Recovering the Past and Capturing the Present: Özdamar's *Seltsame Sterne starren zur Erde*', in Julian Preece, Frank Finlay and Ruth J. Owen (ed.), *New German Literature: Life-Writing and Dialogue with the Arts* (Bern: Peter Lang, 2007), 283–4; Gizem Arslan, 'Animated Exchange: Translational Strategies in Emine Sevgi Özdamar's *Strange Stars Stare to Earth*', *The Global South*, 7, no. 2 (Fall 2013): 195.

11 Emine Sevgi Özdamar, *Der Hof im Spiegel: Erzählungen* (Cologne: Kiepenheuer & Witsch, 2001), 55–61.

12 Liesbeth Minnaard, *New Germans, New Dutch: Literary Interventions* (Amsterdam: Amsterdam University Press, 2008), 71–2.

13 See Gezen, *Brecht, Turkish Theater, and Turkish-German Literature*, 79; Claudia Breger, *An Aesthetics of Narrative Performance: Transnational Theater, Literature, and Film in Contemporary Germany* (Columbus, OH: Ohio State University Press, 2012), 116.

14 Gezen, *Brecht, Turkish Theater, and Turkish-German Literature*, 79.

15 Breger, *An Aesthetics of Narrative Performance*, 112–23.

16 Ibid., 121. See also Laura Bradley, who stresses the effect that Özdamar's fragmented form has of demanding the reader's input. Bradley, 'Recovering the Past and Capturing the Present', 295.

17 See, for example, Leslie Adelson's influential analysis. Leslie A. Adelson, *The Turkish Turn in Contemporary German Literature: Toward a New Critical Grammar of Migration* (New York: Palgrave Macmillan, 2005), 39–77.

18   Arslan, 'Animated Exchange': 192, 201; Withold Bonner, '"Haymatlos" im
     kulturellen Gedächtnis: *Serenade für Nadja* von Zülfü Livaneli und *Seltsame
     Sterne starren zur Erde* von Emine Sevgi Özdamar', *Gegenwartsliteratur: Ein
     germanistisches Jahrbuch,* 15 (2016): 243; Sonja Klocke, 'Orientalisierung der
     DDR? Spuren von antifaschistischer Tradition und DDR Literatur in Emine Sevgi
     Özdamars *Seltsame Sterne starren zur Erde* (2003)', in Inge Stephan and Alexandra
     Tacke (eds), *NachBilder der Wende* (Cologne: Böhlau, 2008), 141.

19   *Oxford English Dictionary*, s.vv. 'montage', 'collage', https://www.oed.com/view/
     Entry/121764?rskey=WjsgSb&result=1&isAdvanced=false%20%E2%80%93%20eid;
     https://www.oed.com/view/Entry/36204?redirectedFrom=collage#eid (accessed 3
     February 2020).

20   See Bernard Banoun, 'Brasch, Brecht, Büchner, Kleist. Einige Beispiele aus Emine
     Sevgi Özdamars Archivmaterialien', *Études Germaniques,* 287, no. 3 (2017); Bernard
     Banoun, 'Document et/ou interpretation: sur quelques collages et dessins d'Emine
     Sevgi Özdamar d'après la mise en scène de *Frédéric, Prince de Hombourg* de Kleist
     par Matthias Langhoff et Manfred Karge, Paris/Villeurbanne/Avignon, 1984', in
     Sylvie Grimm-Hamen, Ingrid Lacheny and Alain Muzelle (eds), *Écrivains et artistes:
     entre échanges et rivalités (XIXe, XXe et XXIe siècles)* (Nancy: Presses universitaires
     de Nancy, 2019); Bettina Brandt, 'Emine Sevgi Özdamar als Theatermacherin:
     eine Vorstudie zu "Karagöz in Alamania"', in Yasemin Dayioglu-Yücel and Ortrud
     Gutjahr (eds), 'Emine Sevgi Özdamar', special issue, *Text + Kritik: Zeitschrift für
     Literatur* 211 (July 2016).

21   Özdamar, oral interview by Hannah Vinter, 10 November 2019.

22   Emine Sevgi Özdamar, unpublished collages, author's private collection, viewed
     January 2019.

23   Brandt, 'Emine Sevgi Özdamar als Theatermacherin', 27–8, 30, 32.

24   Breger, *An Aesthetics of Narrative Performance,* 113.

25   *Encyclopedia of Folklore and Literature,* ed. Mary Ellen Brown and Bruce A.
     Rosenberg (Santa Barbara, CA: ABC-CLIO, 1998), s.v. 'Hamlet'. For discussion of
     the mixture of folk and avant-garde influences in Özdamar's theatre milieu, see
     Brandt, 'Emine Sevgi Özdamar als Theatermacherin', 27–8.

26   Robert Weimann, 'Shakespeare Redefined: A Personal Retrospect', in J. Lawrence
     Guntner and Andrew M. McLean (eds), *Redefining Shakespeare: Literary Theory
     and Theater Practice in the German Democratic Republic* (Newark, DE: University
     of Delaware Press, 1998), 127–8. For more on Weimann's influence on Besson's
     production, see Lawrence Guntner, 'In Search of a Socialist Shakespeare: *Hamlet*
     on East German Stages', in Irena R. Makaryk and Joseph G. Price (eds), *Shakespeare
     in the Worlds of Communism and Socialism* (Toronto: University of Toronto Press,
     2006), 187–8.

27   Robert Weimann, *Shakespeare und die Tradition des Volkstheaters* (Berlin:
     Henschelverlag, 1967).

28 Robert Weimann, *Shakespeare and the Popular Tradition in the Theater: Studies in the Social Dimension of Dramatic Form and Function*, ed. Robert Schwartz (Baltimore: Johns Hopkins University Press, 1978), xvii.

29 Christine Poggi, *In Defiance of Painting: Cubism, Futurism and the Invention of Collage* (New Haven, CT: Yale University Press, 1992), 61–7.

30 Ibid., 67.

31 Margaret Littler, 'Machinic Agency and the Powers of the False in Emine Sevgi Özdamar's *Die Brücke vom Goldenen Horn* (1998)', *Oxford German Studies*, 45, no. 3 (2016): 307.

32 Gilles Deleuze and Félix Guattari, *A Thousand Plateaus: Capitalism and Schizophrenia*, trans. Brian Massumi (London: Athlone, 1988).

33 Ibid., 9.

34 Diane Waldman, *Collage, Assemblage and the Found Object* (London: Phaidon Press, 1992), 11.

35 Littler, 'Machinic Agency', 306.

36 Weimann, 'Shakespeare Redefined', 123.

37 On Besson's *Hamlet* as a subversive play, see Anna Naumann, 'Dramatic Text and Body Language: GDR Theater in Existential Crisis', in J. Lawrence Guntner and Andrew M. McLean (eds), *Redefining Shakespeare: Literary Theory and Theater Practice in the German Democratic Republic* (Newark: University of Delaware Press, 1998).

38 Guntner, 'In Search of a Socialist Shakespeare', 187–8.

39 Arslan, 'Animated Exchange': 192.

40 See Özdamar, *Der Hof im Spiegel*, 25, 56.

41 See Klocke, 'Orientalisierung der DDR?', 142; Gezen, *Brecht, Turkish Theater, and Turkish-German Literature*, 86.

42 For more on the materiality of words in this passage, see Arslan, 'Animated Exchange': 192.

43 Breger, *An Aesthetics of Narrative Performance*, 123.

44 Joseph Beuys, *Das Wirtschaftswertprinzip*, ed. Klaus Staeck und Gerhard Steidl (Heidelberg: Edition Staeck, 1990). For Özdamar's mentions of Beuys, see Özdamar, *Der Hof in Spiegel*, 21; Melih Uslu, 'Emine Sevgi Özdamar's Düsseldorf', *Skylife*, July 2012, https://www.skylife.com/en/2012-07/emine-sevgi-ozdamar-s-dusseldorf (accessed 24 January 2020).

45 'Joseph Beuys: Actions, Vitrines, Environments: Room 10', Tate, https://www .tate.org.uk/whats-on/tate-modern/exhibition/joseph-beuys-actions-vitrines -environments/joseph-beuys-actions-10 (accessed 22 January 2020).

46 Charity Scribner, 'Object, Relic, Fetish, Thing: Joseph Beuys and the Museum', in Bill Brown (ed.), *Things* (Chicago: University of Chicago Press, 2004), 339.

47 Ibid., 334.

48 Georg C. Bertsch and Ernst Hedler, *SED: Schönes Einheits Design: Stunning Eastern Design: Savoir Eviter le Design* (Cologne: Taschen, 1994).

49 Scribner, 'Object, Relic, Fetish, Thing', 338.

50 Bertsch and Hedler, *SED: Schönes Einheits Design*, 50–1, 78–9, 108, 124, 136–7.

51 'Janisal Spiesevollsalz', 'Solzenkuchen' and 'Weizenin' are all featured on the same double-page spread, ibid., 50–1. The 'Steileisbereiter' and 'Eisbecherset' are also shown opposite one another on a double-page spread, ibid., 78–9.

52 For more on Özdamar's contradictory presentation of East and West German objects, see Breger, *An Aesthetics of Narrative Performance*, 118–9.

53 See Frank Hörnigk, 'Müller's Memory Work', trans. Rachel Leah Magshamrain, *New German Critique* 33, no. 2 (2006): 11–2; Breger, *An Aesthetics of Narrative Performance*, 122.

54 Deleuze and Guattari, *A Thousand Plateaus*, 9.

55 Kader Konuk, 'Taking on German and Turkish History: Emine Sevgi Özdamar's *Seltsame Sterne*', *Gegenwartsliteratur: Ein germanistisches Jahrbuch*, 6 (2007): 234–45; Bonner, '"Haymatlos" im kulturellen Gedächtnis', 243–9; Arslan, 'Animated Exchange': 193.

56 David B. Dennis, *Inhumanities: Nazi Interpretations of Western Culture* (Cambridge: Cambridge University Press, 2012), 58–9.

57 Dürer-Komitee der Deutschen Demokratischen Republik, *Dürer-Ehrung der DDR 1971: Dokumente* (Leipzig: VEB E. A. Seeman Buch- und Kunstverlag Leipzig, 1971), 5.

58 Matthias Schultz, 'Der Gott der Farben', *Der Spiegel*, 23 April 2012, http://www.spiegel.de/spiegel/print/d-85157617.html (accessed 3 February 2020).

59 Littler, 'Machinic Agency', 292. On intimacy as a force that disrupts the interiority of the individual in Özdamar's work, see also Margaret Littler, 'Intimacy and Affect in Turkish-German Writing: Emine Sevgi Özdamar's "The Courtyard in the Mirror"', *Journal of Intercultural Studies*, 29, no. 3 (2008): 331–45.

Works cited

Adelson, Leslie A., *The Turkish Turn in Contemporary German Literature: Toward a New Critical Grammar of Migration*. New York: Palgrave Macmillan, 2005.

Arslan, Gizem, 'Animated Exchange: Translational Strategies in Emine Sevgi Özdamar's *Strange Stars Stare to Earth*', *The Global South*, 7, no. 2 (Fall 2013): 191–209.

Banoun, Bernard, 'Brasch, Brecht, Büchner, Kleist. Einige Beispiele aus Emine Sevgi Özdamars Archivmaterialien', *Etudes Germaniques*, 287, no. 3 (2017): 449–61.

Banoun, Bernard, 'Document et/ou interpretation: sur quelques collages et dessins d'Emine Sevgi Özdamar d'après la mise en scène de *Frédéric, Prince de Hombourg* de Kleist par Matthias Langhoff et Manfred Karge, Paris/Villeurbanne/Avignon,

1984', in Sylvie Grimm-Hamen, Ingrid Lacheny and Alain Muzelle (eds), *Écrivains et artistes: entre échanges et rivalités (XIXe, XXe et XXIe siècles)*. Nancy: Presses universitaires de Nancy, 2019, 195–212.

Bertsch, Georg C. and Ernst Hedler, *SED: Schönes Einheits Design: Stunning Eastern Design: Savoir Eviter le Design*. Cologne: Taschen, 1994.

Beuys, Joseph, *Das Wirtschaftswertprinzip*, ed. Klaus Staeck und Gerhard Steidl. Heidelberg: Edition Staeck, 1990.

Bonner, Withold, '"Haymatlos" im kulturellen Gedächtnis: *Serenade für Nadja* von Zülfü Livaneli und *Seltsame Sterne starren* zur Erde von Emine Sevgi Özdamar', *Gegenwartsliteratur: Ein germanistisches Jahrbuch*, 15 (2016): 235–60.

Bradley, Laura, 'Recovering the Past and Capturing the Present: Özdamar's *Seltsame Sterne starren zur Erde*', in Julian Preece, Frank Finley and Ruth J. Owen (eds), *New German Literature: Life-Writing and Dialogue with the Arts*. Bern: Peter Lang, 2007, 283–95.

Brandt, Bettina, 'Emine Sevgi Özdamar als Theatermacherin: eine Vorstudie zu "Karagöz in Alamania"', in Yasemin Dayioglu-Yücel and Ortrud Gutjahr (eds), 'Emine Sevgi Özdamar', Special issue, *Text + Kritik: Zeitschrift für Literatur* 211 (July, 2016): 26–36.

Breger, Claudia, *An Aesthetics of Narrative Performance: Transnational Theater, Literature, and Film in Contemporary Germany*. Columbus, OH: Ohio State University Press, 2012.

Brown, Mary Ellen and Bruce A Rosenberg, eds, *Encyclopedia of Folklore and Literature*. Santa Barbara, CA: ABC-CLIO, 1998.

Deleuze, Gilles and Félix Guattari, *A Thousand Plateaus: Capitalism and Schizophrenia*, trans. Brian Massumi. London: Athlone, 1988.

Dennis, David B., *Inhumanities: Nazi Interpretations of Western Culture*. Cambridge: Cambridge University Press, 2012.

Dürer-Komitee der Deutschen Demokratischen Republik. *Dürer-Ehrung der DDR 1971: Dokumente*. Leipzig: VEB E. A. Seeman Buch- und Kunstverlag Leipzig, 1971.

Gezen, Ela E., *Brecht, Turkish Theater, and Turkish-German Literature: Reception, Adaption and Innovation after 1960*. Rochester, NY: Camden House, 2018.

Guntner, Lawrence, 'In Search of a Socialist Shakespeare: *Hamlet* on East German Stages', in Irena R. Makaryk and Joseph G. Price (eds), *Shakespeare in the Worlds of Communism and Socialism*. Toronto: University of Toronto Press, 2006, 177–204.

Hörnigk, Frank, 'Müller's Memory Work', trans. Rachel Leah Magshamrain. *New German Critique*, 33 (2006): 1–16.

Klocke, Sonja, 'Orientalisierung der DDR? Spuren von antifaschistischer Tradition und DDR Literatur in Emine Sevgi Özdamars *Seltsame Sterne starren zur Erde* (2003)', in Inge Stephan and Alexandra Tacke (eds), *NachBilder der Wende*. Cologne: Böhlau, 2008, 141–60.

Konuk, Kader, 'Taking on German and Turkish History: Emine Sevgi Özdamar's *Seltsame Sterne*', *Gegenwartsliteratur: Ein germanistisches Jahrbuch*, 6 (2007): 232–56.

Littler, Margaret, 'Intimacy and Affect in Turkish-German Writing: Emine Sevgi Özdamar's "The Courtyard in the Mirror"', *Journal of Intercultural Studies*, 29, no. 3 (2008): 331–45.

Littler, Margaret, 'Machinic Agency and the Powers of the False in Emine Sevgi Özdamar's *Die Brücke vom Goldenen Horn* (1998)', *Oxford German Studies*, 45, no. 3 (2016): 290–307.

Minnaard, Liesbeth, *New Germans, New Dutch: Literary Interventions*. Amsterdam: Amsterdam University Press, 2008.

Naumann, Anna, 'Dramatic Text and Body Language: GDR Theater in Existential Crisis', in J. Lawrence Guntner and Andrew M. McLean (eds), *Redefining Shakespeare: Literary Theory and Theater Practice in the German Democratic Republic*. Newark: University of Delaware Press, 1998, 111–9.

Özdamar, Emine Sevgi, *Das Leben ist eine Karawanserei – hat zwei Türen – aus einer kam ich rein – aus der anderen ging ich raus*. Cologne: Kiepenheuer & Witsch, 1992.

Özdamar, Emine Sevgi, *Die Brücke vom goldenen Horn*. Cologne: Kiepenheuer & Witsch, 1998.

Özdamar, Emine Sevgi, *Life Is a Caravanserei – Has Two Doors – I Came in One – I Went Out the Other*, trans. Luise von Flotow. London: Middlesex University Press, 2000.

Özdamar, Emine Sevgi, *Der Hof im Spiegel*. Cologne: Kiepenheuer & Witsch, 2001.

Özdamar, Emine Sevgi, *Seltsame Sterne starren zur Erde*. 2nd edn. Cologne: Kiepenheuer & Witsch, 2003 [2008].

Özdamar, Emine Sevgi, *Sonne auf halbem Weg: Die Istanbul-Berlin-Trilogie*. Cologne: Kiepenheuer & Witsch, 2006.

Özdamar, Emine Sevgi, *The Bridge of the Golden Horn*, trans. Martin Chalmers. London: Serpent's Tail, 2007.

Poggi, Christine, *In Defiance of Painting: Cubism, Futurism and the Invention of Collage*. New Haven, CT: Yale University Press, 1992.

Schultz, Matthias, 'Der Gott der Farben', *Der Spiegel*, 23 April 2012. http://www.spiegel .de/spiegel/print/d-85157617.html (accessed 3 February 2020).

Scribner, Charity, 'Object, Relic, Fetish, Thing: Joseph Beuys and the Museum', in Bill Brown (ed.), *Things*. Chicago: University of Chicago Press, 2004, 330–45.

Stewart, Lizzie and Frauke Matthes, 'Introduction: Emine Sevgi Özdamar at 70', *Oxford German Studies*, 45, no. 3 (2016): 237–44.

Tate, 'Joseph Beuys: Actions, Vitrines, Environments: Room 10', https://www.tate.org .uk/whats-on/tate-modern/exhibition/joseph-beuys-actions-vitrines-environments/ joseph-beuys-actions-10 (accessed 22 January 2020).

Uslu, Melih, 'Emine Sevgi Özdamar's Düsseldorf', *Skylife*, July 2012. https://www.skylife .com/en/2012-07/emine-sevgi-ozdamar-s-dusseldorf (accessed 24 January 2020).

Waldman, Diane, *Collage, Assemblage and the Found Object*. London: Phaidon Press, 1992.

Weimann, Robert, *Shakespeare und die Tradition des Volkstheaters*. Berlin: Henschelverlag, 1967.

Weimann, Robert, *Shakespeare and the Popular Tradition in the Theater: Studies in the Social Dimension of Dramatic Form and Function*, ed. Robert Schwartz. Baltimore: Johns Hopkins University Press, 1978.

Weimann, Robert, 'Shakespeare Redefined: A Personal Retrospect', in J. Lawrence Guntner and Andrew M. McLean (eds), *Redefining Shakespeare: Literary Theory and Theater Practice in the German Democratic Republic*. Newark: University of Delaware Press, 1998, 120–38.

9

Interrogating twilight

Nicholas Royle

In an interrogative mood

Padgett Powell's *The Interrogative Mood* (2009) is a quizzical, wonderfully sustained demonstration that a book can consist of nothing but questions: 'Are your emotions pure? Are your nerves adjustable? How do you stand in relation to the potato?'[1] That is how it begins – or does it? For before that there's the title, which in its subtitle begs a question ('*A Novel?*'), along with a dedication ('For Elena'), and finally an epigraph from Walt Whitman's *Song of Myself*:

> Do you take it I would astonish?
> Does the daylight astonish? Or the early redstart twittering through the woods?
> Do I astonish more than they?

We are already engaged – like the creature in bird-lime 'struggling to be free' in *Hamlet*[2] – in an interrogative mood: What is a novel? What is a book that asks if it is a novel? What is the difference between poetry and prose, when it comes to asking questions? Was it Wallace Stevens or Ludwig Wittgenstein who suggested that questions are remarks? Are Whitman's lines *in* the novel or *outside* the novel, if it is a novel? How does his 'song of myself' relate to the song of Padgett Powell? Who is or are 'you'? Is the 'you' invoked by Whitman the same as the 'you' invoked in Powell's opening questions?

Would it be possible to imagine a work of literary theory ('a critical essay?') written entirely in interrogative mode, in a series of questions, some clearly linked to those preceding them, others seemingly disconnected and heterogeneous? How might it deal with 'literary theories of uncertainty'? Mightn't this phrase be misleading, taken to imply that there are literary theories that are *not* theories of uncertainty? Is it not, in that respect, a bit like the phrase 'unreliable narrator' (*as if* there were any other kind)? And are we talking about theories of uncertainty in literature or about theories of uncertainty that are literary? Can we clearly separate these two things? What would a 'literary theory' look like? Not just, in Jonathan Culler's playful phrase, 'the literary in theory',[3] but theory *as* literary? What does 'as' mean? Is there a way of elaborating Philippe Lacoue-Labarthe and Jean-Luc Nancy's *The Literary Absolute* and advancing new ways of thinking and writing (even 'a new theory') regarding the notion of what Emily Apter calls 'literature as an autotelic medium no longer reducible to the role of adjunct to philosophy or thought'?[4] But then, I think to myself, isn't that what I have been perversely toiling to do for several decades, from *Telepathy and Literature: Essays on the Reading Mind* (1991) to *After Derrida* (1995) to *The Uncanny* (2003) to *Veering: A Theory of Literature* (2011) to all the unidentifiable literary objects flying in and around *Hélène Cixous: Dreamer, Realist, Analyst, Writing* (2020)? Don't these books aim to resist or overflow the category of 'theory' and elaborate on the irreducibly literary dimensions of all theoretical writing? And isn't this also what is going on, in a different guise, in texts which have been – for reasons to do with the publishing industry, marketing, copyright and library database conventions, rather than with any putatively 'internal criteria' of classification – designated as 'novels', that is to say *Quilt* (2010) and *An English Guide to Birdwatching* (2017)?

And what are we to make of the pluralization, 'literary *theories* of uncertainty'? Can there be different literary theories about a shared concept of uncertainty? Or does each literary theory pertain to a different kind, a different understanding or experience of uncertainty? Is there an eco-theory of uncertainty in literature that is discrete from a feminist or a queer or a Marxist or a psychoanalytic or a postcolonialist or a deconstructive theory? Is 'deconstructive theory' not the most absurd, oxymoronic phrase? Or might 'eco-theory' merit that prize? Is all of this barking up the wrong tree? Is there a tree? If Padgett Powell can have a random potato ('How do you stand in relation to the potato?'), can a critical essay (if it is one) make corresponding gestures, with regard to the tree? Or have I already led you to believe that a critical essay cannot pose questions in the same fashion as *The Interrogative Mood*, insofar as the former is concerned with developing an argument or cluster of ideas that would be, precisely, critical, whereas the latter can have a riot of a time, asking whatever questions it fancies, in more or less whatever order it chooses, without the need of any overarching narrative, let alone any argument or abstract? But can a critical essay not, on occasion, make a seemingly random gesture, come up with a surprising rhetorical disjunction, fail to offer a segue, start telling a story or stop poetically in its tracks? Isn't that what you find in many, perhaps all of the most affecting, thought-provoking and memorable critical texts? Anyhow, what are you doing here? Weren't we talking about 'we'?

But in truth, is it so clear that the potato is random? Once you start dwelling on this, not just on the oddity of being asked where you stand in relation to it, but thinking about the word *potato*, its look and sound and texture, isn't it rather tempting to recall Jacques Derrida's characterization, in *Glas*, of what he calls 'the great stake of literary discourse [*le grand enjeu du discours littéraire*]', namely 'the patient, crafty, quasi animal or vegetable, untiring, monumental, derisory [*dérisoire*] too, but on the whole holding itself up to derision, transformation of [the author's] proper name, *rebus*, into things, into the name of things'?[5]

How do you reckon with this Derridean figure of the derisory (from the Latin *dērīsor*, meaning 'derider', 'mocker', from the verb *dērīdēre*, to ridicule, to scoff at, to laugh to scorn)? How do you stand in relation to the Padgett Powell potato? Isn't this *potato* chopped or peeled, boiled, fried or mashed up in the author's name? Doesn't it announce, just as firmly or squishily, the importance of the derisory in Powell's writing, as much as in Derrida's? But then, since when did people consider, seriously consider, the role of the derisory in literary theory? Am I asking that merely derisorily?

And what happened to the tree, putatively the wrong one? Do we need to be barking up it at all, if it is one? Wouldn't it be easier to let sleeping dogs lie? Can we not just give ourselves over to the arboreal serenity of George Herbert's line, 'I reade, and sigh, and wish I were a tree'?[6] But what does it mean to wish to be a tree, especially as an effect of reading? If you could be a tree, would you still want to speak? What kind of tree does Herbert want to be? Is it merely by chance that he has a tree in his name (hErbERT)? If you'd wandered into his tiny church at Bemerton, one lovely spring morning about 400 years ago, and found him there, perusing the font perhaps or admiring the latest flower-arrangement, and if you'd pointed out to him this detail about the tree and the letters of his name, would he have felt you were deriding him? Would he have laughed at the sweetness and gravity of the question? Or would he have just sighed and left it there?

Can there be right trees and wrong trees in literature? How, for example, do we read Wordsworth's lines: 'But there's a Tree, of many one, / A single Field which I have looked upon, / Both of them speak of something that is gone . . .'?[7] What does it mean to speak of a tree as speaking? Especially speaking of a loss or absence? Could we envisage a theory, assuredly uncertain, of trees in literature, especially in poetry? If I spent the next three years, on and off, writing a book about 'tree theory' – an irreducibly but also undecidably literary as well as theoretical treatise (forgive me) – with the working title *Arboreality* or *Arborealism,* and separate chapters on, say, Ovid, Chaucer, Shakespeare, Wordsworth, Dickinson, Yeats, W. C. Williams, Stevens, Plath and Powers, would you appreciate it? Or would such authorial compartmentalizations seem insufficiently in touch with the rhizomatic or dendritic? Too determined by the sylvanity of human wishes? How would such a book deal with the idea of deep time, along with issues of nation and nationalism? That is to say, on the one hand, don't trees rather compel us to think about what is gone, lost in time, immemorial? About what or who was living before us? Surely there's no need to invoke the Gingko in order to acknowledge the imponderable depths of time out of which trees rise? Can you imagine how *Arboreality* (if that is to be its title) would engage with contemporary work in this domain, from Eduardo Kohn's *How Forests Think* to David Quammen's *The Tangled Tree: A Radical New History of Life,* in short with kinds of thinking that shake all our conceptions of the meaning of 'tree'? But then, on the other hand, how easily are trees made to line up in conformity with notions of nation and nationhood? For instance, when you read that 'The trees are in their autumn beauty', aren't you already conscious, at least at some level, that these trees are in Ireland? Wasn't that already clear from the title of that poem, 'The Wild Swans at Coole'?[8] When Whitman wonders about 'the early redstart twittering through the woods', don't you register, if only unconsciously, that these are American woods? Isn't this one of the most fundamental and, as it were, most deeply implanted conundrums of literary theory, whether eco, deco or any other kind? Isn't it indeed too vexed a question even to pursue, I'm now wondering, that most 'literary theory' in English is written in the United States with a predominantly US readership in mind, and that, as a result, non-American (i.e. non-US) literary theory, such as work published in English elsewhere, has a more peripheral status, its role and significance altogether less certain and, it may be, negligible? But if, as I am suggesting, climate crisis and mass species extinction and a few other notable issues of worldwide social and political justice require a thinking about the planet in terms that cannot be contained by notions of nation, national boundaries and national identity, wouldn't this also pertain as much to notions of, say, British or Australian as distinct from US 'literary theory' as it does to the so-called national literatures? As Mark McGurl asks: 'If the idea is to plumb the depths of deep time, why not scrap the idea of "American literature" all together?'[9]

Still, in this regard at least, isn't *The Interrogative Mood* rather characteristic of a literary discourse that shows a salutary attunement to a thinking of longer perspectives (whether deep or less deep time) and consistently illuminates the absurd self-importance and self-aggrandizing of humans, but, at the same time, just as consistently, rather wearyingly assumes the reader's identity as a 'fellow American' and, therefore, creates for itself a kind of unhelpfully self-regarding, artificial readership? That is to say, alongside a powerfully derisory, urgent and (in all respects) *critical* sense of the precarious fate of the Earth and of its human inhabitants ('Are you comforted by the assertion that there are yet people on Earth who know what they are doing? Or, like me, do you subscribe to the notion that people who knew what they were doing began to die off about 1945 and are now on the brink of extinction? That they have been replaced by fakes and poseurs?',[10] 'Would a long view through space and time of human history on the earth resemble the compressed photography you may have seen of maggots working a corpse?',[11] etc.), is there not also a discomfiting – because seemingly blind or rather un-*critical* – valorization of words and phrases that are peculiar to life in the United States, words and phrases that, in their very profuseness, generate for Powell's text a kind of unhealthily enclosed, inward-facing *linguistic zorbing*, I mean words and phrases such as 'shuffleboard',[12] a 'cowhide suitcase',[13] 'the barnyard',[14] 'jawbreakers and Fireballs',[15] 'a big coupe with big running boards',[16] 'Chef Boyardee canned noodles',[17] 'Schwinn bicycles',[18] 'Buster Brown shoes',[19] 'Gojo' and 'Goop',[20] 'rimfire cartridge and centrefire',[21] 'raggedy Ann and Andy',[22] 'Howdy Doody',[23] 'Hershey's Kiss',[24] 'Buicks',[25] 'Texas toast',[26] 'Fudgsicle' and 'banana Popsicle',[27] 'yard sales' and 'pull candy',[28] and 'Juicy Fruit gum'[29]? Do you like this phrase *linguistic zorbing* as much as I do? Is your attraction to it, like mine, partly based on the fact that 'zorbing' is not itself an Americanism, but a word originating from New Zealand?

But were we not speaking of trees, not to mention trees speaking? Doesn't the author of *The Interrogative Mood* actually emerge as a kind of woodsy guy who wants to be seen as following in the spirit or song of Walt Whitman 'twittering through the woods', and perhaps doesn't know or even much care that 'woodsy' is an American word that sounds differently to a non-American ear? Then again, what's not to like (as Americans might say) about 'woodsy'? Isn't it a word that potentially speaks to everyone? Can we (which is to say, at least in principle, readers of English from anywhere in the world) not get in or into the American grain, as Carlos Williams called it, if that is what's required, and ponder, among other things, Powell's many poetic and critical reflections on trees? For how ever else we may want to describe it, isn't *The Interrogative Mood* also a significant work for thinking about arboreality? Just to note half a dozen or so instances: 'Should a tree be pruned?',[30] 'If I told you that I am made depressed by a completely still tree but that I am relatively cheered by a tree with a little wind in it whose leaves flutter or whose branches sway, even a little, would you think me strange?',[31] 'If I said to you "tree wound" and "blood type," would you think there was a connection?',[32] 'Do broken bones knit back together by essentially the same mechanism as a limb grafts to a tree?',[33] 'Do you know that the bark around the base of the limbs of a tree is substantially different from the bark on the trunk of a tree – one of its chief differences, if not the only difference, being that the base-of-limb bark will produce more of itself to cover the wound created should the limb break off or be sawn off at the trunk of the tree?'[34] 'If you were a creature who lives underground, would you prefer to be a creature who lives in a tree or would you hold your ground as it were?',[35] 'Do you know of or perhaps own any dead trees that you are particularly fond of and wish to see stand for longer yet?',[36] and 'Do you feel protective in an unusual way of the turkey oak?'[37]

Could there be thinking or speaking in literary or any other texts *without* trees? Or do we feel that we have moved on from trees and the paper that they furnish? Is a literary text read, felt and thought about on a screen differently from a text on paper? Could it be said to 'speak' differently? What is a screen anyway? Is there not always something of the ghostly in the experience of a screen? Is the increased predominance of screens helping to bring out a spectrality that was always lurking in the literary work? Or is it helping to make literature disappear? In which case, what are literature departments in universities up to these days – with their seemingly happy accommodation of reading on screens, writing on screens – effectively rebranding as a sort of Literary Euthanasia Society? Or, in arguably more upbeat mode, a Literary Exorcism Society?

But aren't all these questions about uncertainty, I mean those adumbrated up to this point, unduly inclined towards the sombre and lugubrious? Isn't there also a fundamental role for pleasure, in thinking about 'literary theories of uncertainty'? Wasn't it Oscar Wilde who observed that 'the very essence of romance is uncertainty'?[38] Will she? Won't he? Do they? What is this like? How long can it last? And can there be humour without uncertainty? Are you sure? Isn't derision a form of pleasure, however contorted and even violent? Do you have any sense where all of this is leading?

It's all very well to suggest that literature is about anguish and to affirm Maurice Blanchot's contention that 'writing is nothing if it does not involve the writer in a movement full of risks that will change him [or her or them] in one way or another',[39] but is it not also necessary, perhaps more than ever, to affirm, to laugh, to sing – if possible – about the pleasure of the text? Wouldn't this idea of pleasure – what Roland Barthes saw as the most intense *jouissance*, an effectively orgasmic enjoyment, or what Leo Bersani liked to call, in his perhaps more overtly hedonistic, earlier writings, *self-shattering*, or what Cixous evokes in wondering 'why we desire so often to die, when we write'[40] – make for one of the most awkward, even taboo aspects of literature from a critical or theoretical point of view? For how is literary theory to deal with it? How could you engage with the compelling, even dangerous uncertainties of literary pleasure in Padgett Powell's *The Interrogative Mood* without getting out of your tree? Isn't one of the most tiresome, turn-off things about literary theory its circumlocutory avoidance of such pleasure or, even worse, its attempt to talk about it, but in (e.g.) the anaesthetizing terms of 'wonder', 'shock' and 'enchantment', by *telling* you rather than loosening up the form, letting it happen, showing it, doing it, like the couple up the tree in Chaucer's 'The Merchant's Tale'?

Am I running out of time to talk about all the non-human animals in *The Interrogative Mood* and the idea (call it a theory, it won't kill you) that if we accept Derrida's contention that 'thinking concerning the animal, if there is any, derives from poetry', whereas this kind of thinking 'is what philosophy has, essentially, had to deprive itself of',[41] the specifically *poetic* character of a novel (if it is one) can be analysed and evaluated on the basis of the text's engagement with this thinking? Hadn't I already run out when I omitted to mention the significance of the early redstart in the Whitman epigraph and then duly failed to go on to broach all the issues of avian and ornithomorphic fascination that you might hope or perhaps fear for from someone who spent several years writing a book (a novel?) called *An English Guide to Birdwatching*?

Do I need psychoanalysis? Is it not perhaps long overdue? In particular, is it not now time seriously to consider the Funniest Question Freud Ever Asks? Do you think it might be when, in writing his remarkable essay on 'The Uncanny', he wonders what to make of literature? Or more specifically when, after spending almost thirty pages trying to situate and 'explain' the funny-peculiar power of literature, he acknowledges that he has been barking up, if not the wrong, at least a funny tree and confesses that 'The uncanny as it is depicted in *literature*, in stories and imaginative productions, merits in truth a separate discussion'?[42] Or is the question that takes the biscuit not the one that comes towards the end of that essay, in a context that *appears* (but nothing makes us more attentive to the strangeness of *appearances* than a critical thinking of the uncanny) to have nothing directly to do with literature, when he returns to the idea of *intellectual uncertainty* (an idea to which he keeps coming back or which keeps coming back to him, and which he keeps failing to disconnect from his theory of the uncanny) and wonders: 'And are we after all justified in entirely ignoring intellectual uncertainty as a factor, seeing that we have admitted its importance in relation to death?'[43] Doesn't Freud's comically performative, self-answering question bring in the all-embracing question of death – in returning himself and his reader not only to a remark made a few pages earlier in the essay ('Biology has not yet been able to decide whether death is the inevitable fate of every living being or whether it is only a regular but yet perhaps avoidable event in life'[44]), and thus to the point of uncertainty as to whether life might be prolonged, for example, in some awful Struldbruggian manner indefinitely, but also, and perhaps less fancifully, more disturbingly and immediately, to the radical uncertainty of dying and being dead (as Cixous so succinctly puts it in her commentary on Freud's text: 'To die is the impossible. To be dead: absolute uncertainty'[45])? Is there any 'literary theory of uncertainty' that doesn't come up, sooner or later, with or against some 'theory of the uncanny'?

And isn't the haunting power of *The Interrogative Mood* not just to do with its derisive eloquence in highlighting the United States as 'a stupid country',[46] or with its poetic thinking of trees and non-human animals, but perhaps above all, at the end of the day, with its uncanniness (uncertainly disturbing *and* humorous) in relation to death? Isn't this uncanniness, as an experience of uncertainty, intellectual or otherwise, what Powell generates, in his disarmingly mild and 'nebbish'[47] way, in letting the flow or mood of everyday questions about how you spend your time in an everyday sort of fashion be regularly interrupted or interrogated by, for example: 'If you contracted a disease that ate away your eyelids, would you shoot yourself?',[48] 'If right now you were on your deathbed but not feeling too bad and could have some one thing brought to you, what would it be?',[49] 'Have you known anyone who has drowned?',[50] 'Can you recall the last thing you said to an acquaintance of yours now dead?',[51] 'If you were to be executed by beheading or hanging, which would you prefer?',[52] 'If there is life after death, would you think one should prepare in any way or does it conversely mean that no preparations whatsoever are in order?',[53] 'Under what circumstances would you kill yourself, and what means might you use?',[54] 'Would you prefer to expire on a fair day or foul, or do you think you'll be past appreciating and lamenting the weather by that point?',[55] or 'Are you still living in such a way that suggests you are waiting for the real living to start at some later and unspecified date? Do you think this sense of delay or stalling would be wiped away were you told you had, say, twenty-two months to live, rock-solid certain you'll be gone in twenty-two months from, say, esophageal cancer – would you set about the *actual living* you have in theory been not yet doing?'[56]

Have we not been interrogative enough by this point?
Isn't it time to call it a day?

Twilight's own

The astonishing daylight of which Whitman and Powell in turn sing, in the wake of the redstart, comes to an end. In his Conclusion to *The Renaissance*, Walter Pater evokes this daylight rather differently when he writes: 'Not to discriminate every moment some passionate attitude in those about us, and in the very brilliancy of their gifts some tragic dividing of forces on their ways, is, on this short day of frost and sun, to sleep before evening.'[57] The day that is a lifetime, or that will have been a lifetime, comes to a close.

In setting out these pages ('a critical essay?') in two parts – the first interrogative, the second reflective – I am concerned with foregrounding a sense and experience of the two, in a sort of dialogue or duet. It is a matter of the *two*, being-two-to-speak, the double, the undecidable and the double bind – to recall *Hamlet* once again, 'like a man to double business bound'[58] – as well as the *meta* (the metalinguistic, the metapoetic, the metafictional etc.). The *meta* is indissociably bound up with this thinking of the two and the double, of what is both and neither. The subtitle of Powell's book, 'A Novel?', is indicative here: the reader relies on a notion of what is outside the text (title and subtitle function in a different and discrete way from what are deemed to be the 'contents' of the book), but at the same time this subtitle can clearly be read as the opening gambit of and in the text. 'A Novel?' is a question that refers to the text as if metadiscursively (from outside), but it is also within, participating in the discourse of the text. Is *The Interrogative Mood* a novel? If not, what is it? The concept of metafiction – so often mistaken as a simple term to designate fictional texts that are 'reflexive', that refer to themselves or talk about their own status as fiction – entails irreducible uncertainty. The 'meta' (metalanguage, metafiction, the metapoetic etc.) is always conducive to an experience of the undecidable. Of special interest, then, is the experience of – and critical response to – the literary text doubling, being beside or next to itself, being able to talk about itself, to refer to itself *as* literature and pose the question of its own existence *as* literature.

I would like to focus on a single word: 'twilight'. I will begin with some reflections on *An English Guide to Birdwatching*, then move on to discuss the particular kinds of twilight ('between cat and wolf') to be encountered in the work of Hélène Cixous, and, finally, I will consider the figure of twilight as it emerges in Jacques Derrida's reading of William Collins's 'Ode to Evening' (1746) and Thomas Gray's 'Elegy Written in a Country Churchyard' (1751).

An English Guide to Birdwatching bears the designation 'A Novel', printed within a splat of seagull shit, on the front cover. At the same time it is, in various respects, a work of literary theory. And it is also, I believe, something other – akin, perhaps, to the figure, mentioned earlier, of unidentifiable literary object. It is a book about English (as its title intimates), and it is almost entirely set in England. It was mostly written in Seattle, however, over a period of some six summers. If the derisible, worn-out, more or less spectralized language of nations and national identity is to be adopted here, *An English Guide to Birdwatching* is an American novel as much as it is a British or, more narrowly, English novel, if it is a novel at all. The book is a sort of double-decker or double text: the first section ('The Undertaking') is (among other things) about a couple of retired undertakers called Silas and Ethel Woodlock, who move down from Croydon to Seaford, a small Sussex seaside town containing many ageing or elderly people like themselves. The second part ('The Hides') is an interconnecting series of observation sites for thinking about language, reality and realism, birds, ornithology and contemporary bird science, anthropomorphism, ornithomorphism, du Maurier's 'The Birds' and Hitchcock's film of the same title, as well as about 'The Undertaking'.

Here is the opening of 'Twilight', a chapter early on in 'The Undertaking':

> How is one, in fact, to spend the twilight of one's years? And since when did people start talking about it like that? True, neither of the Woodlocks could see as well as they used to. Although the retired gentleman prided himself on not needing reading glasses, his vision was certainly weakening. And as for Ethel's, he sometimes wondered if she wasn't actually seeing things. Flaming weird, she'd mutter, but then go all coy and decline to explain herself. There is a comfort in the thought of twilight. It is a charming word at first sight. But then it gathers darker hues. There is, nonetheless, something alluring in the image, a sort of dreamy semi-sleepiness in which things are pleasantly unclear, as if your senses are washed over in a soft mauve-bluish haze, while also enabling incidents of unexpected significance to be picked out, like the clarity of the evening star sparkling over the water or the sharpness of an owl's hoot high up in the woods. Twilight is when animals come out. At least the nocturnal sort. Badgers, for instance, traipse and frolic about the sett, or at least they used to, back in the day when the government wasn't gassing them all.
>
> In the twilight of your life there's no going back. That is the gentle but unequivocal message. You don't come flooding back to morning and the delicious dawn chorus of youth and first love and discovering the world. Nor

is it the afternoon tea-party, when you start to absorb the *tip-top* of the clock of the mantelpiece, the hollow that passed like a ghost through the days of Silas's mum and dad and continues to do so here in the new house, over the fireplace. There's comfort to be drawn, like the flickering of a fire, from the thought of your twilight years, for it's not over yet: there's still light, there's still time. Unless you're a badger and the cull has begun, and you reckon it's coming on twilight and snuffle and push on up towards the fresh air for a good bit of playing, rooting and snouting, only to realise you are actually being throttled and, as you struggle to move another inch closer to the open air and sweet gloaming above, asphyxiated.

Twilight is a phase of softness and tranquillity. It may be cold, but it's still beautiful. Of course these days that evening star is more often than not a satellite: you have to adjust to that. News Corporation: an artificial star crossed in your eyes. But there was, after all, the joy of being by the sea and – something about the new abode neither of them had expected – the full, enormous, clear night skies featuring, nearest and dearest, the shifting radiance of the moon. Naturally in a job like theirs there was plenty of work by moonlight, but in Croydon you never really noticed the night sky, whereas here in Seaford you could lie together in bed at night and listen to the waves crashing on the shingle just a couple of hundred yards off, over and over, and the moon was so strong that some nights you were kept up by it, just like the waves. Perhaps twilight years have to do with an increased sensitivity to that fizzled-out planet or whatever people call it nowadays.

In the twilight of your years you take it easy, in any case, especially after having a rocky year like the last one, stuck in the Mayday virtually on death row, convinced there was no coming home. It makes everything sound so natural, *twilight years*, all in a day's work, life one long holiday and now dusk coming on, prepare with calm and dignity for the big sleep. But what, in this day and age, is this twilight talk all about? If you only looked at the billboards and what is on cinema screens and in the bookshop bestseller charts, you'd think it was to do with teenage vampires. But there's a strong chance, Ethel considered, all that effort to turn it into a teenage love-interest thing was really just a way of guarding against the *twilight of your life*. After all, wasn't the daftness of all those Dracula-type films and books basically just a fantasy of *sexually active* eternal life?

Gazing around at the fellow inhabitants of their new home town, the Woodlocks were not particularly keen to indulge in fantasies sexual or eternal, let alone both.[59]

Unlike 'dusk', 'gloaming' or 'crepuscule', what distinguishes 'twilight' has to do with doubling, with two, the *twi-*, the uncertain *between*. Twilight, the *OED* tells us, is 'The light diffused by the reflection of the sun's rays from the atmosphere before sunrise, and after sunset; the period during which this prevails between daylight and darkness' (sense 1); figuratively, it is 'An intermediate condition or period; a condition before or after full development' (sense 3a), while a 'twilight world' is 'a world characterized by uncertainty, obscurity and decline'. Although it is most often associated with the uncertain time between sunset and darkness, it is also about what Chaucer calls 'dayspring' or, perhaps more precisely, the uncertain time before so-called proper daylight. *An English Guide to Birdwatching* is about *twilight*. It explores the idea that twilight is the condition of literature, especially today, in the twilight of 'today'.

The passage just cited illustrates this in terms of what critics call 'point of view' or 'focalization'. Such terms seem to me outmoded. Rather, I would think of an uncertain telepathic veering (UTV, if you want a technical term for it), whereby the narrative voice weaves or shifts into the voice of Silas and Ethel and out and away and in again: at certain moments we are given to understand that we should read the words in the voice of Silas, at other moments it's Ethel (she who was 'stuck in the Mayday [Hospital] virtually on death row, convinced there was no coming home' [42]), and at the same time there is a (telepathic) narrative voice that is also a doubling or blending of their voices. In these respects 'Twilight' might be seen to illustrate and play about with Derrida's formulation of what he calls the secret of literature, namely 'the altogether bare device of being-two-to-speak'.[60] As soon as the voice of third-person narrative or indirect discourse has begun, as soon as there is an 'I' who is not simply or not at all identifiable with the author, as soon as there is a character whose putatively private thoughts and feelings are imparted to the reader, we are in the twilight. All literary fiction is *twi fi* – twilight listening, watching, reading. Another way of understanding Silas and Ethel is in terms of Sigmund Freud's memorable gloss on Shakespeare's Macbeth and Lady Macbeth: they are 'two disunited parts of a single psychical individuality'.[61] Silas and Ethel Woodlock are repeatedly described (or describe themselves) as being 'on the same page'. Despite their differences, they often appear to be thinking the same thing, even the same words, at the same time.

But this extract from 'Twilight' also suggests that it's not merely a matter of the human: if twilight is the haunt of literature, it is also where we find badgers or (elsewhere in the novel) herring gulls. It's the gulls with their strangely engulfing cacophony occupying 'the night turning into dawn'[62] that start everything off. Elsewhere 'Woodlock' turns into a woodcock (*Scolopax minor*), a 'crepuscular and cryptic creature' described as '[h]uman shadower, being of twilight, old timer in two'.[63] Twilight is when and where species meet, a space of dreamy metamorphosis, the slippage and dissolution of anthropocentrism, *anthropos* in the process or throes of becoming unseen in the Anthropocene. Ethel and Silas Woodlock emerge out of the twilight and disappear into it. As do all the other characters, including Stephen Osmer, who dies of pleasure (in the first sentence of the text that refers to him) while 'writ[ing] in the calm of the early dawn',[64] but ends the novel in the twilight of the preceding evening, dissolving with ibises.[65] If Ethel (née Dunnock) is between narrator and Silas, she is also between sparrow and gull. If Silas Woodlock is between narrator and Ethel, he is also between gull and woodcock.

'Between cat and wolf': this phrase comes from Hélène Cixous, who is playing on the French idiom for 'twilight', *entre chien et loup*, literally 'between dog and wolf'. '*Entre chat et loup*' is a somewhat mad, funny, uncanny trope or veering. Between dog and wolf seems apposite: a dog (day) is not a wolf (night), but one melds into the other – dogs, after all, are descended from wolves. Cixous's twist suggests that, as Eric Prenowitz puts it, 'implicitly the day is simply a domesticated version of the night, not its polar opposite'.[66] A book might be written – if it has not been already – about cats in the work of Hélène Cixous. And a book, too, about the figure of the wolf, taking its point of departure perhaps from her celebrated essay 'Love of the Wolf'.[67] But what of this singular metamorphotographic liminality, 'between cat and wolf'?

It's best to write in the twilight. As Cixous says in conversation with Mireille Calle-Gruber:

> Very often I write at crepuscular hours. Why? I cannot write in the dark, in fact, because I need light. But I take notes which for me are seeds. These are moments of collection, at these moments things gather themselves together. Notes, succinct. And the morning – before daylight. Between night and day.[68]

At which point her interlocutor says, laughing, 'Between dog and wolf', but Cixous demurs: 'You could say between dog and wolf. It's not what I would say.'[69] She resists the idea of externalizing the thing, turning it into a familiar locution. Cixous is concerned with the idea of a time where 'it is as if I were writing on the inside of myself. It is as if the page were really inside. The least outside possible. As close as possible to the body. As if my body enveloped my own paper.'[70] She is immersed in the twilight where, as she puts it, 'the medium, written words, still has the quality of a dream'.[71] Twilight 'is the time of least resistance of everything that is an obstacle to writing: of the self, of organized thought'.[72]

Cixous's book *Dream I Tell You* (2003) begins with a few pages of 'Avertissements' ('Forewarnings' in the English translation) about the material that follows, a seemingly haphazard, non-chronological series of dreams that she has had and noted down over a period of ten years or more. This preface begins:

> They tell me their stories in their language, in the twilight, all alike or almost, half gentle half cruel, before any day, any hour [*Ils se narrent à moi dans leur langue, entre chat et loup, entre mêmes ou presque, entre douceur et cruauté, avant tout jour, avant toute heure*]. I don't wake, the dream wakes me with one hand, the dream hand tugs at the drawer to the left of my bed which serves as my box of dreams, noiselessly takes out the pad of paper and the felt-tipped pen . . . it writes all by itself.[73]

'In their language, in the twilight': Beverley Bie Brahic boldly proffers 'in the twilight' for '*entre chat et loup*': reading Cixous in English makes us acutely aware that there is no translation without the experience of the undecidable. Suppose we were rather to render the French: 'They narrate themselves to me in their language, between cat and wolf, among sames or almost, between gentleness and cruelty, before any day, before any hour.' What slinks away, or hardly shows up in the published translation, is the lingering, uncertain, twilit presence of the cat and wolf, and of the between (*entre*), later in the same sentence (especially in '*entre mêmes ou presque*' and '*entre douceur et cruauté*').

The idiom 'between cat and wolf' (*entre chat et loup*) comes back a few pages later, where it is translated as 'in the twilight hours'.[74] Cixous stresses: 'I have in no way "corrected", censored, touched up the tales [*récits*] set down by my hand in the twilight hours.' Rather, they are just as 'they disported themselves in the preanalytic dawn'.[75] This disporting or frolicking is, prior to the illumination of any psychoanalysis, 'between cat and wolf'. Cixous's strange idiom, between translatable and untranslatable, is just one example of what Derrida has called her 'undecidable writing for which as yet no complete formalization exists'.[76] As he goes on to observe, such is 'literature's secret, the infinite power to keep undecidable and thus forever sealed the secret of what it/she [*elle*] says, it, literature, or she, Cixous'.[77] This is the case, he suggests, even 'in broad daylight [*en pleine lumière*]'.[78] And then a few pages later he comes, in effect, to identify this 'broad daylight' as an 'evening'. Playing on the name of Cixous's mother, Ève, Derrida drifts into English: 'we might *even* say', he says, that '*evening* is the secret watching-over an act of writing [*On pourrait aussi et même*, even, *surnommer* evening *la veillée secrète d'une écriture*]'.[79] Everything is evening, as I once suggested, somewhere or other, years ago.

And since we've drifted into the subject of 'Derrida in English' and since I've already invoked teenagers – specifically the teenage love interest and teenage vampires of *An English Guide to Birdwatching* – permit me to conclude here with a few reflections on a piece of his own (more or less) teenage writing. I refer to what was perhaps 'Derrida's first posthumous publication' (how long we might ponder the vampiric strangeness and anguish of that formulation!), published in the autumn of 2004. This is the essay 'Poetry of twilight in Collins' "Ode to Evening" and Gray's "Elegy Written in a Country Churchyard"', written in English in 1951, for which the young Derrida received a mark of 12.5 out of 20, and the teacher's reprimand, 'Your handwriting should be more *legible*', along with the following feedback: 'Interesting and intelligent. It *does* hit upon some of the deepest differences between the two poems and the meaning of twilight as a literary theme.'[80] In this essay Derrida is especially concerned with the ways in which twilight can be both 'expectation' and 'regret',[81] both 'the beginning of something' (as in Collins' ode) and 'the end of something' (as in Gray's elegy).[82] Twilight is 'a poetic hour',[83] Derrida notes. Whether associated with the past ('something never to come back again') or with the future ('presag[ing] the advent of something new, literar[il]y speaking'[84]), it is a matter for anxiety. 'This anxiety', he writes in conclusion, 'is linked to the unsteadiness and the ambiguity of the world at this hour.'[85]

> Now air is hushed, save where the weak-ey'd bat
> With short shrill shriek flits by on leathern wing;
>   Or where the beetle winds
> His small but sullen horn
>
> As oft he rises 'midst the twilight path
> Against the pilgrim, borne in heedless hum . . .

In his attention to non-human life in Collins's poem, and in considering twilight itself 'like a tired out animal',[86] Derrida's 1951 essay already gives hints of the animal that he is (to follow).

Derrida picks up on familiar comparisons between Collins's poem and Impressionist painting, citing (without naming) a French critic: twilight (or 'the phenomena of Evening') 'dissolves progressively all natural form and destroy[s] the solidity of every object'.[87] We might think here too of Algernon Swinburne's remark that 'Corot on canvas might have signed [Collins's] Ode to Evening' (Swinburne 1880). At the same time, Collins was 'a solitary song-bird', in Swinburne's judgement, and a singular twilight poet:

> There was, above all things, a purity of music, a clarity of style, to which I know of no parallel in English verse from the death of Andrew Marvell to the birth of William Blake. Here, in the twilight which followed on the splendid sunset of Pope, was at last a poet who was content to sing out what he had in him – to sing and not to say, without a glimpse of wit or a flash of eloquence.[88]

Like Swinburne, Derrida is especially attuned to sound, voice, music and the ear. He is interested in the aptness of blank verse in enabling 'the fusing of line into line' (35), and he quotes William Hazlitt's comment in his *Lectures on the English Poets*: 'the sounds steal slowly over the ear, like the gradual coming on of evening itself.'[89] Voice conducts us to the unspeakable. Derrida writes: 'In spite of some isolated noises that cause the silence to be more profound and, so to speak, more perceptible, the "shrill shriek" or the "sullen horn", the poet becomes the character, or more accurately, the very voice of a silent world.'[90] This silent voice, this enigmatic evocation takes us back to Derrida's opening paragraph, where he declares: 'Twilight is the moment when whatever contraries, darkness and light, things and spirit, death and life, sorrow and joy melt into each other as if to give birth to a third element quite unspeakable to us.'[91] With more time we might pursue this ghostly figure in relation to what Derrida elsewhere calls (apropos Mallarmé, Gödel and the undecidable) '*tertium datur*, without synthesis',[92] perhaps first of all through the *as if* and the image of giving birth, including the resonance of Collins's beetle 'borne in heedless hum' – 'as if to give birth to a third element quite unspeakable to us'.

In an interview entitled 'This Strange Institution Called Literature', Derrida 'confess[es] that deep down [he has] probably never drawn great enjoyment from fiction, from reading novels, for example',[93] but he also suggests, a few moments later, that literature is 'the most interesting thing in the world, maybe more interesting than the world'.[94] It is a question of what it is about literature that 'cannot be identified with any other discourse. It will never be scientific, philosophical, conversational'.[95] It has to do with the double and doubling – with what he elsewhere calls 'undecidable fakery',[96] with the dream and twin-engine power of twilight. This power is to be construed less in terms of some 'masculine attribute', as Derrida phrases it, but rather as 'the most disarming feebleness'.[97] If literature is a space of gentleness, it is also, as Cixous puts it in *Mother Homer Is Dead* . . ., 'a land of turbulences and of the perpetual disqualification of states of mind'.[98] Here we might recall the force of Derrida's evocation in his 1951 essay: 'Twilight is torn in half by day and night.'[99] In another recent work, 'Ay yay! The cry of literature' (*Ayaï: Le cri de la littérature* [2013]), Cixous speaks of literature as 'the uncertain that does not lie, the scene that gives the undecidable its rights [*l'incertain qui ne ment pas, la scène qui donne à l'indécidable ses droits*]'.[100] In the twilight writing of Cixous, we are drawn into an experience in which, as Derrida says, 'it is impossible for the reader to decide between the fictional, the invented, the dreamt event, the fantasised event (including the phantasm of the event, not to be neglected) and the event presented as "real".[101] Between: two, twi. Betweenlight.

- Interrogating twilight. Did you see?
- And did you hear?
- When?
- Now.
- A twilight zone?
- No. Twilight's own.

Notes

1 Padgett Powell, *The Interrogative Mood* (London: Serpent's Tail, 2009), 1.
2 William Shakespeare, *Hamlet* [c.1600], ed. Philip Edwards (Cambridge: Cambridge University Press, 1985), 3.3.68.
3 Jonathan Culler, *The Literary in Theory* (Stanford: Stanford University Press, 2007).
4 Emily Apter, 'The Critical Life: Rethinking Biography in an Experimental Mode', in Tom Bishop and Donatien Grau (eds), *Ways of Rethinking Literature* (London: Routledge, 2018), 20–33 (20).
5 Jacques Derrida, *Glas*, (1981), trans. John P. Leavey, Jr, and Richard Rand (London: University of Nebraska Press, 1986), 5. French Version: *Glas I* (Paris: Denoël/Gonthier, 1981), 6.
6 George Herbert, 'Affliction (I)' [1633], in *The Poems* (London: Oxford University Press, 1961), 39–41 (40).
7 William Wordsworth, 'Ode ("There was a time")' [1807], in Stephen Gill (ed.), *William Wordsworth* (Oxford: Oxford University Press, 1984), 298.
8 W. B. Yeats, 'The Wild Swans at Coole' [1917], in James Pethica (ed.), *Yeats's Poetry, Drama, and Prose* (New York: W.W. Norton, 2000), 54.
9 Mark McGurl, 'The Posthuman Comedy', *Critical Inquiry*, 38 (2012): 533–53 (534).
10 Powell, *The Interrogative Mood*, 6.
11 Ibid., 136.
12 Ibid., 2.
13 Ibid., 13.
14 Ibid., 17.
15 Ibid., 18–19.
16 Ibid., 21.
17 Ibid., 23.
18 Ibid., 25.
19 Ibid., 27.

20 Ibid., 31.

21 Ibid., 42.

22 Ibid., 52.

23 Ibid., 66.

24 Ibid., 67.

25 Ibid., 87.

26 Ibid., 90.

27 Ibid., 97.

28 Ibid., 124.

29 Ibid., 147.

30 Ibid., 2.

31 Ibid., 33.

32 Ibid., 61.

33 Ibid., 67.

34 Ibid., 81.

35 Ibid., 83.

36 Ibid., 130.

37 Ibid., 146.

38 Oscar Wilde, *The Importance of Being Earnest* (1894), in Vyvyan Holland (ed.), *Complete Works of Oscar Wilde* (London: Collins, 1980), 323.

39 Maurice Blanchot, *The Work of Fire*, trans. Charlotte Mandell (Stanford: Stanford University Press, 1995), 244.

40 Hélène Cixous, 'Without End, No, State of Drawingness, No, Rather: The Executioner's Taking Off', trans. Catherine A. F. MacGillivray, in Eric Prenowitz (ed.), *Sigmata: Escaping Texts* (London: Routledge, 1998), 20–31 (31).

41 Jacques Derrida, *The Animal That Therefore I Am*, ed. Marie-Louise Mallet, trans. David Wills (New York: Fordham University Press, 2008), 7.

42 Sigmund Freud, 'The Uncanny' [1919], in *The Standard Edition of the Complete Psychological Works of Sigmund Freud,* trans. under the general editorship of James Strachey, in collaboration with Anna Freud, assisted by Alix Strachey and Alan Tyson, vol. 17: 217–56 (London: Vintage, 2001), 249.

43 Ibid., 247.

44 Ibid., 242.

45 Hélène Cixous , 'Fiction and Its Phantoms: A Reading of Freud's *Das Unheimliche* ('The "Uncanny")' [1973], trans. Robert Denommé, revised by Eric Prenowitz, in Hélène Cixous, *Volleys of Humanity: Essays 1972–2009*, ed. Eric Prenowitz (Edinburgh: Edinburgh University Press, 2011), 14–40 (33).

46 Powell, *The Interrogative Mood*, 108.

47 Ibid., 158.

48 Ibid., 33.

49 Ibid., 48.

50 Ibid., 51.

51 Ibid., 67.

52 Ibid., 94.

53 Ibid.

54 Ibid., 116.

55 Ibid., 132.

56 Ibid., 158.

57 Walter Pater, *The Renaissance* [1873] (New York: Modern Library, 1919), 197.

58 Shakespeare, *Hamlet*, 3.3.41.

59 Nicholas Royle, *An English Guide to Birdwatching* (Oxford: Myriad, 2017), 41–3.

60 Jacques Derrida, *Given Time: I. Counterfeit Money*, trans. Peggy Kamuf (London: Chicago University Press, 1992), 153.

61 Sigmund Freud, 'Some Character-Types Met with in Psychoanalytic Work' [1916], in *The Standard Edition of the Complete Psychological Works of Sigmund Freud*, trans. under the general editorship of James Strachey, in collaboration with Anna Freud, assisted by Alix Strachey and Alan Tyson (London: Vintage, 2001), vol. 14: 309–35, 324.

62 Royle, *An English Guide to Birdwatching*, 161.

63 Ibid., 315.

64 Ibid., 12.

65 Ibid., 335–6.

66 Eric Prenowitz, personal email to the author, 16 August 2018.

67 Hélène Cixous, 'Love of the Wolf', trans. Keith Cohen, in Eric Prenowitz (ed.), *Stigmata: Escaping Texts* (London: Routledge, 1998), 84–99.

68 Hélène Cixous and Mireille Calle-Gruber, *Rootprints: Memory and Life Writing*, trans. Eric Prenowitz (London: Routledge, 1997), 105–6.

69 Ibid., 106.

70 Ibid., 105.

71 Ibid., 106.

72 Ibid.

73 Hélène Cixous, *Dream I Tell You*, trans. Beverley Bie Brahic (Edinburgh: Edinburgh University Press, 2006), 1. French version: *Rêve je te dis* (Paris: Galilée, 2003), 11.

74 Cixous, *Dream I Tell You*, 8; *Rêve je te dis*, 18.

75 Cixous, *Dream I Tell You*, 8–9; *Rêve je te dis*, 18.

76 Jacques Derrida, *Geneses, Genealogies, Genres and Genius: The Secrets of the Archive*, trans. Beverley Bie Brahic (Edinburgh: Edinburgh University Press, 2006), 15. French version: *Genèses, généalogies, genres et le génie: Les secrets de l'archive* (Paris: Galilée, 2003).

77 Derrida, *Geneses, Genealogies, Genres and Genius*, 18.

78 Ibid.; *Genèses, généalogies, genres et le génie*, 27.

79 Derrida, *Geneses, Genealogies, Genres and Genius*, 25; *Genèses, généalogies, genres et le génie*, 35.

80 Jacques Derrida, 'Poetry of twilight in Collins' "Ode to Evening" and Gray's "Elegy Written in a Country Churchyard"' [1951], in *Angles on Derrida: Jacques Derrida and Anglophone Literature*, special issue of the *Oxford Literary Review*, 25 (2004): 5–37 (28).

81 Ibid., 33.

82 Ibid., 29.

83 Ibid., 30.

84 Ibid., 36.

85 Ibid., 37.

86 Ibid., 30.

87 Quoted in Derrida, 'Poetry of twilight in Collins' "Ode to Evening" and Gray's "Elegy Written in a Country Churchyard"', 35.

88 Algernon Swinburne, *The English Poets: Selections with Critical Introductions*, ed. Thomas Humphry Ward, vol. 3 (1880): 278–81; accessed at: http://spenserians.cath .vt.edu/CommentRecord.php?action=GET&cmmtid=6466

89 Quoted in Derrida, 'Poetry of twilight in Collins' "Ode to Evening" and Gray's "Elegy Written in a Country Churchyard"', 36.

90 Ibid., 30.

91 Ibid., 28.

92 Jacques Derrida, 'The Double Session', in Barbara Johnson (trans.), *Dissemination* (Chicago: Chicago University Press, 1981), 173–285 (219).

93 Jacques Derrida, 'This Strange Institution Called Literature', trans. Geoffrey Bennington and Rachel Bowlby, in Derek Attridge (ed.), *Acts of Literature* (London: Routledge, 1992), 33–75 (39).

94 Ibid., 47.

95 Ibid.

96 Jacques Derrida, *H.C. for Life, That Is to Say . . .*, trans. Laurent Milesi and Stefan Herbrechter (Stanford: Stanford University Press, 2006), 69.

97 Derrida, 'This Strange Institution Called Literature', 59.

98 Hélène Cixous, *Mother Homer Is Dead . . .*, trans. Peggy Kamuf (Edinburgh: Edinburgh University Press, 2014), 42.

99 Derrida 'Poetry of twilight in Collins', 34.

100 Hélène Cixous, 'Ay yay! The Cry of Literature', trans. Eric Prenowitz, in Tom Bishop and Donatien Grau (eds), *Ways of Rethinking Literature* (London: Routledge, 2018), 199–217 (214). French version: *Ayaï: Le cri de la littérature* (Paris: Galilée, 2013), 73.

101 Derrida, *Geneses, Genealogies, Genres and Genius*, 17.

Works cited

Apter, Emily, 'The Critical Life: Rethinking Biography in an Experimental Mode', in Tom Bishop and Donatien Grau (eds), *Ways of Rethinking Literature*. London: Routledge, 2018, 20–33.

Blanchot, Maurice, *The Work of Fire*, trans. Charlotte Mandell. Stanford: Stanford University Press, 1995.

Cixous, Hélène, 'Without End, No, State of Drawingness, No, Rather: The Executioner's Taking Off', trans. Catherine A. F. MacGillivray, in Eric Prenowitz (ed.), *Sigmata: Escaping Texts*. London: Routledge, 1998, 20–31.

Cixous, Hélène, 'Love of the Wolf', trans. Keith Cohen, in Eric Prenowitz (ed.), *Stigmata: Escaping Texts*. London: Routledge, 1998, 84–99.

Cixous, Hélène, *Rêve je te dis*. Paris: Galilée, 2003.

Cixous, Hélène, *Dream I Tell You*, trans. Beverley Bie Brahic. Edinburgh: Edinburgh University Press, 2006.

Cixous, Hélène, 'Fiction and Its Phantoms: A Reading of Freud's *Das Unheimliche* (The "Uncanny")' [1973], trans. Robert Denommé, rev. Eric Prenowitz, in Eric Prenowitz (ed.), Hélène Cixous, *Volleys of Humanity: Essays 1972–2009*. Edinburgh: Edinburgh University Press, 2011, 14–40.

Cixous, Hélène, *Ayaï: Le cri de la littérature*. Paris: Galilée, 2013.

Cixous, Hélène, 'Ay Yay! The Cry of Literature', trans. Eric Prenowitz, in Tom Bishop and Donatien Grau (eds), *Ways of Rethinking Literature*. London: Routledge, 2018, 199–217.

Cixous, Hélène, *Mother Homer Is Dead . . .*, trans. Peggy Kamuf. Edinburgh: Edinburgh University Press, 2014.

Cixous, Hélène, Hélène Cixous and Mireille Calle-Gruber, *Rootprints: Memory and Life Writing*, trans. Eric Prenowitz. London: Routledge, 1997.

Culler, Jonathan, *The Literary in Theory*. Stanford: Stanford University Press, 2007.

Derrida, Jacques, *Glas I*. Paris: Denoël/Gonthier, 1981.

Derrida, Jacques, *Glas*, trans. John P. Leavey, Jr, and Richard Rand. London: University of Nebraska Press, 1986.

Derrida, Jacques, 'The Double Session', in Barbara Johnson (trans.), *Dissemination*. Chicago: Chicago University Press, 1981, 173–285.

Derrida, Jacques, *Given Time: I. Counterfeit Money*, trans. Peggy Kamuf. London: Chicago University Press, 1992.

Derrida, Jacques, 'This Strange Institution Called Literature', trans. Geoffrey Bennington and Rachel Bowlby, in Derek Attridge (ed.), *Acts of Literature*. London: Routledge, 1992, 33–75.

Derrida, Jacques, 'Poetry of twilight in Collins' "Ode to Evening" and Gray's "Elegy Written in a Country Churchyard"' [1951], in *Angles on Derrida: Jacques Derrida and Anglophone Literature*, special issue of the *Oxford Literary Review*, 25 (2004): 5–37.

Derrida, Jacques, *Geneses, Genealogies, Genres and Genius: The Secrets of the Archive*, trans. Beverley Bie Brahic. Edinburgh: Edinburgh University Press, 2006.

Derrida, Jacques, *Genèses, généalogies, genres et le génie: Les secrets de l'archive*. Paris: Galilée, 2003.

Derrida, Jacques, *H.C. for Life, That Is to Say…*, trans. Laurent Milesi and Stefan Herbrechter. Stanford: Stanford University Press, 2006.

Derrida, Jacques, *The Animal That Therefore I Am*, ed. Marie-Louise Mallet and trans. David Wills. New York: Fordham University Press, 2008.

Freud, Sigmund, 'Some Character-Types Met with in Psychoanalytic Work' [1916], in *The Standard Edition of the Complete Psychological Works of Sigmund Freud*, trans. under the general editorship of James Strachey, in collaboration with Anna Freud, assisted by Alix Strachey and Alan Tyson (London: Vintage, 2001), vol. 14: 309–35.

Freud, Sigmund, 'The Uncanny' [1919], in *The Standard Edition of the Complete Psychological Works of Sigmund Freud*, trans. under the general editorship of James Strachey, in collaboration with Anna Freud, assisted by Alix Strachey and Alan Tyson (London: Vintage, 2001), vol. 17: 217–56.

Herbert, George, 'Affliction (I)' [1633], in *The Poems*. London: Oxford University Press, 1961, 39–41.

McGurl, Mark, 'The Posthuman Comedy', *Critical Inquiry*, 38 (2012): 533–53.

Pater, Walter, *The Renaissance* [1873]. New York: Modern Library, 1919.

Powell, Padgett, *The Interrogative Mood*. London: Serpent's Tail, 2009. (I would like to record my special thanks here to Powell Padgett for permission to cite at length from his remarkable work.)

Prenowitz, Eric, Personal email to the author, 16 August 2018.

Royle, Nicholas, *An English Guide to Birdwatching*. Oxford: Myriad, 2017.

Shakespeare, William, *Hamlet* [c.1600], ed. Philip Edwards. Cambridge: Cambridge University Press, 1985.

Swinburne, Algernon, *The English Poets: Selections with Critical Introductions*, ed. Thomas Humphry Ward, vol. 3 (1880): 278–81. Accessed at: http://spenserians.cath.vt.edu/CommentRecord.php?action=GET&cmmtid=6466

Wilde, Oscar, *The Importance of Being Earnest* (1894), in *Complete Works of Oscar Wilde*, ed. Vyvyan Holland. London: Collins, 1980.

Wordsworth, William, 'Ode ("There Was a Time")' [1807], in *William Wordsworth*, ed. Stephen Gill. Oxford: Oxford University Press, 1984.

Yeats, W. B., 'The Wild Swans at Coole' [1917], in *Yeats's Poetry, Drama, and Prose*, ed. James Pethica. New York: W.W. Norton, 2000.

Index

Printed in the USA
CPSIA information can be obtained
at www.ICGtesting.com
LVHW020211051223
765723LV00013B/674